Voices of Reason, Voices of Insanity

I am extremely impressed by this book . . . I think this book is a very important contribution to the literature. I do not exaggerate when I say that much of it is like a breath of fresh air. I wish I could find a way of making psychiatrists and clinical psychologists read it. They will find it both challenging and liberating. I will certa

Voices of Reason, Voices of Insanity

Studies of verbal hallucinations

Ivan Leudar and Philip Thomas

London and Philadelphia

First published 2000 by Routledge
11 New Fetter Lane, London EC4P 4EE

Simultaneously published in the USA and Canada
by Taylor & Francis Inc
325 Chestnut Street, Philadelphia PA 19106

Routledge is an imprint of the Taylor & Francis Group

Typeset in Baskerville by Keystroke, Jacaranda Lodge, Wolverhampton
Printed and bound in Great Britain by Biddles Ltd, Guildford and King's Lynn

British Library Cataloguing in Publication Data
A catalogue record for this book is available from the British Library

Library of Congress Cataloging in Publication Data
Leudar, Ivan, 1949–
    Voices of reason, voices of insanity : studies of verbal hallucinations / Ivan Leudar and
    Philip Thomas.
        p.   cm.
    Includes bibliographical references (p.) and index.
    1. Auditory hallucinations. I. Thomas, Philip, 1949– . II. Title.
    RC553.A84 L48 2000
    154.4–dc21   99-053679

ISBN 0–415–14786–7 (hbk)
ISBN 0–415–14787–5 (pbk)

Contents

Acknowledgements

We are both grateful to our friends and families for their patience with us while writing this book, and especially to Philippa and Stella. Brian Clark read the manuscript and the following people provided lively comments on the earlier drafts: Charles Antaki, Alan Costall, Rupert Reed, Beny Shannon and Wes Sharrock. But most of all we appreciate the help of all the voice hearers who spoke to us about their experiences.

Permissions

The authors gratefully acknowledge permission to include extracts from the following:

Reprinted by permission of the publisher from MEMOIRS OF MY NERVOUS ILLNESS by D.P. Schreber, translated and edited by Ida Macaldine and Richard A. Hunter, Cambridge, Mass.: Harvard University Press, Copyright © 1955 and introduction to the 1988 edition © 1988 by the President and Fellows of Harvard College.

Reprinted by permission of the publishers and the Loeb Classical Library from PLUTARCH: MORALIA, VOLUME VII, translated by Phillip H. De Lacy and Benedict Einarson, Cambridge, Mass.: Harvard University Press, 1959.

Reprinted by permission of the publisher from *The iliad of Homer*, translated by R. Lattimore, Chicago: Chicago University Press, 1951.

Reprinted by permission 'Schizophrenic freed to kill mother and brother' by Martin Wainwright, copyright © The Guardian, 1996.

Introduction

There is an unusual experience which comes under many names – 'verbal and auditory hallucinations', 'hearing voices' and 'divine signs' being just three of them. It has always been relatively uncommon, and today fewer than 5 per cent of the population will hear voices regularly at first hand and even then it is not an everyday happening, like, say, talking, thinking or imagining. The experience has been noted for more than 2,000 years, and the league of voice hearers is impressive. Pythagoras was a voice hearer, and Socrates heard a daemon nobody else could hear, and this daemon guided his actions. Voices were implicated in religious conversions of St Augustine and Hildegard of Bingen but they are by no means always mystical matters. They can figure in the bereavement process – Galileo, for instance, heard the voice of his dead daughter. Voices are not always benign, however, and they can be frightening experiences – Daniel Paul Schreber's voices boomed abuse at him and threatened him. Voices are relatively common in schizophrenia and they can be consequences of sexual abuse in childhood. Some voice hearers report that voices try to induce them to harm themselves or others. But then, as we shall document, there are voices which are resolutely mundane – Socrates heard the voice telling him which route to take to his friend's house.

The hearing of voices constitutes a significant problem for psychiatry and psychology. Both disciplines categorise voices as (verbal and auditory) hallucinations and they explain them as being due to failures in reality testing. The mechanics of the proposed reality-testing devices vary but the failures typically involve confusing what is objective and subjective, real and imagined, and seen and remembered. Diagnostically voices indicate mental pathology, or at best a discrete psychological error. The problem is that voice hearers do not in fact usually confuse hearing voices and hearing other people speaking. They hear voices even when they know perfectly well that nobody else is speaking. In fact this has been puzzling voice hearers and their fellows since Plutarch's time – how can one hear a voice when nobody in sight speaks? Rather than to presume reality-testing errors our aim is to determine what puzzles voice hearers themselves about their experiences and how they resolve the enigmas the experience offers them.

There are other reasons why hearing voices is an important problem for psychologists. First, many voice hearers accept that the voices are indeed parts of themselves, their own mental states, but then their problem is 'how can the voices which avow feelings alien to me and instigating abhorrent actions be parts of myself?' This raises the problem of how coherent one should consider oneself to be as a person. Psychology should be of help here, and we will consider whether this is so in Chapter 5, using the work of William James and G.H. Mead. Second, some voice hearers claim that they cannot but do as the voices tell them to and they disclaim responsibility for deeds instigated by voices. This raises the problem of the relationship between the intentional and compulsive modes of situated action. We consider this problem throughout the book.

Our aim is not to determine, once and for all and for everyone, what these experiences really are – we shall present no final theory, which would explain them as they were in the past, as they are now, and will be in the future. Instead, we are going to document what these experiences can mean today and what they have meant to people living in different times. (The principle is that it is always good to know first what it is one is explaining.) We will analyse accounts of hearing voices dating from almost as far back as written records allow to the present, but we cannot provide a continuous history of the phenomenon – the information is simply not available. Our strategy has been instead to select well-documented historical and contemporary cases and to consider the traits of the experience as they depend on local epistemes or are independent of them. In other words, our aim is to establish both the historically contingent and the unchanging characteristics of the experiences of hearing voices. Some of the problems we shall be concerned with are:

- Were the voices always individual experiences (as opposed to collective ones)?
- Were they ever common or were they always unusual?
- Was hearing voices always treated as a psychological error or was it sometimes treated as a valid experience?
- Was hearing voices ever seen as compatible with reason or always suspect and even a sign of madness?
- Is it possible to decide whether the epistemes framing voices intrinsically structure the experiences?

Six of the nine chapters are each organised around a specific voice hearer (or a candidate for that status). The individuals we consider in detail are Socrates, Achilles, Daniel Paul Schreber, Pierre Janet's patient Marcelle, one of our own cases (Peg), and Anthony Smith (a young man who recently killed his family, allegedly because the voices told him to do so). Even though we avoid presenting a formal theory of our own, we do consider some influential theories of the phenomenon. These include those of Plutarch (voices are the signs of the divine addressing the men of virtue), of French proto-psychiatrists in the mid-nineteenth century (voices are hallucinations indicating insanity), of Pierre Janet (voices are impulsive actions stemming from one's dissociated past experiences), as well as the more contemporary psychiatric theories (voices are results of failures of reality testing typical of psychosis) and the psychological ones of the socio-cultural variety (voices are a genus of inner speech). We do not consider these simply as theories, true or false, but as accounts in terms of which the experiences are lived by the voice hearers and understood by those around them. So in effect we are concerned with pragmatic effects of these theories rather than with testing them.

At present in the United Kingdom, 'hearing voices' is bound to insanity, to violence or at best to eccentricity. We document this dominant episteme mainly in two of the chapters. Chapter 6 outlines how hearing voices is conceptualised and used in contemporary psychiatry. The experiences are hallucinations; that is, errors of perception, and their global meaning is to indicate serious mental illness. The result is that particular instances of the experience lack any intrinsic meaning worth considering. In fact we shall see that in some versions of this episteme the experiences reflect no more than a confusion about what is real and what is imaginary, and therefore are a dangerous source of psychotic delusions. The practical corollary, not confined to medical psychiatry, is that even though hearing voices is a patient's experience, it is better understood as a psychiatric symptom, by a specialist. Chapter 8 is concerned with the presentation of these experiences in the British national newspapers during the past ten years and with the social and personal effects of these presentations. We find that, like psychiatrists, journalists treat hearing voices as an abnormal experience, but in addition they usually mention it in articles concerning acts of grave violence. Voices are symptoms of insanity and concomitants of violence which is impulsive and for which the voice hearer cannot be held responsible. Admittedly, the newspapers do not always present just the psychiatric version of the experience, but it is always the dominant one – the other versions (e.g. the spiritual, paranormal or mundane ones) are usually acknowledged with irony and in the voices of the insane, their advocates or eccentrics. We are not arguing that these experiences are never confused or confusing, but we do maintain that intrinsically they are no more insane than other psychological faculties such as thinking, imagining or seeing.

Chapter 3 focuses on Daniel Paul Schreber, who in 1903 published *The Memoirs of my Nervous Illness* (not exactly a felicitous translation of the original German title) and became perhaps the most quoted mental patient. Schreber provided detailed descriptions of the voices he heard and we summarise their pragmatic properties. His account of voices was supernatural and not really unique in detail, and the experiences qualified him for psychiatric diagnosis (starting with hallucinatory psychosis, through 'dementia paranoides' and ending with schizophrenia). The chapter is mostly concerned with the court case in which Judge Schreber reasserted his legal rights. The case is fascinating because it is one of the few occasions when a mental patient's version of his experience meets the psychiatric one as a relative equal.

In Chapter 4, we consider hearing voices in a very different psychiatric frame. This chapter concerns a Salpêtrière inmate, Marcelle, whose diagnosis was hysteria and who was Pierre Janet's most famous case of 'aboulia' (a disorder of will). Janet established the concept of 'verbal hallucination' as a dominant category for voices and he conceived of Marcelle's voices as relatively direct re-enactments of an unspecified childhood trauma requiring no interpretation. Unlike Freud, Janet argued that the subconscious was a phenomenon of mental pathology in hysterics and he believed the same to be true of 'verbal hallucinations', so much so that he set aside what his patients told him about their experiences.

But are there really any well-documented historical figures for whom hearing voices was different; that is, not abnormal? There have in fact been many creative and influential individuals known to have heard voices. Socrates is one of the oldest documented cases (by Plato, Plutarch and Xenophon) and it is he whom we shall consider in detail in Chapter 1. We will see that Socrates was guided by a 'daemon' which usually told him what not to do. Such an experience was not common even in ancient Athens, and Xenophon, Plato and Plutarch concluded it was a sign from the divine. Socrates acted on its advice, but with consideration, and was not seen to be insane or a charlatan on its account. Indeed, the daemon was taken to be a sign of his wisdom, and its source, and the particular words of the daemon had ordinary meanings in language. Moreover, Socrates could publicly use the advice the daemon provided to justify his actions and his advice to others. So his situation at the time was very unlike that of Schreber or of Marcelle. Nevertheless, in the nineteenth century, French proto-psychiatrists diagnosed retrospectively that Socrates was insane on account of his daemon. Pinel believed that Socrates' daemon was a hallucination which resulted in occasional catalepsy. In Chapter 1 we document the rise of the medical concept of hallucination and the debate on whether the voices necessarily indicate insanity. Our own analysis of Socrates' experience tells that intrinsically the experience was very much like what some contemporary voice hearers report – it had an auditory quality, it was private, the voice regulated his actions, and was not under his direct control, yet not compulsive. We conclude, however, that even though Socrates' daemon fits our concept of 'hallucination' he himself could not accept this categorisation. Were he to do so, he would have to abandon much of his worldview and practice. Trying to reinterpret the experiences of the ancients according to our own terms is not new. Julian Jaynes, for instance, claimed that during a certain stage of the evolution of consciousness voices of gods did the work which reflexive thinking does for us. Socrates, though, could clearly do both – he could think and he heard the voice, and he thought in response to what his voice told him. In Chapter 2 we therefore turn to the *Iliad* to see whether Homer's heroes' interactions with the gods can indeed be considered 'hallucinations' and how he formulated the gods' influences on heroes' actions. (This can be done without committing ourselves to believing that the *Iliad* is a historical document, like the writings of Plutarch.) We find that it is simply not the case that Homer drew the heroes in the *Iliad* without an intentionality of their own. In all the books of the *Iliad* we find that the characters talk to each other to prepare for action, and there are clear instances of inner dialogue employed to decide what is the proper future course of action. Should the gods be considered as voices or hallucinations? The gods of the *Iliad* are clearly not just voice – they are heard but usually also seen and felt. The encounters between the heroes and the gods are presented as private experiences (as are hallucinations) but they are also rhetorical devices which Homer used to confirm the hero status of his characters. The gods usually guide the actions of the heroes, but they also foretell the future. The former is typical of 'verbal hallucinations' but the latter is not (as we show in Chapter 9). Even should one decide that a god speaking to Achilles is equivalent to having a verbal hallucination, there would still be some crucial differences. Unlike nowadays, the voice personifications in the *Iliad* are not matters for individuals – the gods have identities which are socially given and there are procedures which enable heroes to decide which god spoke on a particular occasion. The daemon spoke to Socrates because of his purity, and similarly in the *Iliad* encountering a god is a privilege and not a sign of confusion or madness. Yet, setting aside the fact that the gods know the future, and that they can affect the world in the way the heroes cannot, they do not actually say anything that a mortal could not.

But are there any more recent cases of voice hearers whose voices are benign rather than pathological? In Chapter 7 we consider the case of Peg. Her case is ambiguous in this sense – at the start of her career as a mental patient she had 'imperative verbal hallucinations' which instigated violence and which she followed compulsively. She could have become a case in the newspaper headlines. Yet subsequent therapy helped her to interpose moral considerations between the voices and her deeds (an idea we borrowed from Pierre Janet). She kept a diary of her voices (some extracts from which we provide) and she learned to engage them dialogically. The result was not an influx of delusions (as Bleuler might have predicted) but instead a new voice, which functioned as a proxy for both her partner and her psychiatrist, and which acted on her behalf.

In the final and the longest chapter, we summarise our work on the pragmatics of verbal hallucinations/hearing voices using extracts from interviews with contemporary voice hearers, some with a psychiatric diagnosis, some without. We find that their experiences are in many cases very ordinary. The voices are most often personified with reference to individuals significant to voice hearers. The talk with voices is typically mundane and relates to voice hearers' ongoing activities (as is the case for ordinary inner speech). The voices are typically oriented towards the voice hearer, without direct access to each other or to other people. Contrary to received wisdom, the voices typically do not impel actions of voice hearers, rather they influence voice hearers' decisions on how to act. Voices are clearly not persons in the sense of being capable of reflection – there could be no voices hearing voices. Finally, we find that voice hearers do not mistake hallucinatory voices for other people speaking. They follow simple, publicly available reality-testing procedures to establish their status.

But are voices really so ordinary? Setting aside those which instigate violence, what the voices say is indeed mostly mundane – they do not reveal profound secrets. What is it then about them that has puzzled philosophers, psychologists and psychiatrists for so long? The problems which Plutarch singled out were why only Socrates could hear the daemon and nobody else, and how he could hear it in the absence of sound. Some contemporary voice hearers also find these problems significant and their experiences do not in certain respects fit the language used to represent ordinary talk. But perhaps the focal problem concerns the politics of hearing voices – that is, what people make of these experiences – as they are caught between the rocks of mystification and pathologisation. Our book aims to bring voice-talk back into ordinary everyday life.

1 The daemon of Socrates

Socrates is not usually seen as a religious visionary. Some would say that he is the father of logic and rationality, and he certainly seems to be the epitome of 'sanity, shrewdness, physical robustness, and moral integrity' (Myers, 1903). It does come as a surprise to those who know him just by this general reputation that he let himself be guided by 'a voice', to which he occasionally referred as 'the daemon', as did others in his time and since. The daemon has been of considerable interest to philosophers for well over 2,000 years; alienists and psychiatrists have become interested more recently. Plato mentioned the phenomenon in several of his dialogues (for instance, in *Apology*, *Crito*, *Euthydemus*, *Phaedrus*, *Theaetetus*) as well as in *The Republic*. Xenophon wrote about it in his *Conversations of Socrates*, and Plutarch dedicated a whole monograph, 'On the sign of Socrates', to the matter. In fact, allowing himself to be guided by a daemon was one of the charges levelled against Socrates at his trial – the daemon was not a god recognised in Athens. The daemon probably cost Socrates his life: it 'stopped' him from defending himself in his trial and from escaping once he was sentenced to death. Thus the daemon is a well-documented phenomenon which is important in understanding Socrates (Nares, 1782; Voltaire, 1773/1994; Nietzsche, 1872/1991). We are interested in both Socrates and his daemon.

In the nineteenth century, the daemon became 'a hallucination' and Socrates was declared insane on its account by practitioners of 'retrospective medicine' (Lelut, 1836; Brunet, 1863; James, 1995). He was in good company; the other prominent figures who have fallen from greatness by a stroke of diagnosis included Pythagoras, Mohammed, Merlin, Joan of Arc, Luther, Loyola and Pascal. Nietzsche wrote the following:

> The Socrates' Daimonion likewise is perhaps a disease of the ear, which he *explains* in accordance with his prevailing moral thinking, but other than how it would be explained today. It is no different with madness and ravings of prophets and oracular priests: it is always the degree of knowledge.
>
> (Nietzsche, 1878/1994, p. 126; emphasis in original)

In this chapter we shall first summarise the early French conception of 'hallucination'. We will then summarise what is known about the daemon of Socrates and finally consider whether it fits this concept of hallucination.

On the history of the concept of hallucination

We cannot assume that the concept of hallucination used in nineteenth-century France was exactly the same as ours; let us therefore briefly consider that concept and then return to Socrates. You may have thought that the concept of 'hallucination' is an ancient one but it is almost accepted wisdom in current psychiatry that the concept was formulated by Esquirol in the early nineteenth century. According to James (1995), Esquirol (1838, 1845) coined a single generic term 'hallucination' for 'visions' and 'ecstasies', and distinguished hallucinations from illusions. Esquirol wrote: 'The activity of the brain is so intense, that the visionary or the hallucinator gives a body and substance to images reproduced by memory, without the senses intervening' (Esquirol, 1838, translated by James, 1995, pp. 84–85).

According to James, there were actually words 'hallucination' and 'hallucinate' in Latin but these meant 'to confabulate' and 'to ramble' without specifically perceptual connotations.[1] (This meaning is still noted in the *Shorter Oxford English Dictionary*.) Esquirol's description of somebody who 'hallucinates' was as follows: 'A man . . . who has the inward conviction of a presently perceived sensation at a moment when no external object capable of arousing this sensation is within the field of his senses, is in a state of hallucination. He is a visionary' (Esquirol, 1838, translated by James, 1995, p. 70). So, as Esquirol saw it, hallucinations were sensations without appropriate external objects (why Esquirol added the word 'perceived' is unclear), and the 'visionary' and the 'hallucinator' were one and the same person.

The term 'hallucination' was not accepted without an argument and with exactly the meaning Esquirol gave it. The controversy ensued over which experiences the term should apply to (the extension of 'hallucination'), as well as over what the correct theory of hallucinations might be.

One recurrent problem discussed by psychiatrists was whether hallucinations can coexist with reason. Many argued that they cannot and that hallucinations are, by themselves, indisputable signs of madness. This means that if Socrates experienced hallucinations he was insane, as were the other 'visionaries'. James (1995) reports that Pinel (1818) thought that Socrates was subject to catalepsy. We shall see that his daemon often stopped Socrates in his tracks, but whether one should consider his contemplation 'catalepsy' is debatable. Lelut, in the now famous *Du démon de Socrat*, argued that Socrates was a victim of hallucinations. He wrote in the first edition of this monograph: 'Hallucination evolves from melancholia and it is a clearest characteristic of madness' (Lelut, 1836, cited in James, 1995). Lelut's definition of hallucinations would not be out of place in a psychiatry textbook today: hallucinations were 'internal perceptions wrongly attributed to the action of external objects' and 'spontaneous transformations of thought into sensations'. Compare this to more recent definitions:

A sensory perception without external stimulation of the relevant sensory organ.

(APA, 1994)

Any percept-like experience which (a) occurs in the absence of an appropriate stimulus, (b) has a full force or impact of the corresponding actual (real) perception and (c) is not amenable to direct or voluntary control by the experiencer.

(Slade and Bentall, 1988, p. 23)

Simply stated, the susceptible patient claims to 'hear' the speech in the absence of the actual speaker.

(Hoffman, 1986, p. 503)

According to Lelut, 'Hallucinations were inherently pathological, and an indisputable sign of madness.' Socrates suffered from auditory hallucinations; only mad people so suffer, ergo he was mad (James, 1995, p. 92).

For Maury (1855) there was no difference between visionaries, ecstatics and madmen of his time. He argued that the apparent rationality of visionaries' hallucinations was beside the point – rational hallucinations were still essentially hallucinations, just like those of the inmates of contemporary French asylums. Maury held that these 'great figures' 'believed in their hallucinations as if they were facts', and the hallucinations motivated their actions. Thus the great projects of Socrates, Mohammed and Joan of Arc to which they attended with such single-mindedness were motivated by hallucinations and insanity.

The French Société Médico-Psychologique met to discuss hallucinations twice in the autumn of 1855 and Brierre de Boismont compiled a report on these two meetings (Brierre de Boismont, 1856). The speaker on the first occasion was Baillarger, on the second Castelnau. Baillarger started by summarising the positions of his contemporaries Buchez and Peisse. Buchez held that we are endowed with physiological faculties of internal vision and internal audition, which can be much more developed in musicians and painters. Their internal visions and auditory images are *prepared* and *voluntary*. In pathological conditions, however, the internal images are *spontaneous* and *involuntary*. In other words, the difference between artistic and insane hallucinations was drawn in terms of control over the hallucinatory experiences or the lack of it. According to Baillarger, Peisse shared this same view of hallucinations but added that the insane hallucinators do not distinguish their spontaneous and involuntary internal perceptions from normal perceptions (of external objects), while the artists do. We are thus told that psychotic hallucinations are false sensations while 'ordinary' hallucinations are not. What is pertinent to us here is simply the attempt to distinguish hallucinations in gifted individuals and in the insane, and that this distinction was formulated in terms of control of the experience and error. It is not absolutely clear to us, however, whether the relevant experiences of artists were really meant to remain conceptualised as 'hallucination'. In general, concept definition has to be distinguished from concept application. Concept definitions regulate which concepts *can* in general apply to an object, but they do not determine which of the concepts will actually be applied to the object. So even if some experiences of creative individuals are very much like hallucinations in the insane, a psychiatrist does not have to call them by that name. To return to mid-nineteenth-century France, it is not clear whether *real* hallucinations had to be spontaneous, not under direct control of the will and mistaken for true perceptions. Or was it sufficient to have perceptual experiences without external objects to hallucinate?

Baillarger also considered the view that hallucinations are no more than internal images preserved by memory and reproduced with a great vividness and confused with perceptions. Not all of those involved in the debate believed that hallucinators necessarily confuse internal perceptions (or conceptions, or sensory memories) with perceptions of external objects; Baillanger did not. He contested the view of Garnier, according to whom hallucinations were conceptions which the ill person confused with perceptions. In Baillanger's view this error was not necessary – the hallucinating person need not be duped by his hallucinations even as they are taking place; he need not believe in their 'objective' *reality*. All we need to do to demonstrate this, Baillarger said, is to turn to fantastic images which precede sleep. One knows perfectly well that they are not real, yet they are hallucinations. The error of confusing two different *kinds* of experience is, according to Baillanger, not an essential element of hallucinations. In fact we shall see in Chapter 9 that contemporary voice hearers rarely confuse hearing voices with hearing other people speak, and that they follow simple reality-testing procedures to establish the status of their experiences.

Thus the arguments about hallucinations were threefold. The first problem concerned the nature of hallucinatory experiences: are they inner perceptions, conceptions experienced as perceptions, or vivid sensory memories? The second problem concerned whether hallucinations necessarily involve mistaking internally generated experiences for perceptions. Either the visions of artists are not hallucinations or the reality confusion is not a necessary aspect of the meaning of 'hallucination'. This is important, since as we shall see, reality confusion nowadays distinguishes true hallucinations from pseudo-hallucinations. The third problem was, do hallucinations and madness go hand in hand?

The paper at the second session of the debate was presented by Castelnau. He and Baillarger agreed that hallucinations are always a pathological phenomenon. But Castelnau quoted the following view of Baillarger: 'But even if a hallucination is always a pathological phenomenon, it is not always a sign of madness; a peasant in Brittany is not a madman even though he believes that a Virgin appeared to him and spoke to him' (Brierre de Boismont, 1856, p. 140, our translation).

Partitioning the concept of abnormal is an interesting way of complicating the argument. Hallucinations are always a 'pathological phenomenon', but they need not indicate insanity. Presumably 'pathology' meant everyday pathology, mistakes anyone could make. Taken this way, clearly not all psychological 'pathology' indicates insanity.

Brierre de Boismont resisted the idea that hallucinations should become uniquely tied to madness. According to James (1995), he did not deny that visionaries were hallucinators, but argued that their hallucinations were compatible with reason and were a result of their time in history. Brierre de Boismont's (1862) book *Des hallucinations* was republished three times and two extensive articles based on it were published in *Annales Médico-Psychologiques*. The book is now extremely difficult to obtain so we shall base our analysis here on the articles. Brierre de Boismont (1861a, 1861b) compared hallucinations of insane and sane individuals ('individus aliénés' versus 'individus raisonnables'). He also considered the hallucinations of Joan of Arc and in 'monomanies tristes'. His aim was to 'neatly distinguish *pathological* hallucinations from the *physiological* hallucinations' (Brierre de Boismont, 1861b, p. 511). We need to note that both were hallucinations – Brierre de Boismont was not attempting to deny that hallucinations of artists and religious visionaries were hallucinations. For instance, he wrote the following about Joan of Arc:

> The voices, the visions, the sensations of touch and smell of Jeanne d'Arc were true hallucinations, in essence identical with those of the insane.
>
> This identity is similar to that between fixed ideas in men of genius and the fools.
>
> (Brierre de Boismont, 1861b, p. 537, our translation)

But he organised hallucinations into two kinds according to their incidental properties of hallucinatory experiences (i.e. those not in the definition of 'hallu-cination'). First, physiological hallucinations were compatible with reason, but pathological ones were not:

> But even though their manifestations are the same in the two cases, their character, their logic, their course, their ending establish sharp differences between them.
>
> *Physiological hallucination* is constantly in touch with the dominant thought, the mother idea, the ideal; it is an echo, an adjunct, a stimulant which decides the success. Whatever its duration, it has the same force at the start and at the end, and it does not trouble the reason.
>
> *Pathological hallucination*, on the other hand, has its origins in diverse causes and mostly false ones; it is almost always associated with delirious conceptions. It invokes most erroneous and contradictory motives. Almost always it is impregnated with childish terrors, or is based on ridiculous exaggerations. It presents remarkable transformations. After time, it causes confusion of ideas and enfeeblement of reason.
>
> These two [kinds of] hallucination have their starting point in mental representations, which exist in all the men, but their different character depends on whether the reason is intact or troubled.
>
> (Ibid., pp. 537–538, our translation)

The second important property of Brierre de Boismont's 'physiological halluci-nations' was that they could be voluntary:

> Without returning to the theory of mental representation and to the identity of sensation, conception and of hallucination, we have the feats of Talma, Goethe, and of Balzac and of many other persons who had hallucinations at will.
>
> (Ibid., p. 534, our translation)

So hallucinations were not in themselves signs of madness any more than are thinking and remembering, even though some people can have bizarre and false memories and some people think delusional thoughts. The madness of some hallucinations was in their involuntariness, delirious content, its falsity, childish terror of the hallucinator; in other words, nothing specific to hallucinating. Brierre de Boismont implied that hallucinations are an ordinary mental function, which can indicate impairment of reason like any other, as did Taime (1878).

The problem for Brierre de Boismont was that it is not difficult to argue that every hallucination is based on an error. We have already seen, however, that this position was not completely accepted by Baillarger – his subjects could have experiences without external objects, but not confuse them for ordinary seeing or ordinary hearing. So where was the error? There is only an error if one says that we *should not* have experiences without external objects – we should not have an over-vivid imagination! In fact, three sorts of infelicities could be involved in hallucinating. First, one could claim that one has an experience when one does not. Second, one could claim to be experiencing an external object when no such object exists. Finally, third, one could claim a *perceptual* experience when one is really thinking, imagining or daydreaming.

There is, however, another, more radical, way to object to pathologising hallucinations. Brierre de Boismont was a Catholic, and he believed in more than what an eye can see and an ear can hear. He objected to subjective experience being treated as merely 'a play of imagination' and somehow less real and valuable than 'objective' perception:

> The adversaries of physiological hallucinations hold that there is an enormous difference between sensations visible to all and those only the hallucinator perceives; the objective is real, the subjective is a play of imagination, a symptom of illness. . . . It is evident that if we deny everything that does not fall on our senses, visions do not have a reason for being and they have to be considered errors of spirit.
>
> (Ibid., pp. 534–535, our translation)

But Brierre de Boismont did not believe that we only perceive '*external*' objects:

> if one admits the existence of the moral world, composed of immaterial beings or spirits, if the conviction in this invisible world is complete, if one

believes, with our wise friend and colleague Pidoux, that it is more stable and more certain than the material world, then the visions will not be any longer listed among the symptoms of madness, and nothing will discourage those who will consider believing in their reality.

(Ibid., p. 535, our translation)

So Brierre de Boismont allowed 'the existence of the moral world, composed of immaterial beings or spirits' and he in fact privileged this realm: 'one believes', he wrote, 'that it is more stable and more certain than the material world'. (We do not believe this, but suspend our disbelief for the duration of this argument.) This moral world can then cause subjective experiences, and as hallucinations are not without an object or causal agency they are not in error. (This, as we shall see, was very much how the ancient Greeks accounted for how Socrates heard his daemon.) Moreover, hallucinatory experiences were not necessarily irrational or idiosyncratic. Why? Because they were socially grounded in some respect: 'One can therefore respond to the preceding objection by saying that subjective perception can have rational integrity, this being so because the individual has a consciousness of the phenomenon which conforms to the communal reason' (ibid., p. 535, our translation).

Brierre de Boismont looked back to some golden age of hallucination: 'In the times when religious beliefs were widespread, physiological hallucinations were found everywhere, in churches, houses, streets' (Brierre de Boismont, 1861b, p. 535, our translation). But we shall see that the available evidence suggests that verbal and auditory hallucinations or hearing voices were always an experience of only a minority of the population even in times with a less materialistic worldview than today.

Brierre de Boismont's position may seem unscientific to us, and so immaterial, but the important thing is that he was not an outsider in his time – he was Secretary of the Société Médico-Psychologique, and his arguments were taken seriously, even if not accepted by everyone. Lelut, for instance, was eventually forced to admit the following:

If you like they were not mad, but they were hallucinators, hallucinators such as no longer exist, nor can exist, hallucinators whose visions were the visions of reason.

(Lelut, 1836, p. 350, cited in James, 1995, p. 92)

If Pythagoras, Numa, Mahomet etc. were not rogues, but believed in the reality of their visions and revelations, which seems beyond doubt, then these were men of genius and enthusiasm, who had partial, isolated hallucinations in a religious and reforming mode which was fostered by the spirit of their age.

(Ibid., p. 346, cited in James, 1995, p. 91)

But as James comments, Lelut found the spirit of antiquity wanting: 'This spirit, incapable of understanding such a form of madness, obliged the hallucinator and

his witnesses to believe in the reality of his false perceptions of whatever kind'
(James, 1995, p. 91).

Let us summarise the conception of hallucination under which Pinel, Maury
and Lelut diagnosed insanity in Socrates. The relatively uncontroversial core of
the definition was that hallucinations were like sensations (for instance, hearing
and seeing something), but they lacked natural external objects which could
be perceived by anybody with eyes and ears. Whether hallucinations had to be
involuntary, confused with perceptions or signs of madness, was contested.

Declaring Socrates insane was certainly a shrewd move which caught wide
attention at the time, but we hope the reader already agrees that it was rather
dogmatic and profession-centred as a diagnosis. According to James (1995), Lelut
and others were claiming for medicine 'areas of experience which had traditionally fallen under the authority of the Church' (James, 1995, p. 86). To warrant
this, James quotes Leuret:

> seeing such obvious cases of madness, considered by theologians as evidence
> of sainthood, the reader will doubtless absolve me from the reproach which
> he might have felt entitled to make, that I have so frequently appeared to
> exceed the bounds of the psychology of the insane.
>
> (Leuret, 1834, p. 339, cited in James, 1995, p. 86)

The sign of Socrates

But why return to the daemon of Socrates? Certainly not to confirm the diagnosis
of retrospective psychiatrists. Our aims are as follows. We want to consider how
easy it really is to project our concept of 'hallucination' into antiquity and on to
the daemon. This may at first seem an easy task; we could only be hindered by
lack of information, and perhaps by the potent poetic dressing of that information
in literary narratives (Athenians did not write objective 'case notes' for posterity –
cf. Foucault, 1991, Ch. 2). But this is not really the most interesting problem.
The question is as follows: What would Socrates have to abandon of his own
worldview to learn our concept of hallucination, use it and accept that his daemon
was a hallucination? We must therefore also consider what the daemon meant
for Socrates and what his contemporaries have to say about it. How did it fit into
Socrates' life in Athens? Our starting point is that we would miss something about
the daemon if we simply said it was a hallucination.

Just because we consider the daemon of Socrates from his perspective does
not mean that we do not have a perspective of our own. We are arguing that
'verbal hallucinations' are usefully seen as an unusual kind of private speech.[2] We
must therefore also consider what our framework has to say about the daemon,
and how our retelling of the experience violates it. What would Socrates have
to abandon of his own worldview to learn our concept of private speech, use it and
accept that this was his daemon?

So did Socrates experience verbal hallucinations? Our sources – Plato,
Xenophon and Plutarch – refer to his experience (after translation, that is) as 'a

voice', 'a divine sign' 'a daemon', 'a divine presentiment', 'a supernatural experience', but never as a 'hallucination'. That term, taking the translators' word for it, is simply absent in their narratives. Thus what grounds could we have for saying that the daemon of Socrates was a hallucination? French proto-psychiatrists of the mid-nineteenth century had no qualms about accepting this (Lelut, 1836), but Socrates himself could not experience his daemon as a hallucination, simply because he did not have the concept. This means, as we shall see, that his 'hallucinations' could not have been the same in every respect as present-day hallucinations. Are we claiming that concepts are involved in the reflexivity of experiences? Not at this point.

But how well does Socrates' daemon fit *our* concept of hallucination? Does it have the correct properties to count as a 'hallucination'? We have seen that the cores of the current and the French mid-nineteenth-century definitions are basically the same: hallucinations are individual, perception-like experiences in the absence of appropriate external objects (cf. DSM-IV, APA, 1994). So if the 'daemon' is an 'auditory hallucination', it should be an *auditory* experience. If we further claim that the daemon was a *verbal* auditory hallucination, we need to show further that its meanings came in discernible words. The daemon should also be a private experience of Socrates. And finally (bearing in mind there was no radio or television in Classical Athens), Socrates should experience the daemon in the absence of any person speaking in his vicinity (this being, for us, the appropriate object).[3] We need also to ascertain if this daemon/experience was under Socrates' control or not, whether he mistook it for a perception open to anybody, and whether the daemon was considered a sign of madness, all these being concerns of the participants in the French debate outlined above.

There is ample evidence that Socrates indeed experienced his daemon in the auditory modality. Xenophon's Socrates described it as 'a divine *voice*' which 'comes to me and communicates what I must do' (Xenophon, 1990b, 4–12, our emphasis). Plato's Socrates said that he was 'subject to a *divine or supernatural experience*. . . . It began in my early childhood – *a sort of voice* which comes to me' (Plato, 1993b: 31c–d, our emphasis) and 'I seemed to *hear a voice* forbidding me to leave the spot' (Plato, 1996c: 242b–c, our emphasis). There is no suggestion in our material that Socrates had visions. On the contrary, Plutarch had Simmias report in the 'Daemon of Socrates' that he

> had often heard Socrates to express the view that men who laid claim to visual communication with Heaven were impostors, while to such as affirmed that they *heard a voice* he paid close attention and earnestly inquired after the particulars.
>
> (Plutarch, 1959: 588c, our emphasis)

Interestingly, there is no information in our sources about the voice qualities of the daemon. Did it sound old or young, male or female, did it remind Socrates of somebody? This does not seem to have been important – nobody asks Socrates about these sorts of characteristics of his daemon. What seemed important was what the daemon said, what it advised and forbade, and perhaps why the great Socrates should accept the guidance of a daemon rather than follow his own reason. We shall return to these issues later in this chapter. The point here is that Socrates' daemon satisfies the first condition of being an auditory hallucination – it is like hearing somebody, but we cannot say any more about its 'auditory' properties.

Note however that Plato wrote 'sort of voice', not simply 'voice' and 'I seemed to hear', rather than 'I heard'. Why? Because the voice sounded odd? There is no evidence that this was the problem. The issue was that the daemon was only audible to Socrates and how this was possible. Plutarch held that hearing the voice of a daemon was not exactly the same as hearing an ordinary person speak. For Plutarch, ordinary 'speech is like a blow – when we converse with one another, the words are forced through our ears and the soul is compelled to take them in' (Plutarch, 1959: 588e). What puzzled Plutarch was how the daemon could possibly have reached just Socrates and not those around him. Plutarch was well aware that the usual medium of communication – the auditory stimulation – was absent when the daemon spoke to Socrates. It reached him 'in some strange way':

> It thus occurred to us . . . that Socrates' sign was perhaps no vision, but rather the perception of a voice or else the mental apprehension of language that reached him *in some strange way*. So in sleep, where no sound is uttered, we fancy, as we receive the impression or notion of certain statements, that we hear people speaking.
>
> (Ibid.: 588c–d, our emphasis)

Why did Socrates hear his daemon when 'no sound was uttered'? Do we know nowadays? Plutarch conjectured that 'What reached him . . . was not spoken language, but unuttered words' (ibid.: 588e). The daemon must have made 'voiceless contact with his intelligence'. Unlike ordinary speech, the contact with daemons 'requires no blows'. Plutarch writes:

> the intelligence of the higher power guides the gifted soul, which requires no blows, *by the touch of its thought; and the soul on its part yields to the slackening and tightening of its movements by the higher intelligence.* No constraint is exerted, as no passion pulls the other way, and the movements of the soul respond easily and gently, like rains that give.
>
> (Ibid.: 588e–f, our emphasis)

Let us leave for a moment the idea that the intelligence of higher power guides a gifted soul and consider the mechanism for communicating without 'blows':

> And as in dreams we fancy that we hear voices and the word of spoken language, and yet here there is no voice, but only meaning, doing the duty of voice; so the mind of Socrates, by the token of a vivid sign, could divine in waking moments the presence of the deity.
>
> (Ibid.: 451ff.)

So according to Plutarch, Socrates' experience of the daemon is in auditory modality, but it is not mediated acoustically. It is rather a spiritual contact, a sign.

Was the experience of the daemon private to Socrates, private as are the present-day hallucinations of madness? By private, we do not mean idiosyncratic in form and meaning, but simply that the experience is not shared with other people *as it takes place*. For instance, several people can listen to a concert or watch a play *together*. Could Socrates ever *hear* his daemon together with someone else? None of our sources ever mentions an event such as this. Socrates' actual contact with his daemon is always presented as his own.

> Socrates . . . happened to be making the ascent toward the Symbolon and the house of Andocides, putting some question to Euthyphron the while and sounding him out playfully. Suddenly he stopped short and fell silent, lost a good time in thought; at last he turned back, taking the way through the street of cabinet makers, and called out to the friends who had already gone onward to return, saying that his sign has come to him.
>
> (Ibid.: 580d–e)

The experience of the daemon involves a withdrawal from social activity and into Socrates' thoughts. But note that even though it is private in this sense, the experience is still socially situated. Socrates is 'lost in thought' *with his companions*. The daemon is both a private and a social experience. Nevertheless, the daemon satisfies the second criterion for being a hallucination: it is a private experience in that it is *not* co-experienced by Socrates and other Athenians.

The final criterion of 'hallucination' is that the experience occurs in the absence of appropriate 'external stimulation' – unlike more ordinary voices the *hallucinated* ones have no speakers. Does the daemon count as 'an appropriate stimulus'? Clearly not to someone who does not believe in the supernatural. We do not, and the alienists and proto-psychiatrists did not either. This being so we can – but do not have to – say that Socrates' daemon was a verbal auditory hallucination. He had 'heard' words without anyone speaking. But what about Socrates and his fellow Athenians? They believed in gods and daemons, but in a very different way than we may today. Winch (1964), commenting on magical beliefs and practices of the Azande, pointed out that they were foundations of their social life and a mundane matter. This is not so nowadays, even for those believing in magic or practising it. For Athenians, a daemon was certainly an agency capable of causing Socrates' auditory experiences. So if Socrates were to accept that his daemon was a hallucination, he would have to say that there are really no such agencies as gods and their children, daemons. But there is ample evidence in our material that this is precisely what Socrates would not do.

One of the charges Socrates faced at his trial was that he did not believe in Athenian gods. Socrates contested the charge vehemently. Xenophon's Socrates said: 'Meletus himself could, if he had chosen, have seen me sacrificing during the communal festivals and at the public altars' (Xenophon, 1990b: 4–12). Plato's Socrates first induced his accuser Meletus to modify the charge and to say that he 'disbelieves in gods altogether' (Plato, 1993b: 26c) and then he 'proved' that this was not so. (The argument was not one of his best.) So what was at stake for Socrates? He asked Meletus whether it was 'teaching them to believe in *new deities*, instead of the gods recognised by the State' (ibid.: 26b), which corrupts the minds of the young, and Meletus agreed that 'Socrates is guilty of corrupting the minds of the young, and of believing in supernatural things of his own invention instead of the gods recognized by the State' (ibid.: 24b–c).

The gods (and daemons) were very much a part of Socrates' and his fellow Athenians' worldview. Meletus never once doubted that gods exist, that one can hear a daemon, or that it was proper to be guided by a daemon. The problem was the social identity of the daemon of Socrates. It was new and it was personal to Socrates. Revealing a voice in ancient Athens may not have resulted in a psychiatric diagnosis and hospitalisation, but it had its own bitter dangers.

Finally, let us reflect on what the daemon considered a hallucination to be in terms of what we referred to as 'incidental properties of hallucinations'. We have already seen that Socrates did not have any control over the experience. It 'came to him' and so it was spontaneous. Did he prepare the hallucination in the way a vivid artistic image might follow a period of intense preparation? Clearly not – the daemon provided him with wisdom which he himself did not possess. Did Socrates confuse his daemon with ordinary auditory perception? He did not do this even though he thought that he was hearing the divine. So using Brierre de Boismont's terms, Socrates' daemon has properties of both physiological and pathological hallucinations – it is consistent with reason but not under Socrates' voluntary control. But even though we can indeed project the concept of hallucination on to Socrates' daemon and say that it was a hallucination, Socrates himself could not do this. Why do we think this? He would have to cease to believe in daemons, their wisdom, and their causal powers.[4] Socrates simply cannot do this and remain who he is – his whole life consists in seeking wisdom in people, not finding it and concluding that wisdom belongs to the gods only. Furthermore, it is not just that Socrates prefers in this one case to understand his experience in a different way than we do. His understanding has many practical consequences. We need therefore to learn more about what the daemon meant for Socrates and his fellow Athenians.

Plutarch's 'On the sign of Socrates' (*De genio Socratis* in the original) provides much relevant material. The monograph had been written around 79 BC and the events narrated take place in late autumn in 379 BC or soon afterwards. The context of the debate we shall analyse is as follows: Caphias has returned from Thebes, which has just been freed from the tyranny of four oligarchic usurpers and a Spartan occupation force. He narrates to Archedamus how this happened. The Theban 'revolution' included many meetings of conspirators and waiting, which was filled with philosophical debate.

One problem they considered was why did only Socrates hear the daemon? We have already noted that Plutarch was puzzled by this. Nowadays most people would probably say that hallucinating is an affliction. Plutarch (and the characters in his book), however, concluded that hearing a daemon was a *privilege*. So why is Socrates granted the privilege? (Why not his wife?) We have already seen that Plutarch argued that what was involved was a higher intelligence guiding a gifted soul. So hearing a daemon may indicate that one is gifted rather than insane, but gifted in what way? Plutarch wrote:

> but whereas some men actually have this sort of apprehension in dreams, hearing better asleep, when the body is quiet and undisturbed, while when they are awake their soul can hear higher powers but faintly, and moreover, as they are overwhelmed by the tumult of their passions and the distractions of their wants, they cannot listen or attend to the message.
>
> (Plutarch, 1959: 588d)

So the giftedness Plutarch means involves being able to resist one's passions. Some men are 'overwhelmed by the tumult of their passions and the distractions of their wants'. Socrates is not:

> Socrates, on the other hand, had an understanding which, being pure and free from passion, and commingling with the body but little, for necessary ends, was so sensitive and delicate as to respond at once to what reached him.
>
> (Ibid.: 588d–e)

> Now the voice that Socrates heard was not, I think, of the sort that is made when air is struck; rather it revealed to his soul, which was, by reason of his great purity, unpolluted and therefore more perceptive, the presence and society of his familiar deity, since only pure may meet and mingle with the pure.
>
> (Ibid.: 451ff.)

Retrospective psychiatrists looked at hallucinations as signs of unreason, but according to the ancients, Socrates heard the voice of the divine because he was a man of reason; he denied his body, sought wisdom and disdained material possessions.

But what are the daemons? We have already seen that they are 'higher intelligences' and 'children of gods'. Does this mean that they are agencies radically distinct from mortals – from Socrates and the other Athenians? Towards the end of 'On the daemon of Socrates', Simmias narrates the following story to Theocritus. Timarchus wanted to learn the nature of Socrates' sign, and so he 'descended into the crypt of Trophonius, after first performing rites that are customary at the oracle'. He remained underground and in darkness for two nights and a day, not sure if he was awake or asleep: 'after an interval someone he did not see addressed him: "Timarchus, what would you have me explain?" "Everything," he answered' (ibid.: 591a). One matter which the voice explains to Timarchus is the nature of the human soul and its relationship to daemons. The narrative deals with the crucial issue of how the daemons relate to the human soul. Human souls are rational but can be infected by passions:

I will explain: every soul partakes of understanding; none is irrational or unintelligent. But the portion of the soul that mingles with flesh and passions suffers alteration and becomes in the pleasures and pains it undergoes irrational.

(Ibid.: 591d–e)

What are the effects of passions on a soul?

Not every soul mingles [with the body and its passions] to the same extent: some sink entirely into the body and becoming disordered throughout are during their life wholly distracted by passions.

(Ibid.)

Passions disorder a soul; it becomes irrational and sinks into the body. A part of the human soul becomes 'submerged' in the body and internal in this sense. But it seems that not all of the human soul has to be body-internal. The souls of some people

mingle in part, but leave outside what is purest in them. This is not dragged in with the rest, but is like a buoy attached to the top, floating on the surface in contact with the man's head, while he is as it were submerged in the depths; and it supports as much of the soul, which is held upright about it, as is obedient and not overpowered by passions.

(Ibid., our emphasis)

The part of a human soul which is pure is not internal to the body and Plutarch calls it a 'daemon':

Now the part carried submerged in the body is called the soul, whereas the part left free from corruption is called by the multitude the understanding, who take it to be within themselves, as they take reflected objects to be in the mirrors that reflect them; but those who conceive the matter rightly call it a daemon, as being external.

(Ibid.)

To summarise, Plutarch argues that how a person lives may result in their soul being divided into two parts. One part is submerged and a slave to passion; the other part is, however, external to the body, wise and called a daemon. What is the function of this daemon? Plutarch's 'voice' explains to Timarchus:

The daemon applies what is called remorse to the errors, and shame for all the lawless and wilful pleasures – remorse and shame being really the painful blow inflicted from this source upon the soul as it is curbed by its controlling and ruling part – until from such chastening the soul, like a docile animal, becomes obedient and accustomed to the reins, needing no painful blows, but rendered keenly responsive to its daemon by signals and signs.

(Ibid.: 592b–c)

The daemon thus controls and civilises the soul entangled in the passions of the body through remorse and shame – it is a moral agency. So the daemon of Socrates is arguably, at least in part, a higher moral understanding and it is the pure part of a person's soul. But the daemon is also external to the person – we have already seen that daemons are 'children of gods' (remember that daemons are wise and people cannot be).[5] We shall see that the daemon also mediates between Socrates and the gods.

It is now obvious why most people on this account do not hear the voice of the divine – this is a moral matter:

heaven consorts directly with but a few and rarely, but to the great majority gives signs, from which arises the art called divination. . . . One daemon is eager to deliver by its exhortations one soul, another another, and the soul on her part, having drawn close, can hear, and thus is saved; but if she pays no heed, she is forsaken by her daemon and comes to no happy end.

(Ibid.: 593d–594a)

What would Socrates himself have made of this account of his daemon? The 'myth of Timarchus' was reported to him, and he is said to have censured the teller 'for recounting it when Timarchus was no longer alive, as he would have been glad to hear it from Timarchus himself and question him about it more closely' (ibid.: 592f).

The third theme in the debate in *De genio Socratis* concerned the merits of being guided by divine signs: Where is the line between fraud and pretence and true divine guidance? Galaxidorus started the argument, implying that claiming guidance by divine signs is necessarily 'humbug and superstition'. Theocritus disagreed, bringing up the matter of the daemon of Socrates, Pythagoras' skills at divination and Homer's depiction of Athena guiding Odysseus.

Heaven seems to have attached to Socrates from his earliest years as his guide in life a vision of this kind, which alone 'showed him the way, illuminating his path' in matters dark and inscrutable to human wisdom, through frequent concordance of the sign with his own decisions, to which it lent a divine sanction.

(Ibid.: 580c)

So the daemon is a sign. Consider the following event narrated by Theocritus. We have heard the beginning of this episode already (Socrates walking to Symbolon, the daemon manifests itself to him and warns him . . .) and we continue it here:

Most turned back with him, I with the rest, clinging close to Euthyphron; but certain young fellows went straight ahead, imagining that they would discredit Socrates' sign, and drew along Charillus the flute-player, who had also come to Athens with me to visit Cebes. As they were walking along the street of statuaries past the law-courts, they were met by a drove of swine, covered with mud and so numerous that they pressed against one another; and there was nowhere to step aside, the swine ran into some and knocked them down and befouled the rest. Charillus came home like the others, his legs and clothes covered in mud; so that we always mention Socrates' sign with laughter, at the same time marvelling that heaven never deserted him or neglected him.

(Ibid.: 580e–f)

The daemon provides just Socrates with a warning about a very ordinary matter. This guidance, however, becomes public, because Socrates acts as a proxy for the daemon: he 'called out to the friends who had already gone onward to return, saying that his sign has come to him'. The acceptance of the warning is not unanimous. Some of his contemporaries took the 'sign' seriously and retraced their steps with Socrates, but the younger companions did not. If we say, along with Lelut, that the daemon was a hallucination, we can also say that he was a person acting under the influence of hallucinations. But did he follow the voice blindly, and what should we say about the conduct of his trusting companions? They did not follow him because he was a fool, but because they considered him to be a bridge to the wisdom of gods. Galaxidoras is interested in why the sign should affect the conduct of Socrates. The daemon knew the future and Socrates considered it infallible, so does this mean that he considered it beyond human reason? No.

'You suppose, then, Theocritus,' replied Galaxidorus, 'that Socrates' sign had some peculiar and extraordinary power, and that he did not, upon verifying from experience some rule of ordinary divination, let it turn the scale in matters dark and beyond the reach of reason? For just as a single drachm does not by itself tip the beam, but joined to a weight in equilibrium with another inclines the whole mass in the direction of its own pull, so too a sneeze or a chance remark or any such omen cannot, being trivial and light, incline a weighty mind to action; but when it is joined to one of the two opposing reasons, it solves the dilemma by destroying the balance, and thus allows a movement and propulsion to arise'.

(Ibid.: 580f)

Theocritus agrees – the daemon does not affect Socrates by its authority only but jointly with other reasoned considerations.

The important point is that the daemon is not completely unique but grouped with other *signs*:

I have it from one of the Megarian school, who has it from Terpsion, that Socrates' sign was a sneeze, his own and others': thus, when another sneezed at his right, whether behind or in front, he proceeded to act, but if at his left, he desisted; while of his own sneezes the one that occurred when he was on the point of acting *confirmed* him in what he had set out to do, whereas the one occurring after he had already begun checked and prevented his movement.

(Ibid.: 581b)

'But whereas others state that it is birds and utterances and chance meetings and oracles which forewarn them, I call it divine, and I think that in using this description I am being both more accurate and more devout than those who ascribe the power of the gods to birds. Furthermore, I have evidence to show that I am not attributing things falsely to God: I have often told friends what God has advised and I have never been found to be wrong.'

(Xenophon, 1990b: 4–12)

So Socrates treats sneezes as 'signs from Heaven' and allows them, like the voice of his daemon, to guide his action. But note that we say 'guide'; the formulation of the manner of influence of signs is clear – Socrates is not acting under their compulsion. Allowing oneself to be guided by sneezes seems odd not only to us after more than 2,000 years of progress, but also to Theocritus at the time. How could Socrates, 'great and superior to the generality of men', be subject to this 'hollow affectation'? How can he 'be upset at odd moments by such external matters as a voice or sneeze, and thus be diverted from his actions and abandon his decisions'? Surely this is not Socrates as he was known then and is today. Galixodorus says that Socrates'

movements are observed to have had an indeflectible force and intensity in all he did, which implies that they were launched from correct and powerful judgement and foundation; for of his own free will to have remained poor throughout his life when he could have had money. . . . His acts are not acts of a man whose views are at the mercy of voices or sneezes, but of one guided by a higher authority and principle to noble conduct.

(Plutarch, 1959: 581d)

[I]t is no sneeze or utterance that guides his acts but something divine. . . . I, on the contrary, should have been astonished if a master of dialectic and the use of words, like Socrates, had spoken of receiving intimations not from 'heaven' but from the 'Sneeze': it is as if a man should say that the arrow wounded him, and not the archer with the arrow . . . for the act does not belong to the instrument, but to the person to whom the instrument itself belongs, who uses it for the act; and the sign used by the power that signals is an instrument like any other.

(Ibid.: 582b–c)

So for his interpreters the daemon of Socrates is not a symptom of madness but the tool which the divine uses to advise and guide him. Is this also the view of Socrates? Yes, he considered his sign infallible. So what would the consequences be for Socrates if he accepted that his daemon was a hallucination? He would have to disbelieve in the divine and its wisdom – Socrates would no longer be himself.

Are the dialogues between Socrates and his daemon pragmatically unique? No. In one of the dialogues, *Crito*, Plato portrays Socrates in an argument about a possible course of action. Socrates has been sentenced to die for corrupting youth and for paying tributes to alien gods. Crito tries to persuade him to escape Athens to save his life; Socrates explains why he cannot. The escape would be an act of unlawfulness. It would contribute to the destruction of the laws of Athens which Socrates has himself validated by his residence. The escape would turn him into a lawbreaker and then who would take his teaching seriously wherever he went? The escape would not help his children. He would achieve nothing by it. Socrates' conduct can be monitored in terms of practical and moral consequences.

Interestingly, Plato's Socrates does not just give his reasons against escaping and for accepting the judgement of Athenians. Instead, he introduces into the dialogue a personification of 'Laws of Athens', and he involves himself, and Crito, in a hypothetical argument with the Laws to explain why he must accept the verdict (Plato, 1993a: 50a–b). Socrates is subject to a Socratic questioning, but it is the Laws of Athens who are the master. The dialogue with the Laws of Athens starts as follows.

> Socrates: Suppose that while we were preparing to run away from here (or however one should describe it) the Laws and communal interests of Athens were to come and confront us with this question: 'Now, Socrates, what are you proposing to do? Can you deny that by this act which you are contemplating you intend, so far as you have the power, to destroy us, the Laws and the whole state as well? Do you imagine that a city can continue to exist and not be turned upside down, if the legal judgements which are pronounced in it have no force but are nullified and destroyed by private persons?' How shall we answer the question and others of the same kind?
>
> (Ibid.)

The participant positioning of the Laws, Socrates and Crito in this dialogue is interesting. The Laws of Athens start by saying, 'Now, Socrates'; they address *him*, not Crito. They challenge *his* possible action. In a sense the Laws of Athens are a personification which regulates the actions of Socrates.

Nevertheless, Socrates does not report to Crito an 'inner' dialogue which he has had, or which he is having, with the Laws of Athens about his actions. His dialogue with the Laws is hypothetical, and formulated for Crito. Socrates formulates possible questions to the Laws as challenges to both himself and Crito. He says 'how shall *we* answer this question?', not 'how shall *I* answer this question?'

Are the Laws of Athens just alien proscriptions to Socrates? No. They provide for the world in which Socrates can come to be and develop. 'Did we not give you life in the first place?' they say, and Socrates agrees. 'Are you not grateful . . . for requiring your father to give you an education in music and gymnastics?' Socrates agrees. The Laws say: 'we have brought you into the world and reared you and educated you'.

Socrates formulates for Crito hypothetical challenges of the Laws to his escaping Athens. The dialogue between Socrates and the personified laws is partly private – the Laws relate morally to Socrates' possible action: escape prison and Athens. So the Laws of Athens regulate actions of Socrates but they are not private or unobservable. He invokes them publicly to assess the course of action he is asked to consider. Laws of Athens are clearly a rhetorical device used by Socrates to justify his course of actions to others. And Socrates also used his daemon as another rhetorical device, whether or not he always had the experience he avowed.

What the daemon of Socrates could do with words

In the final section of this chapter we shall consider the pragmatic dispositions of the daemon of Socrates. We have seen some of them already and we can simply summarise them.

The daemon is an auditory and a verbal experience; it speaks to Socrates. It is personified as a divine agency and it seems not to have properties such as age, gender, or an alignment with somebody known to Socrates. Qualities such as these are at least never mentioned; perhaps they are not relevant to a daemon.

The participant positioning is also clear. Socrates hears only one daemon; it addresses just him and nobody else. Since he has only one voice it is not possible for him to overhear daemons discussing him or anything else. It is not clear if the daemon ever actually asks him to address others. Socrates certainly sets himself up effectively as a go-between between the daemon and Athenians – we have seen that he passes the daemon's warning to them, and not as his own. There is some indication that the daemon itself may speak for the gods.

As we have already said, the experience of the daemon is spontaneous – Socrates does not invoke it. This means that the daemon initiates the dialogues with Socrates. In fact these 'dialogues' are rather one-sided. It does not seem that Socrates talks back to the daemon – he listens, considers and invariably obeys the daemon.

The daemon is strongly restricted in terms of what it does with words – it stops Socrates doing things. In *Apology*, Plato's Socrates formulates the influence as follows:

> The reason for this is what you have often heard me say before on many occasions: that I am subject to a divine or supernatural experience, which Meletus saw fit to travesty in his indictment. It began in my early childhood – *a sort of voice which comes to me; and when it comes it always dissuades me from what*

I am proposing to do, and never urges me on. It is this that debars me from entering public life, and a very good thing too, in my opinion; because you may be quite sure, gentlemen, that if I had tried long ago to engage in politics, I should long ago have lost my life, without doing any good either to you or to myself.

(Plato, 1993b: 31c–d, our emphasis)

Pragmatically the experience is constrained: the daemon 'always dissuades' Socrates from what he is 'proposing to do', and 'never urges' him on. All sources agree on this except for Xenophon. He writes:

'Meletus himself could, if he had chosen, have seen me sacrificing during the communal festivals and at the public altars. As for my claims that a divine voice comes to me and communicates what I must do, how in claiming this am I introducing new deities?'

(Xenophon, 1990b: 4–12)

The daemon communicates what Socrates 'must do'. Is this just ambiguous writing by Xenophon? There is some evidence that the daemon does not just inhibit impending actions of Socrates. Plutarch writes that the daemon can 'sanction' Socrates' own decisions (Plutarch, 1959: 580d). Our conclusion has to be that the daemon talks about actions which Socrates has decided and is about to carry out: Plato's Socrates says to Phaedrus, 'it *checks me when on the point of doing something or other*' (Plato, 1996c: 242b–d). The daemon either inhibits intentions to act or it sanctions them.

What kinds of actions does the daemon regulate and how does Socrates react? The actions regulated can range from trivial to truly important ones. In *Phaedrus* the action inhibited by the daemon seems rather trivial:

Phaedrus: It might be a lot worse! But how so? To what do you refer?
Socrates: 'At the moment when I was about to cross the river, dear friend, *there came to me my familiar divine sign – which always checks me when on the point of doing something or other – and all at once I seemed to hear a voice, forbidding me to leave the spot until I had made atonement for some offence to heaven.*

(ibid., our emphasis)

In *Apology*, the action in question is rather more important. Hermogenes tries to get Socrates to prepare his defence, but Socrates refuses. He first retorts that all his life has been such a preparation. When Hermogenes points out that being right and a good man does not ensure the victory in an Athenian court, Socrates agrees, but then he warrants his refusal to work on his defence by reference to his daemon:

'Yes, but as a matter of fact,' he said, 'twice now, when I was trying to consider my defence, the divine opposed me. 'That's remarkable,' said

Hermogenes and Socrates replied, 'Do you really think it's remarkable that God should decide that it is better for me to die now?'

(Xenophon, 1990b: 0–4)

Does the daemon do anything else with words other than regulate Socrates' actions? Socrates certainly believes that a part of its wisdom is that it knows the future: 'that god has knowledge of the future and communicates it in advance to whomever he wishes – this too, as I say, is a universal claim and belief' (ibid.: 4–12). The daemon's knowledge of the future is one thing which warrants its dissuasions, but there is no evidence that the daemon ever actually *tells* Socrates what the future will be.

Socrates always obeys the daemon – in fact he claims that it never failed him. Even so, the daemon is not an impulsion or even a compulsion. Socrates obeys it for certain reasons. Socrates never reports whether the daemon itself warrants its dissuasions to him. Whether or not this is so, Socrates himself works out the warrants:

'The gods were right to oppose me,' he continued, 'and prevent me from working on my speech, when we thought to find some way to secure my acquittal, whatever it took. Suppose I had achieved this goal: clearly the result would have been that instead of facing the cessation of life as I am now, I would have guaranteed for myself a death made burdensome by illness or old age – and old age is a pit into which flows everything which is intolerable and devoid of pleasure.'

(Ibid.: 0–4)

So why does Socrates do as the voice says? One reason is obviously that he believes, indeed he knows, that the daemon is divine and wise and he is not. It is unwise and immoral to disobey gods, even though one can do so. He obeys the daemon because he reasons about its advice, understands it, and accepts it. This means that when he acts on the guidance of his daemon, he also follows his reason and so is not under any compulsion. Nietzsche (1872/1991) argued that the daemon was what emboldened Socrates to take the position as a critic of Athenians and a voice of reason. He is ignorant and knows this, but the daemon advises and guides him when his intelligence falters.

Does our pragmatic understanding of the sign of Socrates violate his own and that of his contemporaries? On both accounts the daemon guides his actions using language – our description accepts this and what Socrates reports that the daemon tells him. We also accept that such guidance is not just a matter of superior knowledge but also a moral matter. However, we part company with Socrates in that we do not accept that the daemon was a supernatural agency. But to confound the matter, our concept of 'supernatural' and that of Socrates are not the same.

2 The gods of Achilles

The *Iliad* is a poem with disputed authorship. Even if there actually was a Homer, he used much older stories to compose the *Iliad*, stories which his audience knew well. The stories came from a common pool and his characters have marks of ancient tradition – they are not just *his* characters. Eventually the *Iliad* was assimilated into a cycle of written poems which include *Cypria, Aithiopis, Little Iliad, Sack of Ilion, The Returns, Odyssey* and *Telegony* (Bowra, 1930; Lattimore, 1951). The dates given by Greek historians for the fall of Troy are between 1334 BC and 1150 BC – Herodotus placed Homer in around 850 BC. Homer thus talks about his past, not about his present. Nevertheless, the *Iliad* is not a collage of short stories – it is now one poem. The statements in the Greek 'original' are dominated by dactylic hexameter, with phrases included because they are stylistically necessary, not because they are descriptively appropriate (Lattimore, 1951). The *Iliad* though can be translated into prose as, for instance, E.V. Rieu has done.

Homer himself remains anonymous in the *Iliad* – he never mentions his own name or gives a *personal* opinion. Homer's style is of a school, and his language is inherited from his predecessors. Lattimore wrote in the introductions to his translation of the *Iliad*[1] that it is 'a work of art evolved within the scope of a chronicle but it is not the chronicle' (Lattimore, 1951, p. 17). So our analysis below will be strictly of the social actions of *characters* in the *Iliad*, not of fictitious 'real' people at the supposed time of the *Iliad*. The *Iliad* is not a historical or a psychological document. Nevertheless, we carry the assumption that in reading the *Iliad* carefully one can learn much about how Homer constructs the intentionality of his characters – intentionality is a social matter. We also suspect that this intentionality could not have been invented by Homer, it cannot be his literary fancy. The reason is that the conduct of the heroes must have been understandable to his audiences.

We shall not narrate the story-line. There are many ways to read the *Iliad*. For us it is a poem about pride and its consequences. It is also about love and the wrath which ensues when the loved one is lost. Ultimately the *Iliad* is about containing these passions – but neither the gods nor the mortals can contain them in Achilles.

Julian Jaynes' (1976) identification of the voices of gods in the *Iliad* with the present-day verbal hallucinations is well known. What we have learned previously about the sign of Socrates, though, should make us wary of accepting it without an argument. Perhaps saying that verbal hallucinations and voices of gods are one and the same phenomenon is far too strong. We will show that there are indeed some significant similarities between the two, but also differences, and these are fascinating. After all, hearing one's 'voice of madness' and being addressed by 'a voice of god' have quite a different significance – both for an individual and socially. The two are experienced under different descriptions, and they are also situated differently (cf. Hacking, 1995, and Leudar and Sharrock, 1999). This means that their pragmatics are different and we should not set this aside to begin with. We have already seen that Socrates could do very different things with what the 'divine sign' told him than, say, a person in an asylum for the insane can do with verbal hallucinations. We shall argue that the reason for this is twofold – first, concepts are constitutive of actions and experiences, and second, some of their meaning is deictic, exactly as some of the meaning of language is.[2] We must therefore be careful about drawing analogies between the present-day 'voice hearing' and apparently similar phenomena located at different points in history. Ian Hacking's recent discussion of the role categories play in acting and of the pitfalls of projecting our own concepts (of, for example, 'abuse' and 'trauma') into the past is relevant (Hacking, 1995).

Our approach here is therefore informed by what Julian Jaynes did; indeed, we think that he had a stimulating insight when he asserted that hallucinatory voices regulate activities. We could not do what we will achieve in this chapter if he had not already identified hallucinations with voices of gods. But our approach will be rather critical, partly because we start from quite different premises about what reflexive consciousness is and what counts as intentional action. We are also fortunate to have to hand techniques of text analysis which were not available to him in the early 1970s.

The chapter will proceed as follows. We shall first briefly critically outline Julian Jaynes' thesis concerning the minds of heroes in the *Iliad* together with some of its scholarly antecedents. Then we examine in detail 'face-to-face' encounters between characters in the *Iliad* (both gods and heroes). The chapter on Socrates focused on the dangers of projecting the concept of hallucination into the past, which seems to have managed perfectly well without it. Inevitably this issue will be revisited here, but the main focus will be on how social activities are regulated in the *Iliad*. We shall analyse in detail the ways 'voices of gods' guide activities of characters in the *Iliad*, but we shall also analyse how the heroes regulate their own and each other's activities. We conclude the chapter by summarising pragmatics of conversations between Achilles and gods, and by considering how well they fit the category 'verbal hallucination'.

Julian Jaynes on gods and voices

Jaynes worked with two broad themes. One was that the heroes of the *Iliad*, who according to him are not just literary characters created by Homer, lacked reflexive consciousness as 'we' understand it. The other was that voices of gods were a substitute for consciousness and guided the actions of heroes instead of it. Homeric heroes were, as Jaynes puts it, 'noble automata'. Let us start with some quotations. Jaynes speaks boldly:

> There is in general no consciousness in the Iliad. . . . And in general therefore, no words for consciousness or mental acts.
>
> (Jaynes, 1976, p. 69)

> There is also no concept of will or word for it, the concept developing curiously late in Greek thought. Thus the Iliadic men have no will of their own and certainly no notion of free will.
>
> (ibid., p. 70)

These are startling claims. Does Jaynes speak too boldly and what should persuade us that Homeric characters lack consciousness? Just the gaps in their lexicons? Jaynes' argument draws heavily on the analysis of the language of the *Iliad* by Bruno Snell (1953). Snell (following earlier analyses of Homer's language, e.g. Keary, 1884) had pointed out that a psychological lexicon is very different in Ancient Greek, in Classical Greek and in present-day languages. Snell argued that 'What we interpret as the soul, is in the Iliad split up into three components each of which he defines by the analogy of physical organs' (Snell, 1953, p. 15). There is not one word for the mind, but several words fill 'the gap': 'psyche' (which gives life), 'thumos' (generator of motion or agitation, organ of emotion) and 'noos' (cause of ideas and images). Snell also pointed out that in Homer there are many words designating seeing which

> derive special significance from a mode of seeing; not from the function of sight, but the object seen, and the sentiments associated with the sight, give the word its peculiar quality . . . there was no one verb to refer to the function of sight as such, but that there were several verbs each designating a specific type of vision.
>
> (ibid., pp. 3–4)

Snell concluded that

> they [the ancient Greeks] took no decisive interest in what we justly regard as the basic function, the objective essence, of sight; and if they had no word for it, it follows that as far as they were concerned it did not exist.
>
> (ibid., p. 5)

Adkins (1970) wrote that Homeric language does not distinguish between the 'material and spiritual' but he accepted that this does not mean that Homer 'reduces mental and spiritual qualities to material ones'.

We have to accept that the language of the *Iliad* does not have the same psychological action words as we find in most current languages (e.g. intention, plan, will). But does this prove, by itself, that the ancient Greeks were incapable of deliberate and planned actions? Can one not will something without having the verb 'to will', plan something without having the verb 'to plan', or grieve for somebody without having this word? Clearly not always – we can do something (for instance, to cover a figure on a canvas with thin translucent white paint) only to be told by a teacher that the action already has a name ('lazuring'), But this seems to have been indeed Snell's and Jaynes' position, very near linguistic determinism and relativism (cf. Whorf, 1956; Sapir, 1957). Linguistic determinism presupposes a distinction in kind between language and thought. It holds (1) that psychological words refer to *internal* thoughts, and (2) that words have formative influence on the thoughts. Linguistic relativism is a logical consequence of the determinism – different vocabularies will result in differently organised thoughts. Of course, the debate is much more involved that this, but this formulation has to suffice here. One strong point of Snell and Jaynes is that as they read the *Iliad*, they have respect for difference. But we hold that they go too far when they conclude, mainly from lexical evidence, that the intentionality of Homer's characters was radically different from our own.

We seem to be in a quandary – we have already argued that meaning of experiences depends on how they are described (conceptualised), but now we do not accept that psychological *words* are necessary for having particular modes of consciousness. But the quandary is only apparent. We do *not* accept that psychological terms correspond and are used to refer to internal mental states. We agree with the Wittgenstein of *Philosophical Investigations* that psychological terms are used to avow experience rather than refer to internal experiences to which one has privileged access. Such avowals can be done without dedicated words, in fact sometimes without words altogether. One can be demonstrably preparing for an action without the word 'plan' being in one's or one's companions' vocabulary. Adkins (1970) pointed out that one-to-one translation of psychological words between English and the *Iliad* is impossible, and that the best strategy to learn their meaning is to study their use in Homer's works. 'Let us explain Homer in no terms but his own, and our understanding of the work will be the fresher for it' (Snell, 1953, p. 1). Precisely, but the argument applies not just to the use of single words but also to how activities are narrated.

Translation is indeed a real problem. It is not simply that one does not understand the words in Ancient Greek, even though that is one problem. English words can be a problem too. When one uses words such as 'will', 'plan' and 'intention', does one use them to refer to inner mental states? Not in everyone's English. This becomes clear when one compares different translations of the *Iliad* – some translators do use words such as 'mind' and 'awareness'. These are not necessarily bad translations; rather what is at play is a different understanding of psychological action terms by different translators.[3]

Having shown to his own satisfaction that the heroes in the *Iliad* lack consciousness to guide their activities in difficult situations, Jaynes' second move was to make gods do this work: 'the Gods take the place of consciousness.' Voices of gods become the real determinants of the actions of heroes:

characters in the Iliad do not sit down and think out what to do. They have no conscious minds such as we say we have and certainly no introspections. *The beginning of actions are not in conscious plans, reasons and motives, they are in actions and speeches of Gods.* To another, a man seems to be a cause of his own behaviour but not to the man himself.

(Jaynes, 1976, p. 72, our emphasis)

Jaynes used, for instance, Agamemnon's argument that it was not himself, but Zeus who caused him to take away from Achilles his prize and lover Chryseis. Agamemnon does indeed say this but what is he really doing? Is he asserting that Zeus was the *only* cause of his action? Or is he passing moral responsibility for his behaviour on to Zeus? Clearly a detailed textual analysis is in order to determine exactly how Homer formulates the influence of the will of Zeus on the activity of Agamemnon. But the problem is not just the inadequate textual analysis but the model of intentional action Jaynes works with.

To understand Snell's and Jaynes' position we must be clear about what they mean by 'consciousness' and its 'reflexivity'. What they do to sustain the premise that the heroes in the *Iliad* have no consciousness and do not act intentionally is to radically disembody and desituate 'will' and 'mind'. They mentalise intentionality and discount any situated conception of it. The version of consciousness which Snell and Jaynes have in mind is something private, interior to the person and self-contained. Jaynes is an unashamed mental solipsist. According to him, 'experience is lonely'; it is 'a secret theatre of speechless monologues ... an invisible mansion of all moods, musings and mysteries' (ibid., p. 1).

Their reflexivity of consciousness is also of a very specific sort, that beloved to analytic philosophers of mind – 'consciousness of consciousness', 'awareness of awareness'. It is not a reflection on one's beliefs, intentions and activities from viewpoints of other individuals or collectives. It is not social reflexivity; it is rather a prim, logical reflexivity, expressed, for example, in postulates of epistemic logic such as 'if I know something, I also know that I know it'. Logical reflexivity is recursive and so it does provide a sort of infinity to mind, but it is not open to the world and it does not really create new contents of consciousness or new perspectives on the old ones. And indeed this sort of reflexive consciousness is what the 'noble automata' of the *Iliad* lack. But then would everyone agree that the consciousness of humans today is as Jaynes and Snell described it – disembodied, desituated and desocialised? Hardly. In Chapter 5 we will discuss in detail social reflexivity of experience and its significance for experiences of hearing voices. But then Jaynes was writing in the 1970s when cognitivism was seen as a distinct advance over the 'arid deserts of behaviourism'. Jaynes is a disappointed but not quite reformed behaviourist (ibid., p. 15). He draws a sharp distinction between consciousness and reactivity:

Reactivity covers all stimuli my behaviour takes account of in any way, while consciousness is something quite distinct and a far less ubiquitous phenomenon.

(Ibid., p. 22)

Consciousness is not to be confused with reactivity. It is not involved in hosts of perceptual phenomena. It is not involved in the performance of skills and often hinders their execution. It need not be involved in speaking, writing, listening or reading. . . . consciousness does not make all that much difference to a lot of our activities.

(Ibid., p. 47)

What is the function of consciousness in Jaynes's account? It is to regulate stimulus-driven behaviours:

Consciousness operates on any reactivity by the way of constructing an analogue space with an analogue 'I' that can observe that space and move metaphorically in it.

(Ibid., p. 65, our emphasis)

Consciousness functions in the decisions as to what to say, how we are to say it, and when we say it, but the orderly and accomplished succession of phonemes or of written letters is somehow done for us.

(Ibid., p. 27)

The problem with Jaynes' account is that as he defines it, nobody would have reflexive consciousness – neither the heroes in the *Iliad* nor contemporary individuals. We shall conclude in Chapter 6 that reflexive consciousness is not solipsistic but socially mediated and situated. It does not surprise us that Jaynes finds that his version of consciousness is absent from most ordinary activities. This is why we have said that Jaynes is only a partly reformed behaviourist. His theory of action is hybrid: some behaviours are automatic, reflexive and environment controlled; other behaviours are intentional, caused by consciousness. We say that actions are intentional even though they do not originate in advance solipsistic meditations (Costall and Leudar, 1996).

Snell (1953) does admit at one point that Homeric characters are capable of reflection. The example he uses is the following. Agamemnon was delighted when Achilles and Odysseus quarrelled. Not because they did, but because he recollected 'Apollo's prophecy that Troy would fall when the best heroes contended with one another. The basis of his joy, therefore, is reflection' (Snell, 1953, p. 12). The reflection here consists specifically in inferring the not immediately apparent significance of action. Snell, however, goes on to argue that this reflection was not 'genuine' (ibid., pp. 28–29). 'Homer does not know genuine personal decisions: even where a hero is shown pondering two alternatives the intervention of gods plays a key note' (ibid., p. 20).

Social action in the *Iliad*

We can now ask whether the characters in the *Iliad* indeed do not premeditate their actions, and can treat this as an *empirical* question. Contrary to Snell, the characters in the *Iliad* do prepare their actions in advance. This involves them in assessing their present situation and talking through possible courses of action and their likely outcomes. As we shall show, the characters can do this without any help from the gods. We focus here on three sorts of narrative Homer uses to portray premeditation of activities by the heroes. The first is when the heroes debate their future actions collectively. The second is when an individual character prepares activities of another character (or characters) by talking to them. The third is when one character prepares his own activity by talking to himself. Our claim is that activities of mortals can have their origins in decisions of other mortals, as well as being instigated by gods.

Let us begin with collective preparations for activity. In Book X Odysseus and Diomedes are on their way to reconnoitre the Trojan camp when they spy one of the enemy, Dolon, on a similar mission.

> King Odysseus saw him coming towards them and said to his companion: 'Here comes a man from the enemy, Diomedes, maybe to spy on our ships, or else to strip some of the corpses – one cannot say which. Shall we let him pass us by and go on a little way? Then we could make a dash and pounce on him. And if he is too fast for us, you must threaten him with your spear and head him off all the time towards the ships and away from the encampment, so that he may not slip through and reach the town.' They decided to do so.
>
> (*Iliad* X: 340–349)

This text turns around inferring the future course of action of the enemy and choosing what to do in response. Odysseus formulates their situation to Diomedes, and in that formulation he proposes possible interpretations of Dolon's actions (is he spying on our ships, or stripping the corpses? – one cannot say which). He also proposes counteractions which are conditional on what Dolon does. The counteractions are both joint (*we* could make a dash and pounce on him) and individual (*you* must threaten him with your spear and head him off all the time towards the ships and away from the encampment). The reason for counteractions is given (so that he may not slip through and reach the town). Is this episode not a clear instance of planning an activity? It certainly is an instance of practical planning according to Leudar and Costall (1996). It does not matter one bit that the planning is done by Odysseus talking aloud to Diomedes rather than mentally; nor does it matter that the verb 'to plan' is not used. Moreover, the important point to notice is the absence of any god in this scene to decide on how the two heroes should act. Situations in which one character proposes how another character should act are common in the *Iliad*. But wait: why are Odysseus and Diomedes on their mission at all? Is it by the will of a god? In fact, they were sent by an 'Assembly'.

The Assembly was a social institution which presupposed the ability to premeditate and reflect on possible actions. Achaeans in the *Iliad* held them regularly to discuss the problems facing them. They often took action, or abstained from action, on the basis of arguments in Assemblies. Odysseus' and Diomedes' mission of reconnaissance was collectively decided in an Assembly. Nestor proposed it and Diomedes, Agamemnon and Odysseus all played active parts in preparing it (*Iliad* X: 203–255). The hand of gods was nowhere obvious in the deliberations – gods played no obvious role in formulating the intent to carry out the mission. The origin of the action was with the heroes themselves. Does this mean, however, that the gods had no part in the mission? Athene witnessed the council but she did not interfere in the discussions. She did send the heroes 'a lucky omen, a heron close to their path on the right', but she only did so when Diomedes and Odysseus were on their way. The heroes also prayed to Athene, and Homer narrates that she heard them, but no answer is indicated (ibid.: 295–299). Athene does participate in the mission, but only when it is in full flow; she gave Diomedes strength 'to make an extra spurt' (ibid.: 402–405), and she filled Diomedes with fury (ibid.: 482). (She also brings the sortie to a close with a warning to Diomedes which we shall consider in some detail below.) So a god did participate in Diomedes' and Odysseus' mission, but not as a planning agent.

It is not just the clever Odysseus who can premeditate actions. Agamemnon (one of the characters who does not encounter gods personally) prepares the activities of his fellow Achaeans. He said the following to Menelaus:

> I wish you now to run quickly by the ships and call Aias and Idomeneus, while I go to the excellent Nestor and tell him to get up. He might well pay a visit to the outposts, which are so important, and keep the sentries up to the mark. They will pay more attention to him than to anyone for his own son and Idomeneus' squire Meriones are in command. We put them in charge of the whole detachment.
>
> (ibid.: 51–57)

Agamemnon proposes a complex activity which coordinates his own, Menelaus' and hopefully Nestor's actions. Menelaus' part of the plan (to wake up Nestor) is specified as a request, Agamemnon's as a commitment. Nevertheless it would be obscure to deny that planning took place just because it was situated and distributed in a social dialogue. The absence of psychological terms is irrelevant. So it is not always the case, contrary to Jaynes, that '*everything* that happens down below is determined by the transaction of the gods with one another' or that 'human initiative has no source of its own; whatever is planned and executed is the plan and deed of the gods' (Jaynes, 1976, p. 29). In fact the characters in the *Iliad* expect each other to act with foresight and its lack is a failure. In Book I, Achilles declares that he will not fight because Agamemnon stole his prize. He criticises Agamemnon for lacking foresight as follows: 'For surely in ruinous heart he makes sacrifice and has not wit enough to look behind and before him that the Achaians fighting beside their ships shall not perish' (*Iliad* I: 342–344).[4] According to Achilles, lacking foresight implies madness, and the phrase Homer uses, 'to look before him', could well have been translated as 'foresight'. So Achilles sees Agamemnon's lack of foresight rather differently from Jaynes – it is a noticeable individual shortcoming of Agamemnon. Where are the 'noble automata'?

The third way the heroes guide their actions in the *Iliad* is through talking to themselves. The characters who do this include Odysseus (*Iliad* IX: 401–439), Hector (*Iliad* XXII: 98–110), Menelaus (*Iliad* XVII: 90–108), Agenor (*Iliad* XXI: 545–549) and Achilles (ibid.: 29–63). The ability is not unique.

In Book IX Odysseus finds himself in the middle of a battle alone and facing several enemies. He does not react by taking to his heels in blind fear, or by battling against Trojan warriors without a thought. He *formulates* his dilemma in talking to himself and he *resolves* it by considering the honour or the lack of it in the alternatives open to him.

> Now Odysseus the spear-famed was left alone, nor did any of the Argives stay beside him, since fear had taken all of them. And troubled, *he spoke then to his own great-hearted spirit*: 'Ah me, what will become of me? It will be a great evil if I run, fearing their multitude, yet deadlier if I am caught alone; and Cronos' son drove to flight the rest of the Danaans. *Yet still, why does the heart within me debate on these things?* Since I know that it is the cowards who walk out of the fighting, but if one is to win honour in battle, he must by all means stand his ground strongly, whether he be struck or strike down another.' While *he was pondering these things in his heart and his spirit* the ranks of armoured Trojans came on against him, and penned him in their midst.
>
> (*Iliad* IX: 401–412, our emphasis)

Odysseus stays to fight the Trojans and kills several of them. The Trojan Sokos wounds him with a spear but 'Athene would not allow it to penetrate his bowels' (ibid.: 434–439).

Talking to his 'thumos' (the 'spirit' in his 'heart') is occasioned by a dilemma – Odysseus is troubled. His dilemma involves two possible alternative courses of action: backing away and fighting against the odds. The dilemma is first presented in Homer's voice and as arising from the situation in which Odysseus found himself. Odysseus himself then formulates it in talking to 'his own great-hearted spirit'. Once he does this the problem dissolves – he says, 'Yet still, why does the heart within me debate on these things?' And he argues through his dilemma with a generalised maxim he knows: 'I know that it is the cowards who walk out of the fighting, but if one is to win honour in battle, he must by all means stand his ground strongly.' According to Renfield (1975), internal dialogue ('mermerizen') in which Odysseus, alone with himself, seeks to discover proper conduct is an internalisation of a social process: Odysseus 'comes to himself' to the degree that he recognises what society expects of him. But we would add that the maxim is very much a part of his persona – without reflecting on his actions in that way, the character would not be Odysseus.

One more thing is important. Odysseus did not need gods to help him in his reasoning. The son of Cronos is mentioned in the monologue but not in helping Odysseus to formulate his problem or to resolve it. Interestingly, Homer did not allow Odysseus to reach a firm decision on how to act in his internal dialogue. The events decide for him: while he is pondering his dilemma Trojans come against him, and he has no choice but to fight.

The construction of privacy in the episodes with inward-directed speech is also interesting. Odysseus happens to be in the midst of a battle but Homer specifically marks the narrative to show that Odysseus talks to himself and not to other characters. He uses speech-reporting devices: after translation, *'he spoke then to his own great-hearted spirit'*, *'Yet still, why does the heart within me debate on these things?'* and *'he was pondering these things in his heart'*. These phrases are always used in the *Iliad* to introduce private speech. In the second example of private monologue Menelaus debates with himself whether to stand up to Hector or retreat:

> *Deeply troubled, he spoke to his own great-hearted spirit*: 'ah me, if I abandon here the magnificent armour and Patroklos, who had fallen here for the sake of my own honour, shall not some of the Danaans, seeing it, hold it against me? Yet if I fight, alone as I am, the Trojans and Hector for shame, shall they not close in, many against one, about me? Hector of the shining helm leads all of the Trojans here. Then *why does my own heart within me debate this?* When a man, in the face of divinity, would fight with another whom some gods honour, the big disaster rolls sudden upon him. Therefore, let no Danaan hold it against me if I give way before Hector who fights from god. Yet if somewhere I could only get some word to Aias of the great war cry, we two might somehow go and keep our spirit of battle even in the face of divinity, if we might win the body for Peleid Achilleus. It would be the best among our evils.' Now as *he was pondering this in his heart and spirit* meanwhile the ranks of Trojans came on and Hector led them; and Menelaos backed away from them and left the dead man.
>
> (*Iliad* XVII: 90–108, our emphasis)

Menelaus basically resorts to the same code of conduct as Odysseus to work through his dilemma. His options – to back away or to fight – are annotated in terms of honour, but he reaches the opposite conclusion to Odysseus. Quitting a fight does not count as dishonourable when the opponent is someone 'whom some gods honour'. Menelaus leans towards quitting the battle, but he also considers the alternative: fighting. But again, as was the case for Odysseus, while he is pondering his dilemma, events resolve his dilemma for him – Hector advances and he 'backs away'. Is his withdrawal the consequence of his decision or a reaction to the Trojan's advance? Homer does not specify, but we would say that both factors play a role – Menelaus' withdrawal is a matter of both his decision and the situation. Renfield's analysis is also pertinent here – Menelaus' reasoning is grounded in the accepted code of conduct. Menelaus assesses his own actions as his fellows might. His reasoning is clearly socially reflexive with the mirror provided by a generalised 'Danaan' (cf. 'let no Danaan hold it against me' etc.).

How do the gods figure in the episode? Certainly not as planning agents who dictate how Menelaus should act. In the next example of the inner debate a god – Apollo – is actually present. He gives courage to Agenor (who is a Trojan) and stands beside him in person:

When Agenor was aware of Achilleus, sacker of cities, he stood fast, but his heart was a storm in him as he waited, and deeply disturbed *he spoke to his own great-hearted spirit*: 'Ah me! if I run away before the strength of Achilleus in the way that others are stampeded in terror before him he will catch me even so and cut my throat like a coward's. But if I leave these men to be driven in flight by Achilleus, Peleus' son, and run on my feet in another direction away from the wall to the plain of Ilion, until I come to the spurs of Ida, and take a cover there within the undergrowth, then in the evening, when I have bathed in the river, and washed off the sweat, I could make my way back again to Ilion. Yet still, *why does the heart within me debate on these things?* This way he might see me as I started from the plain to the city, and go in pursuit, and in the speed of his feet overtake me. Then there will be no way to escape him and the death spirits. He is too strong, his strength is beyond all others. But then if I go out in front of the city and stand fast against him, I think even his body might be torn by sharp bronze.

(*Iliad* XXI: 550–568, our emphasis)

Agenor vacillates between fighting and running, and weighs the consequences bearing in mind what Achilles might see him doing, and do himself. He assesses his own actions from the point of view of his enemy. In the event he does stand up to Achilles. He strikes him with his spear 'in the leg below the knee'. Even so, he would perish in the counter-attack of Achilles but Apollo saves him (ibid.: 545–549). Thus Apollo affects the episode by encouraging Agenor, and he determines the final outcome. But – and this is important – the decision to stand up to Achilles is Agenor's.

The final episode of 'inward debate' we shall consider involves Hector. The point to notice is that he reflects on his possible actions from the point of view of a specific absent fellow Trojan, Polydamas.

Deeply troubled *he spoke to his own great-hearted spirit*. 'Ah me! If I go now inside the wall and the gateway, *Polydamas will be first to put reproach upon me*, since he tried to make me lead the Trojans inside the city on that accursed night when brilliant Achilleus rose up, and I would not obey him, but that would have been far better. Now, since by my own recklessness I have ruined my own people, I feel shame before the Trojans and the Trojan women with trailing robes, that someone who is less of a man than I will say of me: "Hector believed in his own strength and ruined his people." Thus they will speak; and as for me, it would be much better at that time, to go against Achilleus, and slay him, and come back, or else be killed by him in glory in front of the city.'

(*Iliad* XXII: 98–110, our emphasis)

Hector also considers going out to face Achilles, without his weapons, to promise to give Helen back and all the wealth of the city. But he points out to himself that 'I might go to him, and he take no pity on me nor respect my position, but kill me naked so, as if I were a woman, once I stripped my armour from me' (ibid.: 123–125).

Does Hector himself actually decide to stand up to Achilles? Yes – the inward debate ends with him saying, 'Better to bring on the fight with him as soon as it may be' (ibid.: 129). Yet he realises that the *outcome* of the fight is in the hands of Zeus: 'We shall see to which one the Olympian grants the glory' (ibid.). So a god does plays a role in the event as a determinant of the outcome but not in formulating the intention to act. But the intent to fight Achilles does not in the event determine what Hector does:

> So he pondered, waiting, but Achilleus was closing upon him in the likeness of the lord of battles, the helm-shining warrior, and shaking from above his shoulder the dangerous Pelian ash spear, while the bronze that closed about him was shining like the flare of blazing fire or the sun in its rising. *And shivers took hold of Hector when he saw him, and he could no longer stand his ground there*, but left the gates behind, and fled, frightened, and Peleus' son went after him in the confidence of his quick feet.
>
> (Ibid.: 136–138, our emphasis)

Fear takes over his body despite his courageous intent. The flight and the chase carry on for some time and the gods on the Olympus debate whether 'to rescue this man or whether to make him, for all his valour, go down under the hands of Achilles' (ibid.: 175–176). Their decision is that Hector will die. But even though the *outcome* of the episode – the tragic fate of Hector – is in the hands of the gods, since Hector himself reflects on his actions he has intentionality of his own. We cannot argue the lack of (illocutionary) intent from the lack of control over (perlocutionary) outcome. This is precisely where Feyerabend goes wrong when he argues that actions of Homeric heroes are governed solely by fate, not by decision and will (Feyerabend, 1978, pp. 244–245; Feyerabend, 1987, p. 97). After all, it does not matter whether it is a god, the fate or the laws of nature which hinder us or make our actions possible – the intentionality is sensible (or otherwise) with respect to one or the other.

So at least some individual actions in the *Iliad* are not directly caused by gods, and the heroes' deeds can be their own. But perhaps the events which are narratively crucial to the *Iliad* are always caused by gods? Snell claimed this, when comparing the *Iliad* and the *Odyssey*: 'the two poems are at one in the credit given to the gods whenever some extraordinary performance is at stake' (Snell, 1953, p. 33). But we hope that readers will by now accept that the episodes we recounted so far are crucial to the story of the *Iliad*, yet the gods did not take part in formulating the intentions of the heroes. It is clear that the heroes plan their actions, individually and collectively. There is nothing in how they do this which is alien in the twentieth century. This of course does not mean that gods never guide the actions of the heroes. The aim of the next part of this chapter is to summarise how they do it. The main point will be to see whether such guidance has the same grounds as that by mortals.

The gods and heroes in the *Iliad*

Throughout the *Iliad*, gods affect the ordinary world of heroes in a manner they themselves cannot. For instance, Zeus sends a flash of lightning down among Achaean troops and stuns and terrifies them (*Iliad* VIII: 73–77). Phoebus Apollo comes down 'in fury from the height of Olympus', his descent 'like a nightfall' (*Iliad* I: 43). The heroes themselves realise that gods can affect the world – it is not just the narrator who tells the readers. Phoenix the old charioteer, for instance, claims that he was made infertile by Zeus at the curse of his father (*Iliad* IX: 455–457). Gods can also affect directly, and without the aid of words, the activities of heroes. First, as we have seen already, gods can affect *outcomes* of heroes' intentional actions by affecting the world. In Book IV the Trojan Pandaros shoots at Menelaus. The arrow pierces Menelaus' belt and injures him slightly. According to Homer, Athene deflected the arrow from the flesh and into Menelaus' belt. (Menelaus though had a more ordinary explanation – the metal of his belt stopped the arrow (*Iliad* IV: 112–187)). Second, gods can provide heroes with daring, courage and stamina. We have already seen how Athene filled Diomedes with fury, and gave him strength. (But gods are not the only characters who can do this – men can too. For instance, Hector rouses his men (*Iliad* XI: 289) and Agamemnon's battle fury 'inspires his men' (ibid.: 161–163). Third, gods can determine the actions of heroes by directly affecting their thoughts. Hera 'inserts thoughts' into Agamemnon's head:

> the whole enclosure between ships and the trench by the wall was filled with a medley of chariots and armed men, penned in like sheep by that peer of the impetuous War-god, Hector son of Priam, now that Zeus had given him the upper hand. Indeed he would have had the trim ships alight and going up in flames, *if the Lady Hera had not put it into Agamemnon's head to bestir himself and rally Achaians* before it was too late. . . . 'For shame, Argives,' he cried, 'contemptible creatures, splendid only on parade! What has become of our assurance that we were the finest force on earth.'
>
> (*Iliad* VIII: 249, our emphasis)

Hera does not talk to Agamemnon, she puts an idea into his head (which he then uses almost verbatim to berate the Argives). So the direct divine influences in the *Iliad* set the heroes and gods apart. Such powers of gods are, as we shall see, one reason why the heroes listen to gods.

But the gods also affect heroes by talking. There are many questions we can ask about their encounters. What sorts of things do gods and heroes say to each other, and do the heroes react to the gods' commands as 'automata' or do they obey them for reasons of their own? Can heroes disobey gods? Interestingly, only certain characters in the *Iliad* actually come 'face to face' with gods. They tend to be the heroes, but not all of them: gods never speak to Agamemnon. (But then, is Agamemnon a hero in the *Iliad*?)

Let us first consider how in the *Iliad* a mortal knows that he is speaking to a god.[5] Sometimes there is no problem because the god identifies himself (Apollo does this to Achilles (*Iliad* XXII: 6–10)). But often heroes do not know the gods, the problem being that gods often take the form of mortals. In Book XIII, Poseidon, grieved by the death of his grandson, accosts Idomeneus, who does not know him as Poseidon. This is because Poseidon 'likened his voice to Thoas, son of Andraimon' (*Iliad* XIII: 209–231). The readers, however, know it is really Poseidon because Homer tells them.

Mortals may come to realise that they have spoken to a god only when the encounter is over. Earlier in Book XIII we were told by Homer that Poseidon borrowed 'the form and tireless voice of Calchas' (the seer of the Greek expedition), spoke to two Aiantes and filled them with 'dauntless resolution' (ibid.: 46–62). The eventual recognition of Poseidon proceeded as follows:

> Of the two Aiantes, it was Oileus' son, the Runner, who first knew him for a god. Turning at once to the son of Telamon he said: 'Aias, it was one of the gods that live on Olympus who urged us just now to fight by the ships. He took the prophet's form, but he was not Calchas, our seer and diviner.
>
> (*Iliad* VIII: 46–62)

How did Oileus' son realise that Calchas was really Poseidon?

> 'His heels and the backs of his knees as he left us were proof enough for me – it is not hard to recognise a god. Not only that, but I feel a change in my own heart. I am twice as eager as I was for the fight. My feet and hands are itching to be at them.' 'I feel the same,' said Telamonian Aias.
>
> (Ibid.: 46–62)

The interaction between Poseidon and the two heroes is narrated as an interaction with another human being, and only subsequently does 'Calchas' become a god for the heroes, and even then he is not specifically Poseidon.

The examples so far indicate that gods can be recognised by their appearance – Athene has flashing eyes, Hera has white arms. Sometimes, but less often, gods can also be recognised from their voices. Diomedes, in the reconnaissance episode already partly recounted, 'knew the voice of the goddess speaking' (*Iliad* X: 512). Sometimes the bases of recognition may seem distinctly odd. What can it be about the heels and the backs of knees that is godlike? In any case there are two points to notice and keep in mind: one is that the recognition of a god is not always immediate – sometimes it seems a matter of *post hoc* inference; and the other is that the heroes do not create new personifications – they recognise divinities as established gods with known alignments in the conflict and established dispositions.

Let us next consider the patterns of the participant positioning in dialogues of gods and mortals. There seem to be two basic regularities. First, gods talk to heroes individually, even when other mortals are present. Second, the talk between gods themselves is never actually witnessed by the mortals. In Book V Diomedes is injured and asks Athene for help to continue the fight:

Now Diomedes of the great war cry spoke aloud, praying: 'Hear me now, Atryone, daughter of Zeus of the aegis: if ever before in kindliness you stood by my father through the terror of fighting, be my friend now also, Athene; grant me that I may kill this man and come within spearcast, who shot me before I could see him, and now boasts over me, saying I cannot live to look much longer on the shining sunlight.'

So he spoke in prayer, and Pallas Athene heard him. She made his limbs light again, and his feet, and his hands above them, and *standing close beside him she spoke and addressed him in winged words*:

'Be of good courage now, Diomedes, to fight with the Trojans, since I have put inside your chest the strength of your father. . . . Therefore now, if a god making trial of you comes hither do you not battle head on with the gods immortal, not with the rest; but only if Aphrodite, Zeus' daughter comes to the fighting, her at least you may stab with the sharp bronze.' *She spoke thus, grey-eyed Athene, and went while Tydeus's son closed once again with the champions.*

(*Iliad* V: 114–134, our emphasis)

Homer draws this dialogue away from the battle – only Diomedes and Athene take part in it, and when it ends Diomedes has to 'close again with the champions'. But what distanced Diomedes from the battle in the first place? Was it not the dialogue with the goddess? Similarly, at the close of the reconnaissance episode which involves both Odysseus and Diomedes, Athene does not address both of them but only Diomedes. She warns him to retreat (*Iliad* X: 503–514). This happens as follows:

But he waited, divided in his mind as to what he would best do, whether to seize a chariot, wherein lay the bright armour, and draw it away by the pole, or lift it and carry it off with him, or strip the life from still more Thracians. Meanwhile as he was pondering all this in this heart, Athene came and stood beside him, and spoke to great Diomedes.

(Ibid.: 503–508)

Thus god–mortal dialogues are similar to the inward-directed speech of the heroes – they are set apart from the fury of the battle. The one-to-one god–hero engagement is very much like that between Socrates and his daemon. His companions never co-experienced the daemon with him. This, by the way, means that talking to gods in the *Iliad* satisfies one condition for counting as a hallucination – it is typically an individual experience.

We have, however, already encountered some exceptions to our generalisation. First, gods may fill many heroes with strength all at once – the goddess Strife does this when she puts strength into the Achaeans with 'a great cry and terrible and loud'. Second, Poseidon addressed two Aiantes (*Iliad*: 46–62). He did this as Calchas, and the heroes did not know he was a god when he spoke to them. The pattern is the same in the following episode:

Hera shouted, likening herself to high-hearted, bronze-voiced Stentor, who would cry out in as great a voice as fifty other men: 'Shame on you Argives, poor nonentities splendid to look on. In those days when brilliant Achilleus came into fighting, never would the Trojans go beyond Dardanian gates, so much did they dread the heavy spear of that man. Now they fight by the hollow ships and far from the city.' So she spoke, and stirred the spirit and strength in each man.

(Iliad V: 784–792)

Hera speaks to many Argives at the same time, but – and this is important – *as a mortal*. Athene addresses Diomedes individually in the next paragraph of the *Iliad*. She abuses him and compares him negatively with his father for not fighting. Diomedes responds to her, saying, 'daughter of Zeus who holds the aegis, goddess, I know you, and therefore will speak confidently to you and hide nothing' (ibid.: 814–816). So Diomedes knows Athene for who she is as he speaks to her, and the dialogue is one-to-one, no witnesses. So our previous generalisation needs to be qualified: gods never *talk* to more than one hero at a time *as gods*.

The second feature of participant positioning in the *Iliad* is that god-to-god dialogues are never directly witnessed by heroes. Book V contains the following engagement between Athene and Ares.

But grey-eyed Athene took violent Ares by the hand, and in words she spoke to him: 'Ares, Ares, manslaughtering, blood-stained, stormer of strong walls, shall we not leave the Trojans and Achaians to struggle after whatever way Zeus grants the glory to either, while we two give ground together and avoid Zeus's anger?'

(Ibid.: 29–34)

This was said in the middle of a battle with mortals present, yet Homer does not indicate that the gods were or could be overheard. Similarly in Book VII, Athene and Apollo face each other from different sides in the war and decide 'to stop the fighting for the moment':

'We could rouse the fighting spirit in horse-taming Hector and make him challenge one of the Danaans to mortal combat. The bronze-clad Achaians would be on their mettle and put up a champion to fight a duel with Prince Hector.' This was Apollo's plan, and Athene made no demur.

(Iliad VII: 37–42)

The plan is brought to fruition through Priam's son, Helenus. Homer, however, does not allow Helenus to overhear the discourse between the two gods; instead 'he is able to *divine* what the gods have agreed to do' (ibid.: 44–45). The discourse between gods is thus self-enclosed and only accessible to themselves and to the readers through the narrators.

How do heroes know what the gods say to each other? The discourse between gods is reported by proxies – Iris, for instance, speaks for Zeus and so does Thetis. Gods, though, can see the deeds of Greeks and listen to their arguments. We have seen already that they can hear prayer, but not just prayers – 'And when he [Agamemnon] looked at the ships and his own army, he plucked the hair from his head by the roots for Zeus in heaven to see' (*Iliad* X: 0–33). The gods can see and hear heroes whether or not they are invited. In Book VIII Hector addresses his men boastfully, instigating a sortie:

> Follow close now and be rapid, so we may capture the shield of Nestor, whose high fame goes up to the sky now, how it is all of gold, the shield itself and the cross-rods; and strip from the shoulders of Diomedes, breaker of horses, the elaborate corselet that Haphaistos wrought with much toil. Could we capture these two things, I might hope the Achaians might embark this very night on their fast-running vessels.
>
> (*Iliad* VIII: 191–197)

Without explaining how it is possible, Homer allows Hera to overhear Hector's 'vainglorious' tone from Olympus. Gods can even eavesdrop on god–mortal encounters: Apollo witnessed the above dialogue between Athene and Diomedes (*Iliad* X: 515–520).

To summarise, the typical dialogue involves a single hero with a single god. They may be overheard by another god but not by a mortal. Zeus never speaks directly to mortals but only through proxies. Gods do not speak to many mortals directly at the same time, but mortals can act as proxies for gods and speak for them. The god/hero participant positioning is asymmetric – gods have access to what Greeks do and say, but Greeks cannot see or hear gods together. (The episode in which Paris encounters three goddesses is not a part of the *Iliad*.)

Finally, what do gods do with words and why do the heroes believe them and obey them? If we think about all the god/hero dialogues we have considered so far, in each of them, whatever else may have happened, a god guided the actions of a hero. A god stopped a hero from carrying out an action or he suggested an alternative course of action, and sometimes both. In dialogical terms gods instructed heroes, warned them, encouraged them. Often the guidance is indirect and achieved by judging, mocking and scolding. What interests us at this point is the grounds on which the gods' 'regulatives' work. Achilles disobeys his king Agamemnon – why should he obey Apollo? Let us first reconsider the episode in which Poseidon – in the form of Calchas – 'accosted the two Aiantes, whom he found in little need of exhortation'. The dialogue began with Poseidon/Calchas assessing the state of the battle:

> My lords, you two can save the Achaian army if you keep your courage high, and entertain no craven thoughts of panic. The Trojans have climbed the great wall in force, but irresistible as they seem, I am not concerned for the rest of the front where the bronze clad Achaians will hold them all in

check. It is here that I dread disaster, where that madman Hector, who pretends that his father was almighty Zeus, is storming in their van like a raging fire.

(*Iliad* XIII: 48–56)

This sort of assessment is familiar – it could have been spoken in an inward-directed monologue or at an Assembly. Poseidon/Calchas then exhorts the Aiantes to stand up to Hector and to rally the Achaeans with these words:

If some god could only make you see that this is the place for you two to stand fast and rally the rest, you might yet fend him off from the gallant ships, for all his fury.

(Ibid.: 56–58)

The formulation of the exhortation is interesting: it is as if Calchas himself had no authority to guide the heroes, but a god could. Calchas, even though he is a prophet, cannot say what will happen if Aiantes stands up to Hector, but a god with superior knowledge could. Once the heroes recognise that it was not their prophet Calchas but Poseidon who spoke to them, they obey. Their obedience is not mechanical but intentional, and it consists in accepting the guidance of a god:

'I feel the same,' said Telemonian Aias. 'My mighty hands are itching on my spear; my spirit is roused; and my feet are dancing off. Single-handed I should be happy to meet Hector son of Priam in his fury.'

(Ibid.: 76–79)

The difference from the grounding of the inward-directed talk is that the actions are not warranted, at least in this episode, with respect to Achaean moral code. Instead, the reason for accepting the guidance is the superior power and knowledge of Poseidon – the Aiantes might not have obeyed Calchas. We shall find the same authoritative backing of directives in interactions between gods and Achilles.

We have found that the gods tend to engage individual heroes, and only some of them. This does not mean that the heroes keep their experiences of gods private. On the contrary, unlike contemporary verbal hallucinations, encounters with gods are a privilege, and what a god says is typically used by a hero in social argumentations. The relevance of it is *never* doubted, although the advice of gods can occasionally be disbelieved and not seen as wise (as Priam's wife Hekabe does in Book XXIV: 200–216). The words of gods are regularly used to warrant and account for actions. In Book XVII, for instance, Apollo in the form of Periphas, Epytos' son, reproaches Aineias and Trojans with a lack of confidence, and says:

Aineias, how could you be the men to defend sheer Ilion even against a god's will, as I have seen other men do it in the confidence of their own force and strength, their own manhood and their own numbers, though they had too few people for it? But now Zeus wishes the victory far rather for our side than the Danaans', only yourself keep blenching and will not fight them.

(*Iliad* XVII: 327–332)

Aineias does not keep this 'experience' to himself but calls 'in a great voice' to Hector:

Hector, and you other lords of the Trojans and their companions, here is a shameful thing! We are climbing back into Ilion's wall, subdued by terror before the warlike Achaians. Yet see, some one of the gods is standing beside me, and tells me that Zeus the supreme councellor lends his weight to our fighting. Therefore we must go straight for the Danaans.

(Ibid.: 335–340)

Aineias does not just repeat what Apollo has told him, he uses it freely to warrant an activity – 'we must go straight for the Danaans', he says, and Trojans accept the reasoning. This is very different from what would happen if a schizophrenic asked others to do as his voice advised. The actions in the *Iliad* can be accounted for in terms of guidance by gods, and unlike Agamemnon's lack of foresight, being guided by gods is not a sign of madness. So conversations with gods are private experiences, which are, however, valid in making claims, warranting and providing accounts of activities. Hearing gods is a thoroughly socialised experience which is relevant to context and usable in public argumentation. This is not what auditory and verbal hallucinations are like nowadays.

The voices of Achilles

We now turn to Achilles to see whether it can be sensibly claimed that he was really a voice hearer, bound to follow the gods' orders as an automaton. Homer has him interacting face to face with five deities: Thetis, his mother (four episodes, Book I: 348–429, Book XVIII: 35–135, Book XIX: 3–41, Book XXIV: 21–140), Athene (two episodes, Book I: 188–221, Book XXII: 215–217), Iris (one episode, Book XVIII: 166–217), Apollo (one episode, Book XXII: 6–20) and River (one episode, Book XXI: 211–227). (He also encounters his dead friend Patroclus once, but only in a dream.) We have used the ten episodes in our analysis even though we do not report them all.

Let us start by assuming that what these gods say to Achilles is indeed his hallucinations, but then focus on how it differs from hallucinations nowadays. Perhaps these differences will be so great as to disallow the categorisation. The first important point to bear in mind is that these experiences concern established deities. The five gods whom Achilles encounters have crystallised identities; they are known to every mortal in the *Iliad*, as is their stance in the Trojan war. (Unlike Socrates, Achilles cannot be accused of introducing new deities.) The fact that gods have publicly known dispositions and powers is crucial: it enables others to treat their experience as socially relevant rather than idiosyncratic.

In Book I of the *Iliad* Agamemnon threatens Achilles that he shall 'take the fair cheeked Bryseis' so that Achilles may 'learn well how much greater I am than you' (the *Iliad* I: 184–186). 'Anger comes on Peleus' son Achilles' and:

> within his shaggy breast the heart was divided two ways, pondering whether to draw from beside his thigh the sharp sword, driving away all those who stood between and kill the son of Atreus, or else to check the spleen and keep down his anger. Now as he weighed in mind and spirit these two courses and was drawing from its scabbard the great sword, Athene descended from the sky.
>
> (Ibid.: 188–195)

Achilles is considering two courses of action and he has almost decided to act on his anger and to kill Agamemnon. This is where Athene intervenes, and she does this in character as an ally of the Greeks. The encounter is occasioned by Achilles' anger, a quandary and a moment of decision. But in what sense is it a hallucination of Achilles? The point is that it takes place in the middle of an Assembly with many Achaeans present. They do not witness it, however, and only Achilles is aware of Athene. Homer simply stipulates privacy: 'The goddess standing behind Peleus' son caught him by the fair hair, *appearing to him only, for no man of the others saw her*' (ibid.: 188–221, our emphasis). So the experience satisfies the privacy criterion of hallucination.

But how does Achilles know that he is talking to Athena? He has no problem recognising her by her 'terrible shining eyes'. This means that Athene is not just an auditory experience – she touches him, he sees her, and then he hears her. If she is a hallucination she is not just an auditory one, or just a verbal one either. She comes in all sensory modalities (as do the mortals). In this sense Athena is very unlike the present-day hallucinations, which do not typically happen concurrently in several *coordinated* modalities, and remember that Socrates' daemon was definitely a voice only.

We have seen in Chapter 1 that Plutarch was concerned with how the divine voice could reach only Socrates but not others around him at the time. Contemporary cognitive psychologists are concerned with the same problem, they just solve it differently by saying, 'He did not perceive a real stimulus, he hallucinated.' Homer's characters, however, evidence no such puzzlement – talking with gods is simply talking. No extraordinary channel of communication is indicated by Homer (see n. 5), and the concept of hallucination is not needed. Hallucinations are defined as false perceptions, but the characters in the *Iliad* see nothing false about hearing gods; on the contrary.

Let us continue the analysis of the encounter between Achilles and Athene. Once she is present, Achilles greets her with a threat to Agamemnon:

> He uttered winged words and addressed her: 'Why have you come now, oh child of Zeus of aegis, once more? Is it that you may see the outrageousness

of the son of Atreus Agamemnon? Yet will I tell you this thing – and I think it will be accomplished. By such act of arrogance he may even lose his own life.

(Ibid.: 201–222)

At the start of this episode Athene stayed Achilles' hand by holding him. But she immobilised him only temporarily. She did not *force* him to spare Agamemnon, even though she said that was her aim. She aligned herself with one option which Achilles was already pondering – 'to check the spleen and keep down his anger'. But she wonders whether he will obey her:

> Then in answer the goddess grey-eyed Athene spoke to him: 'I have come down to stay your anger – *but will you obey me?* – from the sky; and the goddess of the white arms Hera sent me, who loves both of you equally in her heart and cares for you.

(Ibid., our emphasis)

In effect she offers Achilles a choice – he can act on his fury or do as she advises: 'Come then, and do not take your sword in your hand, keep clear of fighting, though indeed with words you may abuse him, and it will be that way' (ibid.).[6]

But on what grounds is she to be obeyed? In this instance she appeals to material self-interest:[7]

> And this also I will tell you and it will be a thing accomplished. Some day three times three times over such shining gifts shall be given you by reason of this outrage. Hold your hand, then, and obey us.

(Ibid.)

Why does Achilles actually obey her? He acknowledges that mortals can act against the gods' will, but declares this unwise because he wants to keep the gods on his side (ibid.). But his obedience is reasoned, not an impulsion – gods do not move his body like that of a puppet. Disobedience is possible and Achilles can indeed be in conflict with the gods. In Book XXII: 6–13, for instance, Achilles attacks Apollo. Apollo has to identify himself to Achilles and points out to him the foolishness of attacking an immortal god. Once Achilles knows the god he desists from pursuing him, but not without expressing his anger:

> Deeply vexed Achilleus of the swift feet spoke to him: 'You have balked me, striker from afar, most malignant of gods, when you turned me here away from the rampart, else many Trojans would have caught the soil in their teeth before they go back to Ilion. Now you have robbed me of great glory, and rescued these people lightly, since you have no retribution to fear hereafter. Else I would punish you, if only the strength were in me.

(*Iliad* XXII: 14–24)

Achilles acknowledges the power of Apollo to affect his actions, and the reason he does not press his attack is that he lacks the strength to punish the god – he does not lack the will.

But do the gods exercise their powers arbitrarily? The following example demonstrates that this is not so. In Book XXIV Zeus sends Thetis with this message to Achilles:

> Tell him that gods frown on him, that beyond all other immortals I am angered that in his heart's madness he holds Hector beside the curved ships and did not give him back. Perhaps in fear of me he will give back Hector. Then I will send Iris to Priam of the great heart, with an order to ransom his dear son, going down to the ships of the Achaians and bringing gifts to Achilleus which might soften his anger.
>
> (*Iliad* XXIV: 22–121)

Zeus expects Achilles to obey him because of his anger. But why is Zeus angry? The reasons he gives are that Achilles abused the body of Hector and is refusing to ransom the body, and this violates the heroic code of honour. So the authority of gods is not exercised arbitrarily here – it backs the human code of honour.

The actions of Achilles are not regulated by gods only. One common influence is that of other mortals and in fact much of the *Iliad* is about how his fellows try to bring Achilles to his senses. Another means of activity regulation, as we have already seen, is through inward-directed speech. One instance of Achilles in an inward-directed debate is in Book XXI.

> Now as brilliant swift-footed Achilleus saw him [Lykaon] and knew him naked and without helm or shield, and he had no spear left but had thrown all these things on the ground, being weary and sweating with the escape from the river, and his knees were beaten with weariness, disturbed, Achilleus spoke to his own great-hearted spirit: 'Can this be? Here is a strange thing that my eyes look on. Now the great-hearted Trojans, even those I have killed already, will stand and rise up again out of the gloom and the darkness as this man has come back and escaped the date without pity though he was sold into sacred Lemnos; but the main of the grey sea could not hold him, though it holds back many who are unwilling. But come now, he must be given a taste of our spearhead so that I may know inside my heart and make certain whether he will come back even from there, or the prospering earth will hold him, she who holds back even the strong man.
>
> (*Iliad* XXI: 29–63)

Note that in talking to himself Achilles formulates his puzzlement and reasons a course of action. Like Odysseus, Agenor, Menelaus, Hector and Agamemnon, Achilles is capable of thinking through problematic situations and preparing his actions in talking to himself. Hardly a 'noble automaton'. Being guided by gods, by oneself and by others are not mutually exclusive.

Bowra (1930) also noted that Achilles is capable of reflection and self-reflection. His evidence was that Achilles accepted that he was to blame for Patroclus' death. He knew his quarrelsomeness and anger were the causes. 'He found pleasure in them but now wishes they never existed.' Achilles violates conventions of chivalry and divine ordinances and this is brought home to him by his fellows and by gods. He is capable of guilt but the guilt does not cure him of his anger, nor does it stop him from deeds which Homer condemns as 'shameless'. Homer has Apollo say that he has lost his wits and raves like a lion; he has lost pity and has no truth. The lack of reflexivity reduces Achilles to an animal, if only in a simile.

More recently, Zanker (1994) argued that the behaviour of Homeric characters is not motivated simply by the pursuit of honour (as Adkins had argued) and, for instance, that a sense of empathy motivates Achilles when Priam supplicates for the body of his son. It is empathy, not honour, which motivates the killer to return Hector's body. Zanker asked pertinently what Homeric heroes admire in each other's conduct and what they deplore. What are the grounds of their generosity and are these the same as ours, or different?[8] Agamemnon, for instance, experiences recrimination, thinking of his brother's possible death. He imagines his bones rotting in the earth, and a Trojan boasting that he abandoned him (*Iliad* IV: 155–82). His reaction to himself is mediated by the image of other people's reactions to him, and both of these are recognisable to us. In Chapter 5 we shall see that, according to William James and G.H. Mead, this is an essential characteristic of modern self.

We have seen in the third section of this chapter that the participant positioning in god–mortal encounters was constrained. What are Achilles' encounters with gods like in this respect? In Book I Agamemnon takes Briseis away from Achilles (*Iliad* I: 345–349) and Achilles is shattered:

> Many times stretching forth his hands *he called on his mother*: 'Since, my mother, you bore me to be a man with a short life therefore Zeus of the loud thunder on Olympus should grant me honour at least.'
>
> (Ibid.: 348–356, our emphasis)

So Achilles can initiate dialogues with his mother Thetis (who, in the *Iliad* I: 360–363, hears him 'in the depths of the sea'), but at another time she comes to him uncalled (Book XVIII: 34–36). In fact in most episodes gods address Achilles of their own volition – they come to him in moments of strong emotion and indecision. We have seen that Socrates did not call his daemon; it came to him, he listened and acted on its guidance. Unlike Socrates, Achilles can sometimes initiate interactions with the mother-goddess.

There are other constraints on participant positioning in Achilles' encounters with gods. First, he and Zeus never actually talk to each other directly; their interactions are always mediated by proxies (usually Thetis or the messenger Iris). Second, even though gods debate the merit or the shame of his conduct, Achilles is never a party to these conversations.[9] In Book XXIV, for instance, Apollo and

Hera, on Olympus out of mortal sight or hearing, discuss the shame of Achilles not releasing the slaughtered body of Hector. Zeus arbitrates between them and decides what is to be done. Eventually he sends Thetis with a message to Achilles.

So is Achilles a 'voice hearer'? There are some similarities, but also some differences. The experiences are private like hallucinations, and their pragmatics are focused on regulating his actions. But he is clearly not simply a voice hearer – his 'hallucinations' are in multiple sensory modalities. The grounds of regulation can be the moral code, as in inward debates, but the influences are usually conditional on the authority of gods and their divine powers (we cannot say 'supernatural powers' – gods are not opposed to nature in the *Iliad*). There is thus an element of compulsion in the commands of the gods – but no mechanical impulsion.

The main difference between the gods of the *Iliad* and the hallucinatory voices is a social one. Achilles talks to the gods and this marks him in the *Iliad* as a hero, whereas a person with schizophrenia *has* verbal hallucinations and they are symptoms of his illness devoid of reasonable content. The different social positioning of the experiences determines what one can do with them, even though they are similar in other respects. The gods of Achilles are aspects of Achaean moral and natural order – he could use their pronouncements publicly to guide his actions and to justify them to others. Socrates could also do this, but his problem was that the daemon was not a recognised deity in Athens. Contemporary voice hearers, however, cannot use voices in ordinary public discourses, as we shall see later in the book. Using the distinction of Brierre de Boismont (1861b), if hearing voices of gods by Achilles is to count as hallucinating, then the hallucinations must be of the kind that is consistent with reason at the time, not a sign of insanity. If Achilles were an actual historical person and not a character in a poem, could he accept that the gods he heard were hallucinations; that is, 'perceptions in absence of an appropriate stimulus'? Like Socrates he could not do this – categorising his experiences in this way would mean denying the existence and powers of the gods, but these were one pillar of his and his fellows' worldview.

3   The souls of Daniel Paul Schreber

Daniel Paul Schreber was an eminent German judge from a good family who first went insane in 1884 at the age of 42. He was placed under 'tutelage' at the request of his wife Sabine in November 1894, and this decision was confirmed in March 1900 (Lothane, 1992, p. 56). A tutelage order used to be taken out in Germany to protect an individual from the effects of his or her actions. These included managing one's estate unwisely and conducting oneself so as to lose face. But, as Senatspräsident Schreber himself explained, the actions harmful to other people remained a matter for 'organs of security police', and so a 'tutelage' was not quite the same as a 'section order' is now. The reason Schreber was subjected to tutelage was that, according to his psychiatrist Dr Weber, as a person influenced by 'hallucinations and delusions' he was 'no longer master of his own free will' (Schreber, 1903/1955, p. 475). Schreber appealed against the order, and as a part of his defence he wrote *Memoirs of my Nervous Illness*, using the notes he kept during his illness. The notes are not available but the memoirs were published in 1903 and translated into English by Macalpine and Hunter in 1955, and Schreber became the most frequently quoted patient in psychiatry (Schatzman, 1976). Bleuler (who was not Schreber's psychiatrist) used the *Memoirs* in his *Dementia Praecox* (Bleuler, 1911/1966, 1924/1951). Freud (1911/1972) used them to illustrate his account of psychosis (*Dementia Paranoides*). Klein (1975) and Fairburn (1956/1994) both put Schreber's case to use in their polemics with other psychoanalysts. The interest in Schreber is continuing (e.g. Lothane, 1992; Sass, 1992, 1994; Santner, 1996).

The point of this chapter is not to provide yet another analysis of what was really wrong with Schreber. We will summarise the pragmatic profile of his voices, as we have done for Socrates and Achilles, and we do this as a step in our investigation of experiences of hearing voices in different historical contexts, but our main aim is to use the *Memoirs* to analyse the friction between Schreber's perspective on voices and that of his clinicians. The fact is that the opponents in the Dresden court understood 'voices' in very different ways. For psychiatrists they were perceptual hallucination and symptoms of insanity, for Schreber they were voices of supernatural agencies.

Most psychiatrists see the 'voices' as symptoms to be suppressed – like coughs, aches and measles spots – and many users of psychiatric services do indeed want to be rid of voices. Other voice hearers, however, may want to be able to talk about their exceptional experiences in public. Perhaps the best way to talk about different perspectives on 'voices' is to say that each is an account of the experience and that each categorises it differently. This should allow us to consider both the metaphors implicit in the accounts and their pragmatics: who administers them, for what purpose and with what outcomes. The question about what is the right concept for voices is possibly not the best one – a better one is: Which concept of voices is useful for this purpose? But this pragmatism may well be beside the point: different accounts of voices are clearly not equal now and they were not in Schreber's time. The interesting point about the Schreber case is that it was only in the court that his and psychiatric accounts engaged as anything like equals.

Pragmatics of Schreber's supernatural world

Elsewhere we have conceptualised voices as unusual instances of private speech (Leudar *et al.*, 1997; Davies *et al.*, 1999). We found that like inner speech, much voice-talk is mundane: it is relevant to voice hearers' ongoing activities, and it regulates them through evaluation, direction and prohibition. Indeed, one important problem which has emerged so far in our book concerns the ways in which voices affect the conduct of voice hearers. Nowadays it is often assumed that some voice hearers cannot resist demands issued by their voices. In fact, and contrary to mass media wisdom, we have found in our empirical research that voices typically do not *impel* actions of voice hearers (see Chapters 8 and 9). Instead they may (or may not) influence voice hearers' decisions on how to act. Voices we have examined in our empirical research did not put voice hearers into positions of observers as may happen in passivity experiences. We found that hallucinatory voices influenced the activities of their hearers very much as people influence each other by talking. Everyday requests and warnings provide reasons for or against acting. Whether we act on advice will depend, among other things, on how good was the reason given, on the authority of the speaker and on our mutual trust. Words do not impel actions, but it does happen in everyday life that one comes to be controlled by commands or instructions of another and only thinks later. We have observed this happening in some voice hearers. Voices can also be compulsive and achieve their effects through repetition and fear. But none of these influences are irresistible impulsions. We therefore distinguish between three modes of influence in interaction – impulsion, compulsion and reason-mediated influence. It is the latter two modes of influence, we claim, that are typical of voice-talk. Now the problem is, was this so for Schreber? How did he formulate influences of the supernatural on his conduct; how did his psychiatrists formulate influences of delusions and hallucinations on his conduct? Did the voices impel his actions without a resistance being possible, or did Schreber follow their advice for a reason, perhaps because, like Socrates, he thought them wiser than himself?

Schreber's personifications of the supernatural

Schreber reported interacting with many supernatural agencies – the souls of the dead and living, the sun, birds and God being just some of them. He conceptualised the voices as souls: 'All those souls spoke to me as voices' (Schreber, 1903/1955, p. 51). Schreber believed that the supernatural agencies were real and independent of him, not just subjectively real: 'Everyone who realises that *all this is not just morbid offspring of my fantasy*, will be able to appreciate the unholy turmoil they caused in my head' (ibid., p. 72, our emphasis). There were occasions when Schreber took the people around him not to be real but instead created for him by miracles of his supernatural god. Schreber did, however, realise that only he himself had access to this supernatural world. It was not a supernatural world like that of spiritualists which is socially shared. Nevertheless, some figures in Schreber's supernatural had some similarity to religious figures. So Schreber's conception of reality was eccentric but in his own terms he was not a solipsist, contrary to what Luis Sass (1994) has argued. The reason is that he himself did see the supernatural as independent of himself – his own will, feelings and beliefs.

Voices were 'souls' speaking to Schreber; they were also voices of particular individuals. Some he knew to be 'definitely among the living', others were of dead individuals, 'departed souls, who began more and more to interest themselves in me' (Schreber, 1903/1955, p. 70). Schreber mentioned voices of Dr Flechsig (his second psychiatrist), priests of 'various elevation in the church', 'nerve specialists', members of the 'Students Corps Saxonia' in Leipzig, members of the Student Union, and Dr Hoffman, said to be in the position of leadership on Sirius. Klein commented on Schreber's 'capacity to divide himself into sixty souls' (Klein, 1975), and she held that these 'souls' were introjected fragments of an external object – his therapist Flechsig. Some of the voices were indeed collectively like Flechsig in certain respects – their profession, social standing – and Schreber himself tied them to Flechsig in his text (1903/1955, p. 71). Nevertheless, there were other souls, some aligned with members of his family. He specifically mentioned his mother, father, brother, wife and father-in-law. Schreber, however, did not seem very interested in the souls aligned with the members of his family and they did not figure prominently in the *Memoirs*. (Or perhaps his comments on his family were excised from his memoirs – it is known that they were edited to preserve the face of his wife.)

Other personifications were much more bizarre. The sun spoke to Schreber, and then there were the 'birds'. Schreber not only heard the bird voices, he also saw them (1903/1955, p. 213). To those bird voices which appeared repeatedly, Schreber gave female names (ibid., p. 214).

How did Schreber identify voices? He knew some of them by the sound: 'I recognise the individual nerves exactly by the tone of their voices from years of hearing them.' He also identified voices by their language: 'I know exactly which of the senseless phrases learnt by rote I can expect of each of them, according to whether they are emitted from the camp of the lower god or from that of the upper god' (ibid., p. 208). 'I have no doubt about the identity of the souls concerned because I know the tone of their voices well, and I recognise the phrases I regularly hear from them and which have, so to speak, been crammed into them' (ibid., p. 212).

The modality of Schreber's interactions with the supernatural

Schreber had several modes of interacting with the 'supernatural'. Some supernatural agencies he definitely experienced as voices. To quote him again: 'All these souls spoke to me as *voices*' (1903/1955, p. 51, our emphasis). He specifically reported *hearing* his psychiatrist Dr Flechsig and talking to him when the two of them were apart (ibid., p. 44). Thus the quality of some of Schreber's voices was definitely auditory. But he also experienced souls in 'nerve language', and this he did not hear – he described it as sub-vocal speech and likened it to 'silent prayer' (ibid., p. 46). But even though silent, the 'nerve language' was definitely language (German). It had words, came in sentences and it had pragmatics. Schreber, for example, reported that the sun's 'rays' asked him questions in 'nerve language' and he was able to report the exact words (ibid., p. 48). The voices in 'nerve language' often spoke 'telegraphese', using grammatically incomplete expressions and 'omitting words unnecessary for sense'. 'Nerve language' was therefore like what Vygotsky called inner speech – silent and predicated (Vygotsky, 1934/1962). These properties of Schreber's nerve language were noted recently by Louis Sass (1992; 1994, p. 38). But unlike inner speech, the instances of nerve language were in no way under Schreber's control. Instead they were 'set in motion' in him 'from without incessantly and without respite' by means of 'divine rays' (Schreber, 1903/1955, pp. 46–47). Thus, in common with most voice hearers, he did not consider himself to be the author of what the voices told him. This was expressed in that he called them 'supernatural'; not his illness, not estranged fragments of himself. In other respects, however, the voices *were* 'his', because only he could experience them.

So far then, we have two ways in which Schreber experienced the 'souls' – as a voiced or as a silent language. Was there another way in which he interacted with any of his supernatural agencies? One of the central supernatural figures for Schreber was his dual god – Ariman and Ormuzd. In the *Iliad* Achilles was never spoken to directly by Zeus and Schreber likewise rarely *heard* his god's voice or sensed him in the 'nerve language'.[1] So how did Schreber and his god usually interact? Some interactions with the god were mediated: the god had supernatural powers, and he could affect Schreber's environment through 'miracles'. For instance, Schreber reported hearing crackling noises in the wall, which kept him awake (ibid., p. 37). He endowed these noises with intentionality; in his account they became 'divine miracles' and his voices called them 'interferences': they were the god's intentional actions, the purpose of which was to prevent him from sleeping (ibid., p. 38). Other interactions with the god were mediated by voices, as we shall see below.

Schreber, however, also reported that some of his contact with his god was *direct* (ibid., p. 31). He explained this by the 'influx of god's nerves' into his own body. The direct contact with god, unmediated by language, caused Schreber to bellow. This bellowing was a clear case of impulsion and will be discussed in some detail below. There was, however, no instance where Schreber wrote that he was impelled to act by the supernatural agencies which he heard or which addressed him in the nerve language. We therefore see that it is important to read the *Memoirs* closely to establish which 'supernatural agencies' were and which were not 'voices'; we then find that those which were language did not affect Schreber by impulsion.

Participant positioning

As is typical of contemporary voices, Schreber's were isolated from each other: 'The interesting point is that the souls are separate from each other, not knowing of each other's existence,' Schreber wrote (1903/1955, p. 51). The exception was the god, who was central to Schreber's supernatural world. The god was both remote from him – he interacted with Schreber through proxies (voices which were often personified as 'birds') – or he affected Schreber directly without the benefit of language. The god had access to voices but he was not himself a voice.[2]

Schreber's voices did not attempt to interact directly with other people; like his other supernatural agencies, they were for Schreber only. They sometimes suggested what Schreber should *say* to other people, but they did not try to address others as themselves through Schreber. The voices were not aware of the world – to quote Schreber, 'miracles' 'made [them] immune against all sensation which they would otherwise have when entering my body' (ibid., p. 209). This positioning of voices is consistent with their function being, like that of ordinary 'inner' speech, to regulate activities.

Schreber himself was reluctant to talk about his voices to other people. He had a Messianic mission but he usually wisely withheld his supernatural experiences from the hospital staff, as the entries in his Sonnenstein chart reveal (see Lothane, 1992, pp. 473–475). Bleuler (1911, p. 116) noted this 'reticence' in Schreber and other patients: 'Often they will admit that they are afraid to reveal their experiences because they will be considered pathological, and they themselves "crazy".' Yet it was Bleuler who held that 'hearing voices' was a symptom of mental pathology (but see Szasz, 1996). Schreber's 'reluctance' to talk about voices is rational, but it may have had serious consequences. If the contact of Schreber's voices with the world was minimal, then so was the influence of the world on the voices. It was not surprising that Schreber's system of 'delusions' was resistant to counter-arguments – it rarely encountered them: they really were the 'voices from the underground'. So to summarise the positioning of Schreber's voices: they were focused on him, on his thoughts, plans and current experiences. Their contact with other people and the ordinary world was minimal and this was through Schreber's experiences.

What did Schreber's voices say to him?

Voices gave Schreber information (1903/1955, pp. 51–53). Some of it was mundane – voices told him about Flechsig's family tree and that Flechsig was a member of a drinking club (ibid., p. 56). Much of it, however, concerned the 'supernatural' world to which only he had access. Some voices told him about the god. They revealed to him, for instance, that the god contacts highly gifted people to bless them with creative thoughts (ibid., p. 48). By implication, Schreber was gifted and the contact with the god a blessing. The experience was thus presented in the account as unique and valuable, if rarely pleasant. Voices would explain events and especially his 'supernatural' experiences (ibid., p. 70). In informing him the voices were linguistically creative. They provided Schreber with words to represent a supernatural world that was only accessible to him – 'forecourts-of-heaven', 'fleeting-improvised-men', 'interferences' (e.g. ibid., p. 70). Schreber learned things about the supernatural from the voices (ibid., p. 50). Did he always accept what the voices told him, however? When the information obtained concerned the supernatural, he seems to have done. This conclusion is implicit in what Schreber does *not* say. He reported being informed about the supernatural without indicating doubt. It is not surprising that Weber and Bleuler considered his delusions to have been elaborations of 'hallucinatory contents' – the source of some of his supernatural beliefs was indeed the voices. But when the information provided by voices was mundane Schreber wrote that it would be good to verify mundane information he was given, so indicating a doubt about what the voices said (ibid., p. 56). With regard to the mundane world his ability to engage in reality testing was not affected. This is not to say that it was intact with regard to the supernatural world. Schreber did not say that it would be good to verify the reality of fleeting improvised men, or of miracled events. But then how could these have been tested for reality, since the supernatural world was only accessible to him?

Schreber reported that voices asked him questions, some of which he treated as real questions and not just words: 'They continually *wanted to know* what I was thinking' (ibid., p. 70, our emphasis). The 'rays', for instance, would ask him repeatedly, 'What are you thinking of now?' He would ignore the question: 'My nerves did not react to this absurd question' (ibid.). So far the question–response sequence was what one might encounter in an ordinary dialogue: a question, its consideration, and silence. What would occasionally happen next was more bizarre. Schreber reported that the question he ignored would be answered spontaneously for him: '"He should", scilicet think, "about the order of the world"' (ibid., p. 48). However, this was not a voice answering its own question and Schreber just hearing it. As he put it, the rays forced the answer out of him: 'the influence of the rays forced my nerves to perform the movements corresponding to the use of these words' (ibid.). But note the stilted formulation: Schreber is not uttering these words, the rays forced him to *perform the movements*, and they did not really force *him*, but his nerves. This sort of experience comes under the heading of 'passivity experiences' and what we called impulsion – the movements of one's body against one's will. But was it an impulsion of experience or of an action? We cannot be quite sure because Schreber does not say whether 'performing the movements' meant speaking aloud so others could hear, or sub-vocally, or just hearing the answer. In any case, the rays seem to communicate both through language and by impulsion. The mechanism of impulsion is unclear. The question did not force Schreber to answer, the rays did, but we are not told how.

Schreber did not report specific questions he asked of the voices. He did, however, say that voices *answered* his questions (ibid., p. 72). This implies that he did ask questions but there is no material to analyse them, or the voices' responses.

Did the voices tell Schreber to do things; for example, to carry out ordinary actions (as is typically reported by present-day informants) or perhaps something more serious, like urging him to kill or injure himself? Schreber did not report any such requests, orders or commands. Considering the purpose of the *Memoirs*, this may not be surprising. It would not do to admit that voices attempted to regulate his mundane actions – the point of the court action was to prove that he could take care of his own affairs and to control what is, in a psychiatric view, pathological. Schreber did, however, report that his voices encouraged him to *say* things (ibid., p. 70). 'Why do you not say it?' they would urge him. In the absence of the verbal action (or a response) they occasionally answered themselves, 'as if', Schreber says, 'it came from me'. This seems another instance of impulsion. But again we do not know whether the words came silently and for Schreber only, or aloud and for everybody.

The talk of the voices personified as birds was decidedly odd. Schreber wrote that they uttered 'rote phrases', 'without knowing the sense of the words'. Instead they had 'a natural sensitivity for *similarity of sounds*' and Schreber could stop their stereotyped performance 'by deliberately throwing in similar sounding words' (ibid., p. 211, our emphasis). Then they would, surprised, 'express *in human sounds* the *genuine* feeling, well-being in the soul-voluptuousness of my body, which they share, with the words "Damned fellow" or "Somehow damned", the only words in which they are still capable of giving expression to genuine feeling' (ibid., p. 208). These expressions were used, wrote Schreber, not 'in derogatory sense', but rather as a 'joyous tribute'. So the 'bird voices' uttered stereotyped utterances as proxies of the god, but they also expressed their own evaluations of Schreber's person.

So on the basis of the *Memoirs*, Schreber's interactions with his voices had the following pragmatic characteristics:

- He heard many voices and they were both recurrent and one-off.
- The voices were aligned with individuals personally known to him – with family and acquaintances, with public figures he probably only knew about, with animals, with physical objects, and with supernatural mythological figures. All the agencies were given a paranormal and supernatural patina.
- The dialogical positioning of the voices was the one we commonly observe nowadays – they were isolated from each other, and from the world, and focused on Schreber's current thoughts and activities.

- The voices mostly informed Schreber of mundane affairs and (more often) of the supernatural realm. They also evaluated his person, and regulated his verbal activities. Reversible question/answer sequences were also present.
- The voices affected Schreber's activities in two ways. Some effects were mediated through his reasoning and will, but sometimes the effects on his speech may have been impulsive and able to be controlled by him only as one controls a cough or shivering.

Note that some of these properties of voices would be lost in the metaphorical translation of voices into hallucinations. The pragmatic profile of Schreber's voices is in his memoirs. Schreber reported his interactions with the voices as he would report mundane interactions, developing paranormal and supernatural explanations for impulsions. We did not have to subject his reports to metaphoric transposition – we have simply brought Schreber's reports of what he and the supernatural did to each other together and systematically.

There is, however, one important conflict between the supernatural and pragmatic accounts of Schreber's voices. We do not believe that Schreber was communicating with the supernatural. This is precisely what he believed – he was certain throughout his 'nervous illness' that the supernatural agencies which plagued him were not parts of him, his fantasies or delusions, but this was obviously not how the clinicians saw the matter (cf. ibid., pp. 203–204). Freud (1911/1972) argued that the basis of Schreber's illness was an outburst of homosexual impulse and that the god and the sun symbolised his father. Schatzman argued that the god was an internalisation of Schreber's father's educational practices. Klein claimed that Schreber's voices were internalisations of his therapist Flechsig. More recently Sass argued that his supernatural agencies were his experiences which were externalised because Schreber turned his attention inwards and introspectively (Sass, 1992, see Chapter 6).

It is, however, necessary to keep in mind Schreber's perspective, otherwise some features of his experiences will be incomprehensible. The supernatural account allowed Schreber to dissociate himself radically from the voices, and to present himself to himself and to others as a person in rational control of his actions. The pragmatic account would have forced Schreber to accept the voices as parts of himself, but this would have meant admitting that he had the qualities which he rejected and derided in the supernatural and was responsible for actions he abhorred (e.g. bellowing). On Schreber's own account the souls communicate with him as rays which *enter his body*. So the rays are not for him *signals* which carry messages to him from elsewhere, they are not like sounds or marks on a paper. The rays are the substance of souls. This means that even though functionally the voices are distinct from him, Schreber and the voices, as he puts it, 'share his body', and on occasions the voices can control its movements. Schreber's distinction between himself and the supernatural agencies is not based on physical difference. It is a moral and legal distinction – he is not responsible for what the voices say or what the supernatural does with his body. It is not clear whether

Schreber would reason like this, but he does imply that the border between 'himself' and 'others' has partly moved within his body.

Mixing metaphors in the Court

The case in the Court of Appeal was concerned with whether the tutelage order should be confirmed or discontinued. Quoting from the court decree: 'a person can be placed under tutelage only in his own interest, in order to safeguard him from the threatening dangers of his unreasonable actions, but never to protect other persons, however closely related, from unpleasantness' (Schreber, 1903/ 1955, pp. 484–485). The actions which are disturbing to others were not covered by a tutelage order, they were a matter for 'organs of security police':

> But these 'vociferations' [i.e. the bellowing] have nothing to do with his capacity or otherwise of managing his affairs. They are only a welfare and police matter which in certain circumstances might give the asylum authorities – in their capacity as organs of the security police – the right to keep him in the Asylum against his will.
>
> (Ibid., pp. 489–490)

Thus the 'tutelage' was not quite the same then as a 'section order' is today. It was a precautionary measure 'offered by law' to save the patient 'in civil life from dangers arising out of his lack of will power' (ibid., p. 495). Much of the argument in the Court thus concerned whether Schreber was capable of carrying out ordinary practical activities in his everyday life. The case was really about who knew better what was best for Schreber, psychiatrists or himself. This meant that not all the aspects of Schreber's 'nervous illness' (or insanity if Dr Weber were to speak) were considered in the Appeal Court.

One could argue that a person with a psychiatric diagnosis of psychosis, simply by virtue of the diagnosis, can be deemed to be unable to take care of his or her own affairs. The Appeal Court cited a precedent for this view, but rejected it (ibid., p. 496, and see Lothane, 1992, pp. 283–284). The claim that 'every person suffering from paranoia can be placed under tutelage' was deemed too strong. Would one place under tutelage all members of the spiritualist community? Weber's argument in his submission was indeed that Schreber, as is typical of the patients with paranoia, was not able to act rationally, or at least his sustained capacity to do this was in doubt: 'Despite all assurances to the contrary given by the plaintiff in this respect, one must fear that in pursuing the idea of divine mission he might be led to expenses which he would not incur as a man acting of his free will' (Schreber, 1903/1955, pp. 488–489). Tutelage was necessary to protect him from himself.

But what evidence did Weber produce that Schreber was consistently incapable of acting rationally and in his own best interests? He gave specific examples of Schreber's irrational actions, and of actions where he thought psychiatrists were better qualified to decide what was best for Schreber. But this argument was too weak. Weber needed to prove that Schreber acted under the impulsion or compulsion of his pathological mental states, that this was detrimental to him personally, and that he had no insight of this. Weber did not manage to prove this.

Schreber of course contested the view that his beliefs in the supernatural were delusions, and the voices he heard hallucinations.

> I am quite sure that expressions and phrases like 'fleeting-improvised men' and 'cursed-play-with-human beings', the questions: 'What is going to happen to this cursed affair?', etc., as well as the talk about 'new human beings from Schreber's spirit' did not originate in my head, but were spoken into it from *outside*. This alone would make me assume that the ideas connected with them have some basis in reality corresponding to some historical events.
>
> (Ibid., p. 203)

> I have no doubt that my early ideas were not simply 'delusions' and 'hallucinations' because even now I still receive impressions daily and hourly.
>
> (Ibid., p. 204)

We have to be clear about what the 'outside' means here. Is it the outside of the ordinary world, or the outside of Schreber's supernatural? We could say that Schreber had two outsides, only one of which he shared with other people. Schreber himself accepted that his supernatural experiences had a different meaning for himself and the psychiatrists. In this respect his 'reality monitoring' is intact. The problem which the Court had to decide was in any case whether these experiences, supernatural or not, controlled Schreber's actions to his detriment. The psychiatric submissions claimed that this was so but we have already seen that only some influences of the 'supernatural' on Schreber were impulsive. The effects of voices – auditory or in 'nerve language' – seemed under Schreber's control, and mediated by his will and reason.

One clearly impulsive activity which was considered by the Appeal Court case in some detail was the 'bellowing'. Dr Weber in his 1899 report described it as follows:

> Outwardly most disturbing have been for a long time what the patient himself calls attacks of bellowing, that is to say the uttering of partly inarticulate sounds, partly threats and imprecations against imaginary disturbers of his well-being (Flechsig, etc.).
>
> (Ibid., p. 399)

It is worth quoting Weber at length to see how the bellowing Schreber appeared to others:

> In the garden the patient used to stand for a long time motionless in one place, staring into the sun, at the same time grimacing in an extraordinary

way or bellowing very loudly at the sun with threats and imprecations, usually repeating endlessly one and the same phrase, shouting at her, that she was afraid of him, and that she had to hide from him the Senatspräsident Schreber. . . . Or he raved in his room to such an extent, harangued for some time the 'soul-murderer' Flechsig, repeated endlessly 'little Flechsig', putting heavy accent on the first word, or shouted abuse and suchlike out of his window with such a tremendous force even at night, that the townspeople gathered and complained of the disturbance.

(Ibid., pp. 382–383)

Which of these actions was actually the bellowing? Just the 'bellowing'? Or also standing motionless, grimacing, swearing and so on? The paragraph describes both impulsive bellowing and Schreber's reactions to it. Weber wrote in his submission to the Court of Appeal:

These noisy outbursts occur completely automatically and in a compulsive manner against the patient's will. Though he is able to repress them, if not always at any rate for a time through lively speech, making music fortissimo, and some other *tricks*, they sound not only throughout the greatest part of the day from his living room and in the garden, causing considerable annoyance to his environment, but even at night they can often be heard for hours, causing intolerable disturbance of peace and quiet.

(Ibid., p. 399)

Weber explained bellowing as a reaction against the hallucinations, presenting it as a mechanism to cope with 'hallucinations and disturbances of feeling'. In this he anticipated Bleuler, who wrote that 'peculiarities of behaviour are usually related to, if not direct consequences of delusions and hallucinations' (Bleuler, 1911/1966, p. 95). According to Weber, Schreber also used 'tricks' and 'nonsensical counter actions' to control bellowing (e.g. playing the piano loudly: Schreber, 1903/1955, p. 384), but these were themselves pathological and socially stigmatising. So Schreber's coping strategy, Weber claimed, was actually one of his problems.

Of course Schreber got better with time, and Weber did concede this:

as the accompanying mighty effects gradually decreased and the hallucinatory experiences lost their confusing and directly overpowering influence, the patient was able to a certain extent to put up with them and gradually to find his way back to a more orderly mental life. . . . President Schreber now appears neither confused, nor psychologically inhibited, nor markedly affected in his intelligence.

(Ibid., p. 395)

But in his final submission to the Court of Appeal in November 1900, Weber wrote that Schreber did not realise how far his current beliefs were built on the pathological perceptions he experienced during the acute phase of his mental illness (hallucinatory psychosis): 'his whole thinking and feeling are still under the influence of delusions and hallucinations' and

> He did not, however, realise and recognise the actual products of his altered perceptions and the combinations built upon them as pathological, nor could he rise above the subjectiveness of his views and reach a more objective judgement of events. He could not achieve this, because the hallucinations persisted and delusions continued to be built on them.
>
> (Ibid., p. 395)

Schreber's interests were focused on discovering the order in the supernatural revealed to him by voices. His 'divine mission' led Schreber 'inward' into a private supernatural, not to being an active spiritualist or a preacher. From the psychiatric perspective his orientation was pathological and Weber argued that the healthy aspects of Schreber's person could not be considered apart from the pathological ones:

> the patient is filled with pathological ideas, which are woven into a complete system, more or less fixed, and not amenable to correction by objective evidence, and judgement of circumstances as they really are; the latter still less so as hallucinatory and delusory process continue to be of importance to him and hinder normal evaluation of sensory impressions. As a rule the patient does not mention these pathological ideas or only hints at them, but it is evident how much he is occupied by them, partly from some of his writings (extracts of some are added), partly it is easily seen from his whole bearing.
>
> (Ibid., p. 386)

So Schreber's 'conception of the world is pathological' and he acted under the influence of delusions and voices; he was socially disruptive, harmful to himself, and psychiatrists were required to manage his behaviour (ibid., pp. 387–388). Weber wrote that he 'was forced in June 1896 to segregate the patient at night in a more isolated room and carry this out for a number of months' (ibid., p. 383) and, oddly, he recruited Schreber to support his view of Schreber's conduct: according to him Schreber acceded to being isolated 'without marked resistance, apparently realising that his actions were pathological and causing almost unbearable annoyance to his environment' (ibid., p. 383). Schreber was thus presented not just as a nuisance to others and a victim in need of psychiatric help and management. Weber also accepted that he had some insight into how he affected others:

> he affirms that he cannot control them, that it is a matter of divine miracles, of supernatural happenings, which cannot be understood by other human beings, and these vociferations, based on *physical compulsion*, and very annoying also for his environment, occur so unremittingly that they disturb

the patient's nightly rest in the most painful way and necessitate the use of sleeping drugs.

(Ibid., p. 388, our emphasis)

What did Schreber himself have to say about the bellowings? He accepted that he suffered from the attacks of 'bellowing' and that these were indeed actions which he did not himself will. He wrote:

the muscles which serve respiration (the lung and thorax muscles) were by divine miracle set in motion with such a violence that *I am compelled* to let out the bellow or cry, unless I make quite extraordinary efforts to suppress it, which by the suddenness of the impulse is not always possible, or possible only by constant attention to it.

(Ibid., p. 415, our emphasis)

In my own person the advent of the bellowing-miracle when my muscles serving the process of respiration are set in motion by the lower god (Ariman) in such a way that I am forced to emit bellowing noises, unless I try very hard to suppress them; sometimes this bellowing recurs so frequently and so quickly that it becomes almost unbearable and at night makes it impossible to remain in bed.

(Ibid., p. 205)

So while Weber considered bellowings to be Schreber's (compelled) actions, Schreber held, quite rationally as we shall see, that they were not, even though they involved his body. This is clearly an unusual way to draw a line between conduct and movement, and to distribute the responsibility for an action. But if one accepts that intentions are morally and logically required constituents of actions, Schreber's argument makes sense, and there are analogies in everyday life. Imagine that someone knocks my elbow, perhaps deliberately, so that I spill hot coffee over somebody else. Who is responsible? We would certainly not count the movement of my arm as my deliberate action and so I would not have been held *fully* responsible for the burn. (Yes, I should not have brought coffee into a crowded room.)

Schreber's analysis of bellowing allowed him to put forward his most surprising argument: bellowing was not to be taken as evidence that he was insane, bound to act under the influence of pathological delusions and hallucinations, 'without free will', and thus in need of psychiatric management. On the contrary: he argued that the involuntariness of the bellowing, and his attempts to suppress it, however bizarre and disturbing both may have seemed to others, were precisely the evidence that he, Daniel Schreber, could act rationally and was guided by his own will:[3]

That I neither simulate nor provoke the bellowing purposely – it is after all a real burden for me too – is apparently not doubted by the medical specialist;

he recognises that it frequently requires the greatest effort on my part to prevent the bellowing noise, and that such outbursts occur completely against my own will, *automatically and compulsively*.

(Ibid., p. 415, emphasis in original)

Bellowing was not morally or logically Schreber's act, and so it could not be evidence of *his* madness. Schreber has a point – in the event of our example we would not see spilling coffee as evidence of my malice. So how are bellowings different from having one's elbow knocked? The problem is that, even though Schreber's argument works logically, his 'I' has somewhat contracted and even his body is now not his own. Note also that Schreber's position on bellowings is made possible by his supernatural account. Bellowings are not *Schreber's* 'reflexive reactions to hallucinations' (as Dr Weber held), but a purposeful action of the 'lower god Ariman' on his body. Schreber wrote about bellowing as follows:

> It seems to serve a double purpose, namely to create by 'representing' the impression of a person bellowing because he is demented; and also to drown by bellowing the inner voices which the upper god started so that he could withdraw to a greater distance.

(Ibid., p. 206)

Thus bellowing results from the conflict between different aspects of Schreber's god, but how does he knows about any of this? He warranted the knowing in a footnote as follows: 'That this was the aim was previously often acknowledged quite openly in the phrase which I heard emanating from the upper god: "We want to destroy your reason"' (ibid., p. 206ff., 86). To put the matter from his point of view: Schreber's reason was under attack, but *he* resisted. This resistance was the evidence of his sanity.

It is interesting to note what Bleuler had to say about Schreber's attacks of bellowing. He wrote: 'The patient does something which he really does not want to do.' This clearly applies to bellowing. According to Bleuler, however, the patient 'does not offer any resistance. The patient does not oppose his personality to the impulse; it is still too much bound up with the drive.' In fact, Bleuler wrote that Schreber 'allowed the screaming (which he himself was doing) to pass through'. As we have seen, this is simply wrong – Schreber strenuously resisted bellowing.

As a competent lawyer, Schreber rejected the argument that the attacks of bellowing were a relevant consideration with regard to whether or not he was in need of tutelage. He argued that 'so-called attacks of bellowing can remain out of consideration because pure police matters could not furnish grounds for upholding my tutelage' (ibid., p. 408). Legally he turned out to be correct.

So Schreber's and Weber's accounts of bellowing differed in several important respects. Schreber attributed it causally and morally to a supernatural agency, which was not a part of his person. Bellowing was a malicious action of the supernatural, directed against Schreber, and using his body as an instrument. He was a victim, and a rational one – he resisted bellowing in a rational and socially considerate way. (He would leave a dining-room if he could not control his bellowing.) Weber, on the other hand, saw the bellowings as Schreber's own pathological actions caused by his madness, and his attempts to resist it as mere 'tricks' (rather than a cure). But this of course meant that he could have little empathy for Schreber's struggle with his problems and no insight into it. Schreber did not expect that psychiatrists would 'adopt positively my explanation of the phenomenon'. He appreciated the perspective of his opponents.

Part of the problem is whether Schreber's delusions and voices are to be considered of his person. The answer depends on whether the question is asked in a cognitive, moral or legal sense. As cognitions, delusions and voices are clearly parts of Schreber. Morally he can hardly be held responsible for what he has no control over. The legal situation seems odd. It seems that legally Schreber would have been held responsible for harming others, yet he was provided with tutelage to safeguard him against the effects of his madness. (Harming others remained a matter for the police, not for psychiatrists.) Schreber's own supernatural perspective distances him morally and cognitively from what he interprets as supernatural. The psychiatric perspective seems to have absolved Schreber of blame but insisted on control.

But the point of the legal argument was not just whether Schreber's worldview was pathological (it certainly was highly eccentric) or whether he was preoccupied by the 'supernatural' (he clearly was and knew it). As the Court pointed out, there were many groups of people with irrational and fixed worldviews, such as spiritualists, but one would not think of subjecting them to tutelage. The point of the court case was whether the fixed and bizarre ideas exercised compulsive power over Schreber's actions to his detriment. For Dr Weber, as a psychiatrist, this connection was obvious:

> in the patient's behaviour, in the clean shaving of his face, in his pleasure in feminine toilet articles, in small feminine occupations, in the tendency to undress more or less and to look at himself in the mirror, to decorate himself with gay ribbons and bows, etc., in a feminine way, the pathological direction of his fantasy [i.e. that he is being transformed into a woman] is manifested continually. He takes what one could consider just private eccentricities to be reflections of the hallucinatory processes, which continues in unaltered intensity.
>
> (Ibid., p. 388)

But Weber's main argument for why tutelage should be upheld was Schreber's lack of insight into his condition:

> There is a total lack, as already stated, of the most important criterion of improvement or even recovery, namely the more or less clear insight into the pathological nature of previous events.
>
> (Ibid., p. 396)

The most important moment in judging the capacity of the patient to look after his affairs is and remains the fact that he lacks insight into the pathological nature of the hallucinations and ideas which influence him; *what objectively are delusions and hallucinations are to him unassailable truth and adequate motive for action.*

(Ibid., p. 401, our emphasis)

This is an intriguing view of what constitutes insight. In effect it consumes the opponents' metaphor of voices. To have an insight on Weber's terms, Schreber must accept that the voices he hears are hallucinations, and that his beliefs about the supernatural are delusions. Schreber must accept the psychiatric account of his voices. The sensible reaction to hallucinations is to ignore them, not to dwell on them. Bleuler wrote: 'Thus it is already a sign of improvement when patients succeed in "taking command" of the hallucinations'; but he meant the following by 'taking command of hallucinations' – 'when they are able to withdraw their attention from hallucinations' (Bleuler, 1911/1966, p. 108). The insight in the classical psychiatric account means ignoring one's experience and leaving it to psychiatric expertise. Weber's conclusion was as follows:

It follows from this [the lack of insight] that the patient's decisions at a given moment are unpredictable; he may follow and turn into action what his relatively intact mental powers dictate or he may act under the compulsion of his pathological mental processes.

(Schreber, 1903/1955, p. 401, our emphasis)

His conclusion does not follow without some bridging assumptions. Aside from bellowing, Weber did not provide many instances of Schreber acting under compulsion of voices. Another example of Schreber's irrational acts was publishing his *Memoirs*, which Weber saw as a compulsion:

One finds it quite incomprehensible that a man otherwise tactful and of fine feeling could propose an action which would compromise him so severely in the eyes of the public, were not his whole attitude to life pathological, and he unable to see things in their proper perspective, and if the tremendous overvaluation of his own person caused by lack of insight into his illness had not clouded his appreciation of the limitations imposed on man by society.

(Ibid., p. 402)

Schreber's reply is illuminating. It brings into the open the clash between his supernatural and Weber's psychiatric conceptions of voices/verbal hallucinations and miracles/delusions. Schreber submits:

Of course, I have to realise that for the time being there is little prospect of other people appreciating my basic point of view, least of all in the decision of the present Court case. I therefore used to consider it possible and indeed advisable to exclude every discussion of my supposed hallucinations and delusions from the points at issue in the case, the purpose of which is the contesting of my tutelage.

(Ibid., pp. 411–412)

But now he has a problem:

I have to make the attempt as regards other people, my judges in particular, not really to convert them to my miraculous belief – naturally I could only do this at present to a very moderate degree – but at least to furnish the general impression that the experiences and considerations laid down in my 'Memoirs' cannot be simply regarded as a *quantité negligible*, as an empty fantasy of a muddled head, which from the outset would not justify the effort of further thought and *possible observations on my person*.

(Ibid., p. 412, emphasis in original)

The Appeal Court's position was as follows:

It is true as the contested judgement [of the district court] criticises in his manuscript, that he occasionally uses offensive strong language. But these expressions do not originate from him, but occur only where he relates the content of the conversations the voices held with him. It was not his fault that these voices frequently used expressions not fit for drawing rooms. Beside, his 'Memoirs' were not written for flappers or high school girls.

(Ibid., pp. 486–487)

The Appeal Court decided that even though Schreber was indeed 'insane', his derangement was not all-encompassing. The Court saw the domain of Schreber's madness and his 'lack of insight' as restricted to his religious 'fixed ideas' (ibid., p. 498). There was thus no reason to deprive Schreber of his legal rights.[4]

4   Pierre Janet on verbal hallucinations

The case of Marcelle

Marcelle will be remembered as Pierre Janet's foremost case with 'an essential characteristic of hysteria, the absence of will' (Janet, 1901, p. 88). We are interested in her because she was a 'voice hearer' and because Janet used her case to formulate the concept of 'verbal hallucinations'. He used this term as a more accurate name for 'hearing voices' (Janet, 1891). His early work, *Automatisme psychologique*, was published in 1889 when he was only 30 years old. It contains a brief account of hallucinations and other 'impulsions' in a chapter on dissociation (*désaggrégation*), but Marcelle herself is not mentioned. Our chapter is based on Janet's references to her in three of his works: a two-part article in *Revue Philosophique* in 1891, 'Études sur un cas d'aboulie et d'idées fixes', and two books: *The Mental State of Hystericals* published in 1892 and *Psychological Healing* published in French in 1919 and translated into English in 1925 (Janet, 1919). This means that even though the case we present here of Marcelle is detailed, it is without a doubt not based on everything that Janet ever wrote about her. Moreover, even though both *Mental State of Hystericals* and *Psychological Healing* recapitulate, sometimes verbatim, what Janet wrote about Marcelle previously, the settings change as do Janet's ideas about hallucinations. The second limit of this chapter is that we shall not provide an explicit account of how Janet's views of hallucinations and their context developed over time, even though that would certainly be an interesting project.

According to Ellenberger (1970, p. 337), Janet once considered doing his doctoral thesis on hallucinations. Reading the three works it soon becomes clear that he lost specific interest in hallucinations, unlike, for example, Ball (1882), Baillarger (1886) or Binet (1884a, 1884b). He did not dedicate a monograph to hallucinations or even an explanation of their own. Nevertheless, his occasional comments on hallucinations seem to us original and deserve attention. The reason is that the frame in which he considered hallucinations was different from what is common nowadays. First, Janet noted hallucinations mainly as a symptom of hysteria, so strictly speaking he dealt with them in a very particular population of patients, and grouped them with different symptoms than do most contemporary psychiatrists. Second, like the other symptoms of hysteria, he eventually explained spontaneous hallucinations as actions which originate in 'fixed ideas', and which are incomplete in certain senses and inadequately controlled through reflections in 'inner speech'. Janet also referred to hallucinations as 'false sensations', but he concluded that treating hallucinations only in this way was superficial:

> A hallucination as I have tried to show a good many times, *is in reality an action, an impulsive action.* The main characteristic of the visual or auditory hallucination is not that the subject sees or hears something which has no objective existence. This is a minor consideration.
>
> (Janet, 1925, p. 287, our emphasis)

The important feature of Janet's psychology in general was that he was concerned with what one would nowadays call *pragmatics* of the abnormal, unlike Freud, who was more interested in its *semiotics*. The hallmark of Janet's psychology was his stress on action.[1] He wrote:

> The scientific study of psychology is only practicable if we look upon all the phenomena of mind as actions, or grades of action. The mind appears to consist of an aggregate of tendencies. It is composed of dispositions to produce definite series of movements in response to stimuli applied to the periphery of the body. But these tendencies are activated to a different extent in different cases.
>
> (Ibid., p. 224)

Janet treated hallucinations as both 'false sensations' and 'impulsive actions'; so did he work with two *alternative* conceptions of hallucinations? This is one tension in his work to which we shall return.

The idea that hallucinations are incomplete, impulsive actions contrasts with their conceptualisation in contemporary cognitive psychology and psychiatry (see Chapter 6). The problem is that if we approach hallucinations as just false perceptions then their relationship to actions, and especially to the compulsive ones, becomes difficult to explain.[2] Our final point here will be to establish whether Janet's approach made it easier for him to deal with the relationship between hallucinations and actions, and especially with their supposed compulsivity (some voice hearers claim they carry out voice commands without a question – see Chapters 6 and 9).

It is clear, then, that to understand Janet's view of Marcelle and of her 'verbal kinaesthetic hallucinations' we need to know more about his psychology – about his theory of action, suggestion and fixed ideas. Our aim is to bring together Janet's reflections on hallucinations and use them to decentre our study of 'hearing voices'.

Let us return to Marcelle and summarise Janet's 1891 vignette of her and her family. Her father suffered a complete paralysis in his last two years of life but showed 'no problems of speech or delirium'. He died aged 50 when Marcelle was a teenager. The family on her mother's side presented a history of mental illness. Her maternal grandmother died in an insane asylum suffering from 'delirium of persecutions'; her maternal aunt was also interned at an asylum – at Vaucluse – and her mother suffered from 'weakness of spirit'. Janet commented that she would lose her *sang-froid* easily when she visited her daughter at Salpêtrière. Marcelle had six brothers and three 'bizarre' sisters. She was the youngest child and she 'united and intensified in herself the various deficiencies of her family'. As a child she was intelligent but subject to endless caprices and tantrums. When aged 14 she suffered an attack of typhoid fever and was delirious for a month. This illness left profound effects on her and Janet located the onset of her 'actual illness' to this point. According to him, Marcelle changed her character and conduct in a way 'noticeable even to strangers'. She was also incapable of intellectual effort and stopped learning. She was sad and avoided moving. She became 'uncivilised' in her manner instead of speaking to people of all sorts, as she had done in the past. She would not speak to her acquaintances and often isolated herself in her room. Janet characterised her state as one of 'inertia and melancholia' and said it was made worse by her father's death shortly after the typhoid attack. By the age of 19 Marcelle would stay motionless for long periods and was incapable of the simplest acts. She refused to eat and made repeated tentative attempts at suicide. In 1889 she was interned in Salpêtrière in the care of Dr J. Falret (to whom Janet referred as his 'maître'). Marcelle was introduced to Janet in 1890 (Ellenberger, 1970) and he published his first paper concerning her case a year later, in 1891. Janet's vignette of Marcelle and her family is strictly psychiatric: what he tells his readers allows him to trace Marcelle's problems partly to her inheritance – the weakness on her mother's side – and partly to her twofold trauma – physical illness and bereavement.

In the Salpêtrière, Marcelle presented Janet with all the signs of hysteria. In *The Mental State of Hystericals* she is mentioned side by side with Mary Reynolds (Weir Mitchell, 1888), both being good cases of hysterical amnesia. The difference between the two women was that Mary Reynolds forgot her past (Hacking, 1995), but Marcelle's memory for childhood was 'clear, exact, rich in details'. What deteriorated was her memory for the happenings from the age of 15 where, as we have seen, Janet placed 'the beginning of her malady'. The memory for the contemporary past is 'limited to some few salient events'; 'Marcelle cannot tell us what happened the day before' and 'a word from her tells the situation: "Is it possible that I have been here a whole year?"' (Janet, 1901, pp. 88–89).

But Marcelle was not in a constant state of amnesia. Janet wrote that she had 'cloud periods' with 'very little psychological strength' as well as occasional 'lucid moments'. Like Mary Reynolds, she alternated between these two states which left 'very different remembrances' (ibid., p. 107) and in her lucid periods she found it difficult to remember what took place in the cloudy periods. In *Automatisme psychologique* Janet used the conception 'doubling of personality' to explain a similar switching in his better-known patient Leonie. He did not, however, postulate a doubling of Marcelle's personality, as Azam (1882) may have done – he saw different states of one and the same person. Hystericals have periods during which the thick veil which prevented them from understanding things is rent asunder and they have lucid intervals, as Marcelle once told us. During these *lucid intervals* . . . suggestibility has considerably decreased or has even disappeared; no more automatic or impersonal acts, no more hallucinations in contradictions of real sensations.

(Janet, 1901, pp. 271–272, our emphasis)

However, even though Janet characterised these lucid periods as 'remission in the illness' they were not quite returns to normality because Marcelle's conduct in lucid periods was affected by the fixed ideas originating in the cloudy period (Janet, 1925, pp. 801, 861–862). Janet asserted that even in lucid periods she acted like a 'somnambulist' or a person moved by post-hypnotic suggestions. As a result, in some respects he knew Marcelle better than she knew herself, even during her lucid periods. Janet is in the position of authority regarding her conduct and its meaning, just as a hypnotist is with regard to a person who has been hypnotised.

Marcelle also presented Janet with some of the physical signs of hysteria established by Charcot (1991) – Janet mentioned contractures ('which often arrested her arms, leaving them in the strangest positions': 1901, p. 190; 1925, p. 802) and anaesthesias of all body parts, even the most intimate ones (1925, p. 801).

But what most interested Janet about Marcelle was her 'aboulia' – she was his 'great aboulic patient' (1901, p. 123). He defined this condition in general as 'alterations' and 'the diminutions of will'. For Janet – as for Briquet (1859), whom he quotes – aboulia was a crucial 'stigma of hysteria' and one of the 'lesions in the weakening of mind' (1901, p. 117). Marcelle herself had 'singular difficulty' initiating motions by herself as well as those which Janet requested her to carry out: 'all voluntary movements of the arms, legs, tongue, and lips present the same hesitation and the same powerlessness' irrespective of the objects of movements (1901, pp. 124–126).

But her problem was not physical – rather it was psychological and specifically intellectual. Marcelle had problems directing her attention, and even though she could read aloud she had problems understanding what she read. In fact she had a general problem understanding what she saw or heard if it happened to be something new and unfamiliar (ibid., pp. 128–130). Thus both her attention and understanding of ordinary events in her 'cloud periods' seemed poor to Janet.

One therapeutic technique Janet eventually developed was 're-education of will and attention' through what he called 'gymnastics of attention' (1925, p. 862). But Marcelle was one of Janet's earlier cases and he did not exercise her will and attention' systematically. In fact, in her case he did not advise spontaneous efforts to exercise attention and intelligence, even in lucid periods:

We yielded, curious to see how *a person of her kind* would listen to a scientific explanation, and told her in the simplest way possible what a visual field is. *To our great surprise, she understood very well*, and made very correct remarks on the drawings before her. All this was very fine for her. She, *however*, soon stopped in the midst of a sentence, fixed her eyes on the ground, and was suddenly overcome with a spell of melancholy, with complete aprosexia, which lasted till next day. *A little mental fatigue had in an instant destroyed all the progress so painfully obtained.*

(Janet, 1901, pp. 133–134, our emphasis)

So what kind of person was Marcelle for Janet? His intellectual assessment of her as we see it was that in her cloud periods she was effectively feeble-minded, and in her lucid periods any intellectual effort would render her unduly mentally fatigued. Janet's vignette of Marcelle's family is relevant here – it ties her intellectual enfeeblement to her heredity. Janet the clinician, is, on the other hand, the source of 'moral' and 'intellectual' education, as Tuke was in the York retreat (Foucault, 1967).

However, Marcelle's 'enfeeblement of will' did not affect all her movements or all her 'intelligence of ideas'. She was able to repeat actions and ideas: 'automatic acts are preserved but the voluntary new acts are difficult to carry out' (Janet, 1901, pp. 138–139). She could not talk to unknown people, including Janet when she first met him – 'It took her two months to learn to speak to us. She now speaks to us with perfect ease' (ibid., p. 141). Janet found the selective locus of Marcelle's aboulia on new acts significant. He concluded that 'she cannot synthesise new acts out of old components but since this is not necessary in conserved automatic acts, these remain possible' (ibid., p. 143). But Janet also observed that even automatic acts could occasionally present a problem, since 'the future is never the exact repetition of the past, a conscious act is never completely automatic' (ibid.). Marcelle could in fact carry out completely new acts but only when they were *suggested* to her:

> We suggested to Marcelle, while in a somnambulic state, that, at a given signal, a blow on a table, she should take my hat and hang it on a peg. This done and apparently forgotten when she woke, we said to her softly: 'Mlle. Marcelle we wish you would take our hat away from here and hang it on a peg.'
>
> (Ibid., pp. 144–145)

Marcelle agreed – but she could not carry out the verbal instruction; only when the signal was given did she accomplish the action. But even then she does this under Janet's control and not herself intentionally. So the problem was not with the physical movement. Janet argued that the two acts – carrying out an instruction and acting on a suggestion – were different in their intentionality. Suggested acts are, according to Janet,

> done quickly and without a reflecting. She does not even know what she has in her hand as we stop her on her way; she does not know why she took the thing . . . the suggested act, so well performed, is with all these patients an isolated, subconscious act, in no wise connected with the personality of the subject.
>
> (Ibid., p. 145)

By implication, voluntary acts involve premeditation, reflection and integration in the personality. Janet refers to these globally as 'synthesis', which he contrasts with dissociation. We shall say more about Janet's ideas on suggestion below.

But aboulia does not simply involve being unable to carry out new actions. It had a sister condition in which patients may act against their own will: 'impulsions' were for Janet also 'disorders of will' (1889, p. 420). But what exactly are impulsions? Janet sketched out the concept in *Automatisme psychologique*. His patients would report a feeling that they were 'allowing themselves to be carried along, as if by a strange force. ... The subject declares that the impulsions take place despite himself, even though he knew, and could have resisted if really necessary' (ibid.).

Impulsions should not be confused with reflexes. Reflexes are, roughly, reactions to the environment while the 'strange force' of the impulsion comes from within a person. Impulsions can be partly matters of consciousness, and indeed Janet was most interested in those which occurred during wakefulness, when his patients could perceive them, reflect on them and comment. His list of impulsions started with simple involuntary body movements (such as tics and choreic movements of St Vitus dance – Janet cited Maudsley (1867) here as an authority) but he focused on 'violent and unexpected desires' which can result in 'absurd or criminal deeds' studied by the Nancy School. The patients sense that such desires are 'ridiculous and reprehensible', and they resist them. But 'the desire to carry out the act returns more precise and implacable' (Janet, 1901, p. 421). When the patient eventually yields and

> the act is accomplished, then he breathes out, calms himself, rejoices, but not of the act he has done – this always fills him with horror. Though he is relieved by not having to feel that terrible torture anymore and he can retake the control of his free spirit.
>
> (Ibid.)

The point Janet makes about impulsive desires is that the patients themselves describe them as alien – they have no interest in the actions forced on them nor in the desires which are in contradiction of their 'profound and cherished sentiments'.

Janet commented that 'these impulsions are an interesting form of incomplete dissociated acts, which are *half known* by the subject' (ibid., p. 428, our emphasis). By this he meant that his patients were aware of the alien desires and could reflect on them – in this respect the impulsive acts were known to them – but what they did 'not realise is that the acts are suggested by internal phenomena the existence of which they do not suspect'. But what exactly were these 'internal phenomena'? Janet could not really know this himself precisely – these phenomena were his unresolved research problem at the time. According to Janet, the origin of compulsive desires was to be found in a 'second consciousness' – at that time Janet meant by disaggregation 'the formation of successive or simultaneous personalities in the same individual' which are to some extent isolated from each other but one of which can produce automatic phenomena in the other. In fact, he used 'dissociation' and 'doubling of personality' to explain the conduct of spiritual media, possession, automatic actions of criminals as well as hallucinations (ibid., pp. 376–385).

Implicit in Janet's account is that impulsive desire is a function of both the sub-personality (or a more circumscribed fixed idea) and the person herself. The former contributes the desire, the latter a moral orientation of this desire – and remember that in Janet all of these are activities. (The moral orientations which Janet reports are typically those of censure.) In a sense then, impulsive desire is a unity in tension and it can be more complex than a simple unalienated one.

Impulsive desires are, then, experienced by patients, but not as their own. They contradict their personalities and cannot be integrated into them, even after having been experienced repeatedly. It is thus not surprising, as Janet noted, that his patients could not provide reasons for impulsive desires. Now how does Janet uses the concept of impulsion to explain hallucinations? In *Automatisme psychologique* he writes:

> The impulsions exist sometimes in another form which seems a bit different; instead of presenting itself as an act, or at least as a desire, a wish, it is a simple idea equally fixed and obsessive, but which does not seem to have a disposition to cause any act. *These ideas often manifest themselves in the form of hallucinations of hearing.*
>
> (Ibid., pp. 428–429, our emphasis)

So 'hallucinations' are simple 'fixed and obsessive' ideas and Janet seeks one general explanation for them and for the other two species of impulsion – impulsive desires and impulsive actions. The problem is exactly the same as for the impulsions: the abnormal experience 'is not integrated in the personality, it is alien to self which would like to repel it' (ibid., pp. 429–430). The quote makes it clear that even though in *Automatisme psychologique* Janet's hallucinations were impulsions, he did not see them to be causes of impulsive actions.

We willl look at some examples of hallucinations which Janet used in his arguments in *Automatisme psychologique*. He described the following episode of spontaneous voice hearing in another of his patients, Leonie, who suffered a crisis and whom he could not calm down:

> Suddenly she stopped and told me in terror: 'Oh! Who spoke to me just now in this way? It frightened me. Nobody spoke to you, I am alone with you. – But yes, there on the left.' And she moves there and wants to open the cupboard placed to her left [to see] if anybody is hiding there. 'So what do you hear?', I asked her. 'I hear from the left a voice which repeats: "Enough, enough, be quiet, you bore us."'
>
> (Ibid., p. 430)

On another occasion during somnambulism Leonie refused to do as she was told. She was listening to the same voice and it told her: 'Come on, be sensible, it should be said' (ibid.).

Leonie's hallucinations do indeed almost satisfy Janet's criteria of impulsion:

- They are experienced by her (a subconscious hallucination may seem to be a semantic contradiction, but see n. 4).
- They are not under her control and appear spontaneously – she did not call them up.
- She does not understand their origins nor can she explain them, at least to Janet's satisfaction.
- Being impulsions, hallucinations should be repetitive, but this is not obvious in Janet's examples.

What were the origins of Leonie's hallucinations? Janet wrote that the utterances evidently originated in Leonie's 'inferior personality existing below this layer of consciousness' (ibid.); so verbal hallucinations were not necessarily expressions of individual isolated fixed ideas – they may originate in sub-personalities. To prove this point Janet reported an experiment somewhat similar to those which Morton Prince conducted with Miss Beauchamp (Prince, 1920). Janet instructed Leonie 3 (one of her alters invoked in hypnosis) to say 'Bonjour' 'to the other' (meaning Leonie), and then to wake up. As a result Leonie heard the word 'Bonjour' and asked him, 'So who said "Bonjour"?' Janet called her experience 'a hallucination of subconscious origins' and he compared the spontaneous hallucinatory voice and the experience induced by suggestion, concluding that the two were essentially the same phenomenon, with one exception:

> But this time, I could also hear the word 'Bonjour', because *her mouth pronounced it perfectly* although very low. This hallucination of subconscious origins was due, in this case, to hearing true automatic speech analogical to the writing of mediums.
>
> (Ibid., p. 431, our emphasis)

Strictly speaking, Leonie did not hallucinate at all – she *heard* Leonie 3, just as Janet did, even though Leonie was absent for her, and only for her. She at best thought she hallucinated. The point is, however, that Janet did nevertheless refer to Leonie's experiences as 'a hallucinatory voice' and that he explained it as *really* consisting in her hearing her own automatic talk. Another example of the same phenomenon he provided was

> the degenerate patients of Saury, who utter obscenities on impulsion and despite themselves, but sometimes they sense these through their muscular sense before they pronounce them, and 'they figure that they are hearing a strange voice localised in this or that place.'
>
> (Ibid., pp. 428–431)

Thus already in *Automatisme psychologique* Janet considered that the significant point about 'hearing voices' was that they were 'matters of language' and that patients 'hearing voices' sensed their own automatic speech.

The problem which Janet (1891) discussed for several pages was that not all experiences of 'hearing voices' have clear auditory qualities. Some do:

> Here for example is one persecuted [person] who complains of being tormented by her sister Josephine: 'It is unbearable, she said, that Josephine can enter everywhere! When I was in Ville-Evrard, she placed herself in the space under my bed, from where she insulted me constantly. Now I live at Salpêtrière and Josephine is still there, in the thing below the sick bed when I sleep, and in the thing below the worktable when I work. – Do you think Josephine could enter here? Certainly, I can hear her voice well, I recognise her; let me go up to the attic room and I will show you that Josephine is there.' This description is typical: the patient hears a true voice with a recognisable timbre, a specific exterior location, etc.: these are hallucinations of the sense of hearing.
>
> (Janet, 1891, p. 277)

Janet noted that this 'voice' had clear auditory qualities, so much so that the patient could attribute it to her sister. In fact, a patient's report of such an alignment seems for him to have been persuasive evidence that the verbal hallucination was auditory. But Janet also noted that other patients' voice-hearing experiences did not fit easily under the heading 'auditory hallucinations'. One of his patients described this as follows:

> It speaks to me all the time, said one of them, it told me that it is necessary to go and ask the pope for a pardon. – Do you know who speaks to you? – No I don't recognise it, it is not a voice of anybody. – The voice, is it far or near? – It is neither far nor near, one would say that it is in my chest. – Is it like a voice? *Not really, it is not a voice, I do not hear anything, I sense that I am spoken to.*
>
> (Ibid., our emphasis)

Silent voices are difficult to categorise as hallucinations since they do not have an obvious sensory modality: 'When one describes an hallucination, it is necessary before anything else, we believe, to indicate what sense is involved, to which category of sensations it attaches itself' (ibid.). Janet reported that alienists referred to voices without auditory qualities as 'psychic hallucinations', which according to him explained nothing. The phenomenon was also given the name 'epigastric voice', which to Janet indicated no more than the usual place of occurrence. Janet turned to Charcot (1881) and Seglas (1888, 1889) to provide him with a starting point for his account of 'silent voices'. According to him, Charcot postulated three types of language – 'auditive, visual or motor, and the last name he gave to the language composed of tactile or muscular images through which we go to speak' (Janet, 1891, p. 276).[3] Seglas then used Charcot's scheme to define 'a species of verbal hallucinations which are a specie of language' (ibid., p. 277). Janet wrote that in Seglas' scheme there were

> auditory hallucinations of language . . . visual hallucinations of writing, and finally the third category will be formed by the hallucinations of those tactile and muscular sensations which constitute Charcot's motor type. And these hallucinations which Mr Seglas calls 'verbal psycho-motor' will be precisely the epigastric voices of the aliened.
>
> (Ibid.)

Janet supported Seglas with the following empirical observations. He noted 'real movements of the mouth and the tongue corresponding to the words which the subject *pretends* to perceive mysteriously' (ibid., our emphasis) and also that some of his patients could not speak when hearing voices:

> this patient T. could not begin, when I asked her, to speak at the same time she sensed her voices: 'There is', she said, 'something happening which is stopping me from talking at the moment.' The patient could not come to have at the same time two images of the muscular sense type of language.
>
> (Ibid., 278)

Janet did not, however, accept Seglas' name for this type of hallucination – 'psychomotor verbal hallucinations'. He spends some time clarifying what 'sense' is involved in experiencing them:

> in the present case it is important to realise that there is not at all a psycho-motor image but a sensory image so important that we'll call it muscular image or even better *kinaesthetic image*. We therefore divide hallucinations, like sensations, into auditory, visual etc. . . . and *kinaesthetic*.
>
> (Ibid., p. 279, our emphasis)

Thus drawing on Charcot and Seglas, Janet invented a conception of 'verbal hallucinations', which could in principle be either auditive or kinaesthetic (and sometimes even visual). But according to him, the hallucinations in the two modalities were not equally frequent:

> these auditive hallucinations are rare. Generally these verbal hallucinations are the reproduction of kinaesthetic sensations, the same one experiences when speaking oneself. It is a simple inner language repeating monotonously ever the same idea.
>
> (Janet, 1901, pp. 388–389)

This then is Janet's conception of verbal hallucinations. Now let us return to Marcelle, who had hallucinations in all sensory modalities except for taste, smell or touch (ibid., p. 387). She had visual hallucinations:

She sees black animals move before her; her bed appears to her covered with mice, which she thinks will gnaw her wrist. She sees people pursuing her, they have terrible faces, and she is in great fear. Such visual hallucinations may be recurrent and reproduce exactly 'the same scenery, the same personages, the same attitudes'.

(Ibid.)

She had hallucinations of movement:

One day she attended an electricity seance of Mr Charcot, and she saw a patient afflicted by chorea. She told me on her return that she did not want to go to that service again, because it made her more ill, and gave her St Vitus dance. 'I feel', she told me, 'my right arm moving all the time, it does not stop except when I watch it.' Well, that was perfectly false, her arm did not move but she represented to herself that it moved.

(Janet, 1891, p. 278)

And she had auditory but *non-verbal* hallucinations: 'She has sometimes hallucinations about hearing. She tells us that she hears noises, music; sometimes she starts, turns her head in the direction of the noise, and appears to listen' (Janet, 1901, p. 387).

Note three points about these non-verbal hallucinations. First, as Janet presented them, they were true hallucinations: Marcelle had no insight that she was hallucinating rather than perceiving something; she treated them as being in her environment, and guided her actions by them. Second, note that one point of interest for Janet was that some of the hallucinations were repetitive and some were relatively direct reproductions of original experience. Third, the source of these non-verbal hallucinations, where known, was not necessarily traumatic.

Janet paid particular attention to Marcelle's verbal hallucinations. These were 'much more frequent and important' than visual hallucinations. They could be auditory but they were usually, Janet claimed, kinaesthetic perceptions of inner speech:

During these attacks *Marcelle hears someone call her* and would even get up at times to answer. Maria heard and recognised her husband's voice. But we must say that these *auditive hallucinations are rare*. Generally these verbal hallucinations are the reproduction of kinaesthetic sensations, the same one experiences when speaking oneself. It is a simple inner language repeating monotonously ever the same idea. . . . *Marcelle keeps repeating to herself* that her mother and everybody bears her ill will.

(Ibid., pp. 388–389, our emphasis)

Like her visual hallucinations the verbal ones were repetitive. In fact they involved speaking to herself. But did all Marcelle's inward speech become a verbal hallucination? If she spoke to herself deliberately in the cloud period would she necessarily experience this as a verbal hallucination in her lucid period? Not in Janet's account: the inner speech which could metamorphose into hallucinations was automatic and 'despite herself', that which she did not accept as her own. Marcelle therefore reported her experiences to Janet simply as hearing what a voice told her, but Janet had a different version of her experience – she spoke to herself automatically.

Janet found two errors in Marcelle's version of her experiences. First, she believed that somebody was talking to her, but it was herself speaking. This error – mistaking one's own self-directed speech for somebody else's – is essential to Janet's theory of verbal kinaesthetic hallucinations. The error is basically of a 'reality-testing' variety – subjectively generated experience is confused for an objectively generated one. Second, Marcelle also confused her kinaesthetic experience for an auditory experience. This error could be attributed to most patients who reported *hearing* voices (rather than sensing them in some unknown way), but as we have seen, not all of them did this – so this error was 'optional' in the account. Now Marcelle could have mistaken her own inner speech for auditory experience and yet accepted that the voice was a hallucination. So the category of experience mistake is not necessarily of a reality-monitoring variety.

Thus Marcelle's voices were for Janet very much matters of language. And since his approach was consistently pragmatic it is not surprising that he paid particular attention to the 'voices' which told Marcelle to do things:

> Alongside with the ideas of persecution, we notice other utterances of a great importance. *These are kinds of commands or prohibitions simple and fast which repeat themselves with tenacity in their minds.* Her most important ones are the following: 'You have to die . . . it is necessary to die as fast as possible', or even: 'Do not eat, you do not need to eat . . . do not speak, you do not have a voice, you are paralysed, etc.', ill-omened commands, which, as we have seen, do not repeat with clarity except during the periods of cloud, but which have a very great influence on the rest of the life.
>
> (Janet, 1891, p. 279, our emphasis)

So the verbal hallucinations which command are repetitive, like hallucinations in general; but where are their origins? In Leonie's case Janet put their origin in her dissociated alter, Leonie 3. Marcelle's voices on the other hand are really memories, repetitions of past experiences:

> almost all of these ideas, and probably all of them, if one knew the patient better, in some memory of the past life. These ideas do not seem to me to be invented in the current moment in which they are formulated; they are nothing but repetitions. The most visual hallucinations which tormented Marcelle during the winter, were also exact reproductions of a scene which had taken place last year. The fixed ideas of death, of not eating, are repro-ductions of desperate decisions taken some years ago.
>
> (Ibid.)

Here Janet tied Marcelle's command hallucinations to the decisions she had herself made *in the past* and which did not make sense to her now in the present. This is one important point about Janet's account of hallucinations: they are matters of the person's past, unchanging memories. They oriented to the past, not pertinent to the present or the future:

> Today *these ideas reproduce themselves unrelated and without reason.* She has completely forgotten, I am convinced, her old despair and has no desire to die. The dreams of suicide present themselves today *without rapport to her present situation* and Marcelle despairs of these thoughts of suicide which impose themselves on her like a remains of the past. She does not know any more why she does not want to eat. . . . We always find in the fixed ideas the characteristic automatic repetition of the past, without relationship to the present, without present logic.
>
> (Ibid., our emphasis)

This quotation draws out another property of impulsions. Not only are they alien to the person experiencing them, they are also 'without rapport to her present situation'. Impulsions are definitely not simple reflexes (which can be glossed as reactions to the environment). Note though that Janet ignores that impulsions and their consequences cannot be utterly abstracted from the here and now. Marcelle placed one voice she sensed under her bed, and to carry out the commands of other voices Marcelle made use of what the environment afforded her – the staircase on which she floundered was not a memory.

A further important point is that Janet did not consistently narrow the causes of hallucinations to a particular class of past events. Some memories which 'parented' hallucinations were clearly traumatic. These included Marie's self-immersion in freezing water to stop her periods[4] and Marcelle's one-time decision to kill herself and whatever that decision was supposed to resolve for her. Other such events, however, were hardly traumatic. To add to our previous examples, the following voices of Marcelle originated in a mundane social episode which could hardly have been so traumatic and shameful to have to be hidden:

> A young girl came to be brought to the same room as Marcelle, and like her was a bit ill. As is common among the aliened, she sought to make acquaintance with her neighbours. This person approached Marcelle and wanted to chat, but she was met with an outburst of a bad temper from our patient and started saying loudly: 'Oh! Miss, you are giving me an evil eye, you are frightening me.' This sufficed to modify the crises in Marcelle. For the next few days her voices repeated: 'The whole world is afraid of you, all the world shuns you etc.' The ideas of persecution have, relative to their parents, the origin in the same genre.
>
> (Ibid., p. 280)

We expected an explanation of why the memory of the young girl's words became dissociated in Marcelle's mind and was relived in hallucinations, but Janet (1891) did not provide it. The point is that he did not over-use the concept of trauma. Young (1995) was correct to place Janet in the history of 'trauma' conception but it seems reasonably clear that at least where hallucinations were concerned their parent causes were not for him necessarily traumatic. But since hallucinations were dissociated impulses, not all dissociation could be a matter of trauma. The point implicit in all this is the following: traumatic events are often said to be *re*-narrated in memory so as to attenuate their hurt (Freud, 1950). Janet's examples of Marcelle's hallucination are, however, relatively direct representations of the parent events, very much unlike in psychoanalysis, but not just there. We have seen this in Freud's analysis of Schreber's hallucinations (Freud, 1911/1972) but also in that of Schatzman and Louis Sass (Schatzman, 1976; Sass, 1992), where his hallucinations required painstaking interpretation. According to Ellenberger (1970, p. 344), Janet specifically objected to Freud's method of symbolic interpretation, calling it metaphysics (see also Micale, 1994). In the example introduced above, Marcelle over-generalised the parent event in her hallucination but she did not re-symbolise it. This is the point about Janet's account of experiences of hearing voices: he saw them as relatively direct repetitions of his patients' past experiences, which are not re-symbolised and remain relatively fixed in succeeding re-experiences. At one point Jane considered that memories change simply by virtue of being split off and isolated (Janet, 1910) but he did not seem to pursue this point. The repetition of split-off experiences without a change is clearly crucial to Janet's account: to maintain that voices are expressions of *fixed* ideas, the ideas have to remain fixed. They do not change because they are dissociated from the rest of the personality and are not accommodated to the situation. The consequence of this is that Janet was less privileged than Freud in therapeutic transactions – there was no 'real meaning' or 'code' which only clinicians could know.

But of course we know already that not all 'voices' are repetitive – the advice given by the daemon of Socrates was apt and relevant to new situations (see Chapters 1 and 9, and cf. Leudar *et al.*, 1997). Were Janet's patients, and Marcelle in particular, different? Janet possibly listened to them selectively – he certainly discounted some of what Marcelle told him:

> *Marcelle pretends*, in fact, that, during the cloud, she is told a lot of things. *She exaggerates a little*. It seemed to us that these frequent inner speeches were but little varied, being insistently repeated, like the deliriums of an hysterical crisis. *We establish*, first, in these speeches ideas of persecutions, a quite important fact with this kind of patients. Marcelle keeps repeating to herself that her mother and everybody bears her ill will. . . . These ideas vary only according to the person she has to do with.
>
> (Janet, 1901, p. 389, our emphasis)

So we do not know everything which the voices told Marcelle. Clearly she reported more to Janet than he told us, but she 'pretended' and 'exaggerated'. Her voices were *really* only slightly altered repetitions of her past experiences. Janet does occasionally slip into assimilating Marcelle's experiences into his theory.

One of the questions we started this chapter with was how Janet accounted for actions in response to hallucinations. We have seen that in *Automatisme psychologique* Janet categorised hallucinations as impulsions but did not see them as sources of impulsive acts. Indeed, he wrote that hallucinations did not 'seem to have a disposition to cause any act' (1889, p. 428), but he himself provided examples of patients who habitually did as the voices told them:

> One heard a voice which repeated to him: 'Do not move or you are lost', and he stayed immobile in an apparent stupor. Another heard a voice which commanded him to throw ten francs into the Seine.
>
> (Ibid., pp. 428–429)

By the time he wrote *Psychological Healing*, Janet had changed his position and accepted that hallucinations not only are actions but also result in actions:

> In hallucinations, too, there are dispositions, present actions, and preparations for future actions. Irene runs away from the tap; when she sees a glass of water she makes gestures of terror and disgust; at meals she insists on having a bottle of water which has been brought from elsewhere.
>
> (Janet, 1925, p. 224)

So how did Janet explain the actions in obedience to voices? There were some obvious lines of argument open to him:

- perhaps no special explanation is required at all since commands of hallucinatory voices work exactly like other verbal commands;
- voices could cause actions in the same way as post-hypnotic suggestions;
- voices could be accompanied by impulsive desires and it would be these that cause actions.

We shall see that Janet developed the second position. In the 1891 article he accepted that hallucinations affected Marcelle's subsequent conduct. But Janet was not explaining actions which were necessarily temporally contingent on verbal hallucinations (like those of Irene) – Marcelle only did in the lucid *period* what the voices told her to do in the cloud period: 'the phenomena which happened during the period of cloud have an extremely serious influence in the intervals of lucid thought' (p. 280).

> The fixed ideas of the cloud period are expressed in the subconscious movements during the lucid period. For instance after a period of crisis in which she hears voices telling her she must die, her actions are directed to that end without her knowing – 'One day she steered towards a stairs, she stopped

on the first step, and then moved away not understanding why she came there: it was a subconscious movement due to the ideas of suicide which were *previously* dominant.'

(Ibid., p. 281, our emphasis)

Following these internal chats, we note a third consequence of the cloud period, which is that despite herself, *during the lucid periods, she carried out the commands given to her during the cloud periods by her hallucinations.* Voices told her: 'You do not have speech anymore, you cannot speak anymore' or: 'You cannot eat', and she cannot speak anymore or obstinately refuses to eat. She recognises that it is absurd, makes me all sorts of possible promises, everything is useless; when she sits at the table she clenches her teeth and cannot open her mouth.

(Ibid., p. 283, our emphasis)

The problem which interests us is: actions of exactly what *kind* were caused by Marcelle's voices? When she did as the voices told her were these voluntary acts under her control? We have seen already that Janet characterised Marcelle's actions during the period of cloud as 'automatic and impersonal'. Now the actions in response to voices are also such actions – some as subconscious, others as against her will and none of them understood by Marcelle herself, and therefore they are not fully intentional and rational. We need to find out more about Janet's theory of action, but before we do so let us note that the hallucinations of the cloud period were also sources of delusional beliefs:

Then comes the period of interpretation: 'If she can't eat, then it is because she does not need to; she does not have a stomach like the other times; she is not hungry, she has a cardboard stomach; she is completely changed, etc.' These interpretations, expressed with doubt and hesitation to explain her resistance, will completely naturally transform themselves during the next crisis of cloud into hallucinations and once the patient entered this vicious circle the crises will be stronger and stronger and the intervals of lucidity lesser and lesser.

(Ibid.)

Janet saw hallucinations as a source of delusion, as did Dr Weber in Schreber's case. He moreover observed that these delusions could become 'parent events' of new hallucinations. Janet (ibid.) did not say whether Marcelle's delusional interpretations were split off even from their parent fixed ideas or whether they augmented them – strictly speaking he should not have admitted the latter if he wanted to keep his fixed ideas fixed. In fact he accepted elsewhere that fixed ideas grow, but slowly:

They grow, they install themselves in the field of thought like a parasite, and the subject cannot check their development by any effort on his part, because they are ignored, because they exist by themselves in a second field of thought detached from the first.

(Janet, 1901, p. 267)

In Janet's account therefore, hallucinations can be sources of dissociation as well as its consequences. Let us return to Janet's treatment of *actions* in response to hallucinations. According to him these are like actions of a person who received a post-hypnotic suggestion during somnambulism:

> I have made the following observations: During the somnambulism I gave Marcelle the following posthypnotic suggestion, but I chose a rather difficult act which could not be executed crudely and without consciousness. I told her to remove an apron which I had on, which was for her, being so timid, a complicated and serious act. On waking up she did not do so, but she stopped talking, she regarded me with serious air; in one word she took on the attitude which characterises her when she is tormented by an obsession. If I interrogate her, she responds: 'It is again one of my ideas which is tormenting me.' She was completely persuaded about the identity of my suggestion with her fixed ideas and saw no difference at all. . . . *We can see then that these two things, obsessions and post-hypnotic suggestions, are strongly analogical; the laws known of one can be used by us to understand the others.*

(Janet, 1891, p. 284, our emphasis)

Fixed ideas and impulsions for Janet were therefore like suggestions, even though they resulted from natural causes rather than experimental interventions (1925, p. 278). So to understand how Janet explained actions in response to voices we need to know more about his conception of action in general and of suggested action in particular.

Janet considered suggestion to be a distinct psychological phenomenon.[5] It was not to be explained as an emotion (p. 222) or as 'social influence' (p. 215). And despite the fact that 'the majority of suggestions are made through speech, or by signs which correspond to speech' (p. 214) and even though 'there is certainly some analogy between a suggestion and a command, for both phenomena are based upon the fundamental association between the verbal sign and the corresponding action' (p. 244), Janet distinguished 'suggestion' from the ordinary communicative use of words: 'the command may be carried out after deliberation, acceptation, and decision, whether these operations are repeated in the case of each specific command, or whether they have been made once for all as regards certain categories of commands' (p. 245).

The suggestions, on the other hand, lack the 'deliberations, acceptation, and decision'. He illustrated the difference with the following example:

> A woman to whom I was trying to make a suggestion interrupted me, saying: 'That's not caught on this time.' Yet she had understood me perfectly well,

she had accepted the idea I had expressed, for she added: 'You tell me to do this, and I will do it if you like, but I warn you that what you say has not caught on.' She felt that the action would be done voluntarily after acceptation, but that it would not develop spontaneously as had done actions following previous suggestion.

(Ibid., p. 216)

The point about suggestions is that they are incomplete actions (p. 224) and what distinguishes them from complete actions is that they are not done 'deliberately' and 'after acceptation'. According to Janet all actions (even the incomplete ones) begin with the activation of tendencies, and much of his theory of action is succinctly summarised in the following quotation:

These tendencies, these dispositions to the performance of aggregate of co-ordinated movements, may remain in a 'latent condition' or may be 'activated' more or less completely by passing through the stages of 'erection,' 'desire,' and 'effort,' in order to reach at length the stage of 'completed action' or 'triumph.'

(Ibid., p. 229)

Suggestions may be carried out as 'co-ordinated movements', or to 'triumph', as Janet put it, yet they will still be incomplete. We have already seen that suggestions lack 'deliberateness', 'acceptation' and 'decision'. And the 'completeness' Janet had in mind was certainly not just the matter of observable behaviours or in instrumental success because, in this respect, even suggestions can be complete:

Between desire and effort, and sometimes between effort and completed action I have placed a very interesting stage of activation. *This is characterised by the complete or almost complete performance of the movements proper to action, a performance complete enough to generate the illusion of the action in the spectator or the performer: and nevertheless characterised also by certain insufficiency,* so that action cannot produce the appropriate outward effects, since there is a more or less complete suppression of those perfectionments of the action which would render it psychologically real. This is the stage of 'quasi-action' (Baldwin), or of 'ludic action.'

(Ibid., our emphasis)

In extreme cases of hysteria, suggested actions can be carried out utterly without awareness, 'unwittingly'. 'Subconscious actions' for Janet were those whose insufficiency was pushed to the extreme and involved lack of the memory for action itself (ibid., p. 229; and see Janet, 1910).

So what 'perfectionments' could make evolving tendencies 'psychologically real'? According to Janet, 'the action has to be adapted to the outer world and it has to be also adapted to our own individuality' (1925, p. 225); and every action is 'an addition to our personality, which not only preserves the memory of action, but assimilates the action and considers it as a part of itself' (p. 226).

The incomplete actions – including those in response to verbal hallucinations – are defective in their lack of adaptation to the personality of the 'doer', they do not harmonise with the 'subject's individual tendencies', and their 'insufficiency relates especially to the subjective modifications of the individual, to the adaptations of his personality to his action' (p. 229).

By completeness of an action therefore, Janet meant much more than just accomplishments of movements or instrumental success, but how did he propose that ordinary actions achieve the adaptation to the outer world and psychological completeness, both of which are missing in suggestions and actions in response to hallucinations?

> in the case of every action there must occur a series of psychological operations which, first of all, transform the action so as to harmonise with the tendencies and the interest of the doer; and, secondly, transform the individuality of doer in so far as the memory of action becomes part of the individual's archives, and in so far as the personality of the doer is augmented and transformed by the addition of this new element.
>
> (Ibid., p. 226)

Completing an action psychologically therefore involves both transforming it and also adjusting the personality of the doer to it. But how is this achieved? In 'inward conversations', says Janet – it is significant that well before Pavlov (1928), Vygotsky (1934/1962) or Luria (1961) he stressed the pivotal role of internal speech in regulating activities.

Actions involve activation of tendencies. According to Janet this activation can be 'arrested' and the doer may 'assent' to a tendency or he may withhold the 'assent'. Janet is not using 'assent' here metaphorically – he indeed meant dialogical assent: 'a reaction to a special kind of stimulus, such as a *question*. It matters not whether the question is asked by the subject himself or is put to him by another' (1925, p. 234). The assent can be given without consideration – impulsively – but the important type of assent is 'reflective assent': 'the essence of reflection is arrest, a slowing down of assent, which allows the subject to test the awakened tendency by a comparison with a number of other tendencies' (p. 236).

Janet argued that reflection was essentially an inward conversation 'of *ideas* which in verbal form represent competing tendencies'. But why conversation of ideas and not of words or sentences? Ideas as Janet defined them are divorced from actions – their 'tendency to evoke deeds is enfeebled' (p. 234). Inward conversations of ideas were thus possible without actual action taking place. Janet defined the conceptions of 'will' and belief in this frame. *Will*, according to him, is 'an assent which relates to an immediate action whose conditions of execution are actually realised' (p. 234), and 'All belief is an assent that bears upon the conditional performance of actions' (p. 235). What this means is that acting without will may involve acting out a tendency without arresting and giving it a reflexive assent. And the 'reflexive assent' is formulated in inward conversations which prepare the individual for action:

The presentation of alternatives and the estimate of their comparative worth must be regarded as imaginative trials of the action in the form of internal speech. Such a trial gives rise to social reactions within us. In these internal discussions, we recall moral rules, praise or blame the various witnesses and ourselves, or revive the memory of similar actions and their favourable or unfavourable consequences.

(Ibid., p. 239)

However, it is important to bear in mind that the inward conversations do not just select and inhibit tendencies – they transform them. They complete them psychologically and adapt them to the environment:

The decisions that are the result of such a work [of reflection] are by no means identical with voluntary actions and beliefs that are the outcome of immediate assent. They are essentially different, for the original tendency had been transformed; it had undergone evolution through adapting itself to all the commands it has encountered in the course of the reflective process.

(Ibid., p. 240)

According to Janet, actions and beliefs based on reflections are more determined and stable – voluntary actions become 'resolutions'. It is in reflections that actions are adjusted to the personality and the personality is adapted to action (ibid.). We have noted above that impulsions are not reflexes, but it is clear that Janet's complete actions are not 'situated actions' (see Costall and Leudar, 1996). Their adaptation to the environment is achieved mentally and not as a matter of situated improvisation. Janet's inward conversations can, however, do the work which Freud assigns to the ego and the superego, and do this without being compartmentalised and in a more flexible fashion.

So how are the actions in response to hallucinations explained by Janet? Voices are phenomena of cloud periods. Patients act on them as if on suggestions given by hypnotists. The actions in obedience of voices are incomplete – they are split off from the personality of the doer and they do not fit into the current environment. The reason for this is that the voice impulsions are not arrested and reflected on in inward conversations. Instead they are given an 'impulsive assent' and are allowed to 'triumph'. The point to note is that in Janet's account there is no gap between command hallucinations and actions – the action is the unfolding of the disposition in the hallucination. This is in the spirit of Pragmatism, and recalls both Dewey's profound critique of the notion of 'reflex' (Dewey, 1896) and Mead's notion of transaction (Mead, 1938/1972; see also Chapter 9). Moreover, it is obvious that Janet's view of hallucinations as incomplete actions does make it easier to explain their compulsiveness.

To summarise some salient points about Janet's account of hallucinations:

• Hallucinations are impulsions; that is, incomplete activities.

- They are definitely pathological experiences. Not only are they the phenomena of cloud periods but they also have pathological consequences both in lucid periods (suggested actions) and in cloud periods (delusions).[6]
- Hallucinations as dissociated fixed ideas are repetitions of past experiences which were not necessarily traumatic.[7]
- Hallucinations are relatively direct repetitions and Janet does not attempt to interpret them symbolically.[8]

So let us at last return to Marcelle. All we know about her and her experiences of voices comes to us from Janet. It is obvious that Marcelle reported to Janet some experiences of hearing voices which he does not pass on – claiming that she exaggerates a little. The point is that to some extent Janet seems to have filtered Marcelle's hallucinations to retain those which made sense to him in the frame of his theory. Hallucinations are impulsions and, like other impulsions, they are repetitions of past experiences which had become dissociated. There is no point in speculating about what Marcelle reported to him which he does not pass on – she is not our case, she was Janet's.

Marcelle reported that at least in some cases her voices had auditory quality, but Janet maintained that she sensed them kinaesthetically. This is possibly because Marcelle's voices were anonymous and none of them seemed aligned to individuals known to her. Janet was willing to accept that the voices were *auditory* verbal hallucinations when the patients reported that they sounded like an identifiable figure.

Marcelle heard voices which told her to do things that included commands to harm herself. She also experienced voices which abused her. Janet attributed the origins of her voices to 'parent events' in the past, the memories of which became dissociated from the rest of Marcelle's person. Not all these 'parent events' were obviously traumatic, however. Marcelle's dissociation is a matter not just of the nature of what is done to a person but also of their inherent weakness. Marcelle acted on her voices impulsively but she could also resist their commands. Did she converse with her voices? Janet does not analyse any such conversations, but remember that Marcelle's voices were herself talking to herself automatically.

5 Pragmatists on self

Voice hearers do not experience voices as their own talk. Achilles of the *Iliad* heard gods, Socrates was advised by a daemon, Schreber did not experience Ariman's messengers as parts of himself, and Marcelle's voices were strangers to herself. None of them said 'this voice is me' or 'this is me speaking', yet it is arguable that voices are voice hearers' own speech. This is what Pierre Janet proposed – hallucinatory voices are the voice hearer's own *automatic* and so partly subconscious speech – and subsequent research provided some evidence for his proposal (Gould, 1949; Cacioppo and Petty, 1981; Green and Preston, 1981). Yet this is not how voice hearers experience voices, and we will investigate their reasons for denying authorship of the voice-talk in Chapter 9. These include the following:

- Voice hearers do not intend the voices to speak but the voices do so anyway (and vice versa).
- They cannot control the voice-talk as they can their own speech (e.g. stop it, change it or correct it).
- The experiences, such as the effort and movements involved in speaking and the coordinated sound of one's voice, which normally accompany speaking are missing in 'hearing voices'.
- The sentiments the voices utter may be alien or abhorrent: 'This is not me!'

These are good reasons for disowning the voice-talk, but then the problem is, who is it speaking? This is the beginning of an enigma for a voice hearer – this voice I hear is not me talking, yet, even when other people are present, only I experience it. Some voice hearers solve this problem by assuming that voices come from supernatural agencies and address them and nobody else. Schreber believed himself to be singled out in this way – his 'nervous illness' allowed him to hear what others could not. Plutarch's account of the daemon of Socrates was also of this sort, even though the reason why Socrates heard voices was his purity and wisdom and not a nervous illness. But this supernatural solution creates a problem. If the gods speak only to me, I had better be sure that they are the right gods and that I am in a warranted position to hear them – this was so for the heroes of the *Iliad* but not for Socrates or Schreber – otherwise what beckon are exile, madness and death.

But if the voice hearer rejects the supernatural account the enigma of voices becomes pressing – these voices which I and only I hear must come from me, yet I do not experience them as mine. How can there be parts of me which are not me? One solution to this problem is to accept the clinicians' version: the voices are hallucinations and so symptoms of mental illness. Only in this sense are voices aspects of oneself – as symptoms of one's illness. The question 'who is speaking?' is answered by 'nobody, it's just hallucinations', and 'what do the voices mean?' is answered by 'they mean your illness, nothing else'.

Another solution is to disregard the romantic ideal of the coherent self and to adjust the conception so that it does not necessarily encompass all of one's experiences. (This of course does not mean abandoning the effort to maintain some unity in one's life in the face of social discontinuities.) Then voices might well become a part of my person without belonging to that which I experience as me. Hearing voices should be approached from the perspective of each voice hearer – how do they individually formulate their relationship to voices? In Chapter 9 we will also investigate in detail contemporary voice hearers' own accounts of how their voices are real or unreal to them. In this chapter, however, we will remain with the accounts of specialists who have studied voices as 'mutations of self' (cf. Sass, 1992, Ch. 7). Such mutations are said to involve alienation from one's experiences: from an observer's point of view they belong to a person who, however, does not accept them as their own. In this sense hearing voices involves dissociation of self – voices are experiences which are somehow split off from the voice hearer's flow of experience, yet only partly, because they are not fully unconscious, as Janet had shown (see Chapter 4). In this chapter we bring into the book the work of two pragmatists – William James and G.H. Mead – to formulate this perspective more clearly. We do not aim to present complete critical summaries of their accounts of self and conduct (see Ayer, 1968; Wilshire, 1968; Bird, 1986; Joas, 1985); instead we will focus on how the two psychologists explained continuity, unity and identity of self on the one hand, and its fragmentations on the other. It is important to understand that in no way are we testing Mead's and James' models of self against the phenomenon of voices – they did not set out to explain hearing voices and could simply declare it to be irrelevant. Our aim is rather to use their vocabularies and distinctions they introduced into self to understand voices. Their accounts may provide an interesting additional perspective on voices, or they may not.

William James on consciousness of self

Let us start with William James' *Principles of Psychology* (James, 1891). In the chapter 'Consciousness of self' he wrote the following:

> What the particular *perversions of the bodily sensibility* may be, which give rise to these contradictions [of the unity of the me], is for the most part *impossible for a sound-minded person to conceive*. One patient has another self that repeats all his thoughts for him. Others, *among whom are some of the first characters in history, have*

familiar daemons who speak with them, and are replied to. In another someone 'makes' his thoughts for him. Another has two bodies, lying in different beds. Some patients feel as if they had lost parts of their bodies.

(p. 377, our emphasis)

Perhaps James did mean to refer to Socrates in this paragraph. If he did, then like the French alienists, he saw Socrates' voice as a pathological phenomenon. He grouped it with what would nowadays be first-rank symptoms of psychosis, and considered all of them to be 'mutations of self'. Each of the experiences was mentioned because it involved a disunity of self: the patients declared that their acts, utterances, their thoughts and even their bodies were not their own. How did James account for these disunities of self? He wrote that they were due to 'perversions of the bodily sensibility'. In order to make sense of this we need to find out something about how he related 'bodily sensibility' to continuity, unity and identity of self.

James distinguished 'empirical self' (a problem for psychologists) from a pure ego, which, according to him, is not experienced directly but is instead conceptually implicit in experience (and hence a problem for philosophers); we shall be concerned with the former. His initial definition of the empirical self was 'the sum total of all that he can call his, not only his body and his psychic powers' (1891, p. 291). This means that some aspects of self were for James not bound by the body – they were, as he put it, 'extra-corporeal'. He did write that this was self-defined 'in its widest possible sense', and he subdivided it into 'material', 'social' and 'spiritual' selves. It is unfortunately customary for the commentators on James to ignore the former two kinds of self and to focus on the 'spiritual self'. This is not surprising, especially since James was at his most original in formulating 'spiritual self', but in our view the bias makes the commentaries on his account of self incomplete and much less interesting nowadays.

Material self includes a person's body but extends beyond it. Our families are, according to James, parts of ourselves. 'When they die, a part of ourselves is gone. If they do anything wrong it is our shame' (1891, p. 292). James further included under material self one's work product, possessions and property, as well as the body and the family. *Social self* also goes beyond the individual – James succinctly defined it as 'the recognition which he gets from his mates' (p. 293). So far then, James' conception of self is surprisingly contemporary despite being over a hundred years old – self is not just a mental phenomenon but also a social and material one, and it does not exactly coincide with the body. Moreover, unlike G.H. Mead (1934), James did not totalise social self in the conception 'generalised other'. According to James, 'a man has as many social selves as there are individuals *who recognise him and carry an image of him in their mind*' (1981, p. 294, our emphasis). (Note that even James' very broad initial definition of self was not broad enough – the self now depends on recognitions by others, not just on what 'he can call his own'.)

James argued that as those individuals performing the recognition fall into classes, so do one's social selves – 'He has as many different social selves as there are distinct *groups of persons about whose opinion he cares*' (1891, p. 294, original emphasis). A person can, then, have several social selves but this division is not arbitrary and reflects the varieties in a person's social engagements. So according to James, the discontinuities in me partly reflect the discontinuities in my social life. Using contemporary terminology we could say that James saw social selves as socially situated. He wrote: 'he generally shows a different side of himself to each of these different groups' (ibid.).

James' social selves – being a friend, employer, customer, lover – depend on recognition by others, and this implies that they are formed in varied social relationships, and invoked and situated in them. Different characters could possibly develop in a person's life history, yet only some of them will, and different social selves can come to conflict when they demand incompatible activities (1891, pp. 293–295). An interesting point is that James established these facts about struggles for social self mainly with recourse of common sense and without a detailed analysis, and he did not ask whether different social selves enter into dialogues, whether one social self could change another one just in a mental engagement, or whether only involvement with other people achieves this. We will return to the relationship between common sense and technical aspects in James' arguments later in the chapter. What matters now is that James did not see the fragmentation of social self to be pathological – it reflected the richness of a person's social life and the variety of her social positions in it – and he did not use the discontinuities in *social* self to explain 'doubling of personality', or 'possessions and mediumships' (in which he was interested) or 'hearing voices' (which is our topic). These pathologies involved discontinuities of spiritual self caused by failures of memory.

James' social selves were not static. He distinguished between *actual* and *potential* self and tied the latter to ideals – according to him, a potential self is worthy of aspiration if it receives an approving recognition from 'the highest *possible* judging companion'. According to James, the *growth* of the social self involves 'the substitution of higher tribunals for lower, this ideal tribunal is the highest, and most men, either continually or occasionally carry reference to it in their breast' (1891, p. 316). Moreover, the tribunals one faces are not abstract principles:

> probably no one can make sacrifices for 'right' without to some degree personifying the principle of right for which the sacrifice is made, and expecting thanks from it . . . [but individuals] differ a good deal in the degree in which they are haunted by this sense of ideal spectator.
>
> (Ibid.)

So the history of social self is partly a matter of recognition by others, and partly indexical to judgements of imagined but personified tribunals.

Could such tribunals be not just personified but also concretised and experienced as voices in some individuals? There is certainly a pragmatic similarity between the two. Voices may, like James' tribunals, judge and evaluate voice hearers and their deeds (see Nayani and David, 1996; Leudar *et al.*, 1997).

Schreber's voices did this. The point is, however, that James did not see the inner tribunals to be pathological. On the contrary, they were for him the seeds of personal and moral development. Yet although in his account the structuring of self into 'me' and the 'judge' is not pathological the structuring into 'me' and the 'voice' is. The difference might well be that the inner tribunals can be accepted as aspects of myself (as the voices of my consciousness), while hallucinatory voices usually cannot – Schreber's voices were not parts of himself even though they could enter his body physically. Hearing voices is more comparable to the situation of K in Kafka's *Trial*. The court judging K is definitely not internal to his person or benign. It is personified, but cannot be known directly but only through its messengers. Its judgements do not result in personal development for K but exclusion. Schreber's supernatural judges were also malign, but can we just declare this? Are there no voices which comment on what their hearers do in a positive way?

James did not see social and situational fragmentation of self to be a matter of individual pathology, but it would be a mistake to think that his views align him with contemporary 'post'modernists, who regard unitary and lasting self as an illusion. The continuity of a person was for James chiefly maintained by *spiritual self*. For him this was relatively the most enduring and intimate part of self, the focus of personal coherence, and its central nucleus.

So what is this spiritual self? James characterised it as the 'self of all the other selves', 'the active element in all consciousness' and as a 'source of effort and attention, and the place from which appear to emanate the fiats of the will' (1891, p. 298); thus 'spiritual self' seems to have a similar meaning to the more familiar term 'agency'. James maintained a dichotomy between self as a public social object, and self as a psychological process, visible only to itself. The *social* selves, we have seen, depend on recognitions provided to me by other people, as well as on their memories of me, and so one's social self seen as a whole is necessarily fragmented, situated and contingent. *Spiritual* self, on the other hand, according to James is private, continuous and relatively lasting.

Spiritual self is the *stream of thought* which, as James pointed out, is phenomenally continuous. There may be actual objective discontinuities in it, which are detectable by other people (doctors for instance see one unconscious under the effects of anaesthetic), but James argued that these gaps are edited out of our personal experience – 'thought', he wrote, 'is sensibly continuous' (ibid., p. 225). But there is a problem – the stream of thought may be continuous, but it is a continuous *change* (ibid.). Yet the basic feeling characteristic of being a person is that one remains the same, within time-limits of course and barring dramatic events. So how can the 'stream of thought' and the 'self' be the same? Equating the spiritual self with some of the stream of thought provided James with a phenomenally continuous self, but one which would be continuously changing and without a fixed identity. James' solution was to privilege the present segment of the stream of thought (he called it the 'I') and to allow it to inspect introspectively other segments of the stream of thought (some of them being accepted as 'me' and others disowned as 'not me'). So spiritual self is not just a stream of thought, but a stream which can inspect itself – we abandon 'the outward looking point of view', and 'think of subjectivity as such', [we] 'think of ourselves as thinkers' (ibid., p. 296). James considered dividing 'consciousness' into 'sciousness', which would be a pure stream of experience which just happens and which can, however, observe itself, and thus become consciousness and reflexive spiritual self.[1] Despite his well-known experiments with introspection, James was not actually entirely persuaded by what he characterised as a common-sense assumption that such consciousness could 'think its own existence' and observe itself as it happens:

> But this condition of the experience is not one of the things experienced at the moment; *this knowing is not immediately known. It is only known in subsequent reflection* [our emphasis]. Instead then the stream of thought being one of *con*-sciousness, 'thinking its own existence along with whatever else it thinks,' (as Ferrier says) it might be better called a stream of *Sciousness* pure and simple, thinking objects of some of which it makes what it calls a 'Me', and only aware of its 'pure' Self in an abstract, hypothetic or conceptual way. Each 'section' of the stream would then be a bit of sciousness or knowledge of this sort, including and contemplating its 'me' and 'not-me' as objects which work out their drama together, but not yet including or contemplating its own subjective being.
>
> (Ibid., p. 304, emphasis in original)

James' spiritual self is therefore reflexive and this involves the present consciousness inspecting the former segments in the stream of thought: 'seeing and thinking' them as 'me' and 'not-me' (ibid., pp. 400–401). So for James the continuity of a person was a matter of phenomenal continuity of the stream of thought with the identity of spiritual self being maintained through introspection and dependent on memory. The point to notice is that the present 'I' may become a 'me' (or 'not-me') in the future, and the present 'me' (or 'not-me') will have formerly been an 'I'. The continuity of spiritual self then involves the transformation of agency (the 'I') into, let us say, 'objectivity' ('the me') in our reflections and memories.

The reflexivity of the spiritual self as James defined it was thus very much a psychological matter – it is not socially mediated, but rather a matter of remembering and an inward perception. Before we comment on this any further let us briefly consider whether in James' account social selves are also reflexive. Remember that social self is a social recognition of oneself by others and their memories of one, but it also involves judgement by internalised tribunals. Such judgements are clearly an instance of social reflexivity, but this is not the only sort which James provided for social self. He wrote:

> These images of us in the minds of other men are, it is true, things outside of me, whose changes I perceive just as I perceive any other outward change. But the pride and shame which I feel are not concerned merely with *those* changes. I feel as if something else had changed too, when I perceive my image in your mind to have changed for the worse, something in me to which

that image belongs, and which a moment ago I felt inside of me, big and strong and lusty, but now weak, contracted, and collapsed.

(Ibid., pp. 321–322)

Social self therefore consists of an image which others have formed of me and which I note. So like the spiritual self, social self can be reflexive, except that the image is in one person and its reflection on it is in another person. The image aspect of my social self is extra-corporeal and belongs to the person who is providing me with the recognition, but it is 'I' who 'see and think' this image as 'me'. In fact, according to James, I not only *perceive* the image another has of me, but also react to it emotionally. Social self as James formulated it is not just situationally fragmented – a person may have many social selves – but each is also distributed between the person whose social self it is and the one who is providing the recognition. The reflexivity of self (not just of spiritual self) is for James both a psychological and a social matter with its social aspects being both internal to the individual and 'extra-corporeal'.

There are two problems with this spiritual self as an account of self which knows itself. The first one is simply an omission – James did not hold that the stream of thought *always* reflects on itself, but he did not specify when it does. The second problem is potentially more serious – it is not obvious why the spiritual self defined in this way should be experienced as having a fixed identity. Why should the 'I' 'repeatedly egotistically appropriate', to use James' words, parts of the stream of thought to one and the same 'me'? Setting aside the possibility that this is simply a matter of grammar (see Muhlhäusler and Harré, 1990), one can simply ask what remains unchanging to the backward glance of the 'I'. James certainly regarded this as a real problem. He quoted Ribot (1885), who held that what remains unchanging is the 'feeling of life' (1891, p. 375), but he also looked for an answer through introspection and found, as we shall see, that what was unchanging was proprioceptions 'in the head or between the head and throat' (ibid., p. 301).[2]

James based much of his account of spiritual self on philosophical analysis, but he also based it on introspection and tried to 'think his own existence along with whatever else he thought'. He asked himself: What does *my* feeling of 'central, active self' actually consist of? To his introspection it appeared as follows. He was 'aware of a constant play of "furtherances" and "hindrances"' in his thinking, 'checks and releases, tendencies which run with desire, and tendencies which run the other way' (ibid., p. 299). But these were not simply mental matters; by introspecting, James was tempted to conclude that his spiritual self was really 'a feeling of bodily activities whose exact nature is by most men overlooked' (ibid., p. 302). He related his introspective experiences to Wundt's 'apperceptions' – the feelings from our bodies:

> The images of feelings we get from our own body, and representations of our own movements distinguish themselves from all others by forming a *permanent* group. We excite the sensations of movement immediately by such impulses of the will as shall arouse the movements themselves; and we excite the visual

and tactile feelings of our body by the voluntary movement of our organs of sense. So we come to conceive this permanent mass of feelings as immediately or remotely subject to our will, and call it the *consciousness of our self.*

(Ibid., p. 303, emphasis in original)

Surprisingly, therefore, introspection told James that his 'spiritual self' was not all spiritual, but embodied (or perhaps less happily *embrained*), with the body maintaining its continuity. This was possibly a profound phenomenological discovery by James, but perhaps it was an artefact of introspecting. Wilshire (1968), claiming James for the history of phenomenology, commented that James' use of introspection misdirected his attention to the brain and the head as embodiments of self rather than to the whole of the living body, and so the introspection distorted his findings. Wittgenstein (1976, pp. 412–413) saw an even more profound problem:

> But what can it mean to speak of 'turning my attention on to my own consciousness'? This is surely the queerest thing there could be! It was a particular act of gazing that I called doing this. I stared fixedly in front of me – but not at any particular point or object. My eyes were wide open, the brows not contracted (as they mostly are when I am interested in a particular object).

Wittgenstein has a point – it is not obvious what anybody does when they say they introspect, even William James. Are they observing their consciousness, as they should according to the psychological meaning of the term? For psychologists, introspection means an examination of internal mental processes, but Wittgenstein's comments indicate that this may be quite simply a nonsense. Introspection may sensibly involve remembering and inspecting one's past, but does it really involve looking inwards at something in principle not observable by others? Not according to Wittgenstein. Introspection may involve *not* seeing what is in front of one, but, as Wittgenstein pointed out, what James got out of his introspection was nothing to do with the self:

> Here we have a case of introspection, not unlike that from which William James got the idea that the 'self' consisted mainly of 'peculiar motions in the head and between the head and throat'. And James' introspection showed, not the meaning of the word 'self' (so far as it means something like 'person', 'human being', 'he himself', 'I myself'), nor any analysis of such thing, but *the state of a philosopher's attention when he says the word 'self' to himself and tries to analyse its meaning.* (And a good deal could be learned from this.)

(1976, pp. 412–413, our emphasis)

How could James possibly know that what he experienced in his introspection – the movements in his head – was anything to do with his spiritual self rather than with the activity of introspecting? The conclusion must be that James' account of spiritual self as consisting of continuous bodily adjustments is suspect, because he arrived at it with a nonsensical method of investigation – introspection. It could still just be true, but there is a another problem concerning introspection and spiritual self. James did not just use introspection as his method of empirical investigation; he also provided spiritual self with an essentially introspective reflexivity to assure the continuous identity of self. Wittgenstein's criticism clearly applies to introspections carried out by any spiritual self, just as it did to the psychological introspection James carried out in the interests of scientific psychology.

Can James stand up to these criticisms? To some extent. First, introspection was not the only method of investigation he used. Second, some of the introspection he used involved examining his past, rather than looking within himself. Third, and perhaps most importantly, the introspective reflexivity of seeing inwards was not the only sort of reflexivity he allowed for the spiritual self. According to him, spiritual self is 'not cognised only in an intellectual way', it is felt directly (James, 1891, pp. 288–289). The relation to oneself, for James, is not only a matter of intellectual reflection, it is also a matter of *self-feeling*. James spent some time discussing self-complacency, self-satisfaction and self-love and characterised these as 'direct and elementary endowments of our nature' and 'worthy to be classed as a primitive emotional species as are, for example, rage or pain' (ibid., pp. 306–307).

An interesting argument concerning James' use of introspection has been put forward by Louis Sass (1992, p. 223). Discussing Schreber's case, Sass considered that introspection as 'looking within' is not an impossible nonsense – one can 'look inwards' and turn to systematic self-examination – but he considered that such immersion in one's own subjectivity is 'an abnormal way of disposing one's attention' and actually pathogenic. According to Sass (1992), inward reorientation involved in introspection puts 'states of consciousness and willing at a remove', resulting in their loss of meaning and intentionality. According to Sass, it is this inward turn, which James postulated to be essentially involved in spiritual self, that in fact produces schizophrenic delusions as well as verbal hallucinations, which Sass characterised as 'externalisations of involution' (Sass, 1992, p. 233). This seems to us too strong a claim and one difficult to warrant. Not everybody who turns to self-contemplation ends up hearing voices and even people who are not introverted may hear voices. Sass has to argue that schizophrenic introversion results in voices with specific characteristics. But his characterisation of voices of schizophrenics is based on case materials which reflect traditional construals of voices in psychiatry rather than on the ground-floor experiences of individuals with schizophrenia.

Mead on the socially reflexive self

James identified himself as a psychologist, so studying self and people's experiences of themselves were legitimate problems in their own right. But he was also a pragmatic philosopher and he believed, along with John Dewey, that the mind originated human activities (see Dewey, 1909). So what was there for the self drawn so intricately by James to do? He assigned a social function to self, namely to mediate the effects of the actions of others on a person: 'But if a man has given up those things which are subject to foreign fate, and ceased to regard them as parts of himself at all, we are well-nigh powerless over him' (James, 1891, p. 312).

The self as a means of social control over an individual was clearly not focal to James' interests, but it was very much the point of G.H. Mead's socially reflexive self. Mead distinguished consciousness from self-consciousness and his aim was to account for social genesis of self-consciousness and for its social functions. Socially reflexive self, according to him, both emerges in coordinated social activities and allows new forms of social actions to emerge (Mead, 1934, pp. 194–196).

Mead formulated the problem as follows: 'the self has a characteristic that it is an object to itself and that characteristic distinguishes it from other objects' (ibid., p. 136) and 'how can an individual get outside himself (experientially) in such a way as to become an object to himself?' (ibid., p. 138). We have seen that this was indeed a problem which also concerned William James. Their answers were, however, different. James' was mainly psychological, while Mead argued that the reflexivity of consciousness develops as a consequence of the individual's involvement in social activities. According to Mead, one becomes an object to oneself by adopting reactions of others to one's conduct (rather than through introspection). Mead formulated the socially reflexive self using two central concepts – 'generalised other' and the 'I/me' dynamic.

Generalised other is in the first place a social instrument which Mead used to explain coordination in joint activities. It is an account of how society enters individuals so that they act in a manner relevant to social activities. Mead's account of self is very much about communication. There are several respects, however, in which his model of communication does not fit effortlessly into contemporary pragmatics. One is the following: most models of communication do not see the speaker to be among the targets of her own message (e.g. Grice, 1957; Searle, 1969; Levinson, 1988). The default case in conversation is when I am addressing you (singular or plural), not us, and you are expected to react to what I say, not I.[3] This was not so in Mead's model of social action. He wrote: 'A person who is saying something is saying to himself what he is saying to others; otherwise he does not know what he is talking about' (1934, p. 147), and 'one responds to that which he addresses to another, and that response of his *becomes a part of his act*' (ibid., p. 140, our emphasis).

The word 'otherwise' in the first quotation is not quite persuasive. A cognitive account of communication might counterclaim that one knows what one is saying as a private meaning before it is expressed in words. A radical pragmatist might assert that one can only know the meaning of what one is saying from its uptake by others (cf. Austin, 1962a). Indeed, whether one is included among the targets of what one says, and in what way, depends on the situation, and it is an occasioned accomplishment (see Leudar and Antaki, 1996b). So there is probably not a general answer to the question, but Mead was making a general point – social acts (including talking) do not simply consist in individuals expressing their intentions; they are also characterised, perhaps in general, by an element of a reaction to oneself from the point of view of another. But then how does reacting internally to one's own actions result in coordinated social activities?[4] Mead proposed that individuals react to their own acts *in the same way as others might do*; the reactions to oneself are not idiosyncratic. According to him, an individual 'inspires' in himself the beginnings of others' parts in common activities. Social interaction in general, and dialogue in particular, involve 'participation in the other. This requires the appearance of the other in the self, the identification of the other with the self, the reaching of self-consciousness through the other' (Mead, 1938/1972, pp. 150–151). The generalised other is thus a set of individual-internal reactions which arises in group activities and serves as a internal proxy for external social agencies.

Can we make a use of the I/generalised other manifold, which Mead introduced into self, to understand the hearing of voices? For instance, can we think of voices as 'generalised other'? Some voices do indeed fit this categorisation – those which react to the activities of voice hearers, and regulate and evaluate them (see Leudar *et al.*, 1997). The prohibitions which Socrates heard were of this sort – the daemon reacted to actions which Socrates was about to carry out, and proscribed him from continuing. Furthermore, categorising voices as generalised other draws our attention to one of their properties we might otherwise miss – they do not seem to be themselves socially reflexive; for instance, they do not comment on what they themselves say (see Chapter 9). Mead's analysis implies that *it is confused thinking to regard voices as persons*.

Other voices, though, do not behave as they should if they were generalised other, or its fragments. Voice hearers report that voices may come spontaneously and not only in reaction to their conduct or thoughts. Reactions of generalised other should be activity-specific, but it is not at all clear that voices are always reactions of an individual typical to a position in an activity. Some are clearly individual-specific in that a voice is aligned with a particular person (real or fictional, dead or alive) and it does not express 'generalised or universal' attitude (see Leudar *et al.*, 1997). Most seriously, however, some voice hearers report hearing two concurrent voices expressing opposite attitudes. This experience is certainly not recognisable as *generalised* other.

Let us return to Mead's account of self. In *Mind, Self and Society* Mead used the same words as James – 'I' and 'me' – but not in the same way. Whereas James considered the proposition that the 'I' is not available to immediate experience to be an interesting possibility, Mead was committed to it. Mead argued that 'the "I" of the present moment is present in the "me" of the next moment' (1934, p. 174) but he amplified that the 'I' 'gets into his experience only after he has carried out the act. Then he is aware of it' (ibid., p. 175).

So how did Mead define 'I' and 'me'? The 'I' was the response of (the biological) organism to the attitudes of others, or more precisely 'the answer which the individual makes to the attitudes which others take toward him when he assumes an attitude toward them' (ibid., p. 177). The 'me' on the other hand was 'an organised set of attitudes of others which one assumes' (ibid., p. 175). Put together, 'he had in him all the attitudes of others, calling for a certain response; that was the "me" of that situation, and his response is the "I"' (ibid., p. 176). But a response requires a distinct point of view, so what is this 'I'? According to Mead, the responses of 'I' also stem from the 'primitive human impulses' provided by evolution (ibid., pp. 347–349).

'I' and 'me', however, were not presented by Mead as a dualism; they stood in a dialectic relationship – the 'me' responds to the actions of the 'I', the 'I' responds to the attitudes of the 'me', and both change in the process. Mead characterised the 'I' and 'me' as different phases of 'self'. Yet he also claimed that there was one crucial difference between reactions of 'I' and 'me' – those of the 'me' are stereotypical and predictable, those of the 'I' are not. The 'me' is a 'conventional, habitual individual' (ibid., p. 197).[5] He regarded 'me' as giving social and conventional form to 'I'. The knowledge of social attitudes of others, internalised in 'me', was for Mead a certainty, but the responses of the 'I' were 'more or less' uncertain, partly because they were a function of the situation. The argument was that since 'I' appears only retrospectively, as a memory once the response has taken place, so it must be uncertain prior to action, and become clear through it, in a 'me'.

In fact, Mead's account of self is even more intricate than our exposition might so far suggest. The first complication is that individuals do not react reflexively to *all* of their own activities, just to some.[6] Only some actions inspire social reactions and only some reactions constitute the generalised other. He wrote:

> When the activity is an organised one in which the different roles because of their organisation all call for an identical response, as in an economic or political process, the individual assumes what may be called the role of the *generalised other*, and the attitude is a universal or rational attitude. The rational attitude which characterises the human being is, then, the relationship of the whole process in which the individual is engaged to himself as reflected in his assumption of the organised roles of the others in stimulating himself to his response.
>
> (Mead, 1938/1972, p. 445, emphasis in original)

So according to Mead one reacts to oneself only in some activities, and the generalised other consists of *rational* reactions and represents 'universal or rational attitude'. Thus the account is constrained to activities in which there is a common reaction (to what one does) and Mead's generalised other represents the rationality of a particular activity. Mead himself distinguished two modes of activity: habitual actions and actions which are under control of reflexive consciousness.

Habitual actions include just 'moving about in a world' and social habitual actions (such as offering a chair to a person who comes into the room). They are characterised by 'a certain amount of sensuous experience' but they do not involve 'thinking' – 'an organism which acts habitually is, and no doubt must be, adjusted to the world'. We have seen this distinction between habitual and thought-out actions already. Julian Jaynes gave voices in antiquity the role of regulating activities when habits failed (Chapter 2). Similarly, in Mead's account, impulsive and instinctive actions are controlled by 'me' (and by 'generalised other'), which are given a similar function to that which Freud gave the superego. The term 'superego' is not mentioned in *Mind, Self and Society* but there are references to 'Freudian psychology' (Mead, 1934, pp. 209–211) and one to Freud (ibid., p. 255n). In both cases Mead was concerned with social control of creative and pathological impulses from within the individual. He acknowledged that not all human conduct is conventional and that the extent of conventionalisation differs from activity to activity. So, in his account, how does novelty enter our actions? For Mead, it 'comes in the action of the "I"'. Mead likened artistic production to 'impulsive conduct'. According to him, in impulsive acts the 'me' does not determine the expression of the 'I'. (So in a sense his account is very similar to the much earlier one of Janet, with impulsive actions corresponding to his automatisms.) And here came Mead's first reference to psychoanalysis: 'If we use a Freudian expression, the "me" is in a sense a censor. It determines the sort of expression which can take place and it gives the cue.' But in 'impulsive conduct', as in artistic work, the 'me' does not exercise control. So Mead acknowledges that 'me' acts like Freud's 'superego' and that 'social control involves the ascendance of the "me" over the "I"'. Mead, however, had no great respect for psychoanalysis and was ambivalent about its concepts. He wrote: 'in the more or less fantastic psychology of the Freudian group, thinkers are dealing with the sexual life and with self-assertion in its violent form'. Discussing how social control can operate through self-criticism, Mead acknowledged Freud in a footnote as follows:

> Freud's conception of the psychological 'censor' represents a partial recognition of this operation of social control in terms of self-criticism, a recognition namely, of its operation with reference to sexual experience and conduct. But this same censorship or criticism of himself by the individual is reflected also in all the other aspects of his social experience, behaviour, and relations – a fact which follows naturally and inevitably from our social theory of the self.
>
> (Ibid., p. 255n)

So Mead saw his own approach as very much wider than that of psychoanalysis, which for him was in effect restricted to abnormal psychological conditions and to control of sexual impulses in ordinary life.

Habitual action, as Mead saw it, is not asocial – it affects other individuals because 'from the point of view of the observer it is a gesture' (ibid., p. 43). Like James, Mead drew on Wundt, this time on his conception of gesture. Gesture, he wrote, 'is that part of social act, which serves as a stimulus to other forms involved in the same social act' (ibid.). The most primitive form of social coordination for Mead was the 'conversation of gestures'. He believed this mode of coordination does not require reflexive consciousness (ibid.) and individuals do not react to their own gestures, only to those produced by others actually involved in the activity.

Mead also held that speech was one class of gestures to which the individuals producing them also react:

> In human social conduct certain gestures, notably the vocal gestures, arouse in the individual who makes them a response that is of the same nature as that which they call out in those with whom they are engaged in co-operative activity. *In vocal gesture, in speech, one has already indicated to one's self what one indicates to the other with whom one is conversing.* One finds one's self already in the attitude of the other. It is this common response, excited in the organism, which is the inner nature both of the others and of one's self.
>
> (Mead, 1938/1972, p. 150, our emphasis)

In fact by the end of the argument Mead restricted the self-reflexive gestures to speech, 'the language of hands' and possibly 'language of expressions of countenance'. 'Emotional aspects of our acts', on the other hand, were not self-reflexive:

> We do not normally use language stimuli to call in ourselves emotional responses which we are calling out in others . . . we do not assume that the person who is angry is calling out the fear in himself that he is calling out in someone else. The emotional part of our act does not directly call out in us the response it calls out in the other. . . . We are not frightened by a tone which we may use to frighten somebody else.
>
> (Mead, 1934, pp. 148–149)

So the reactions of 'me' are not emotional. Mead's stricture on emotional reflexivity restricts the application of his conception of self to the experiences of hearing voices. Voices are often *emotional* reactions to what the voice hearer does, but they would not be if they were Mead's 'me' or 'generalised other'.

The second intricacy in Mead's account is that, like James, he allowed social self to fragment and did not see this as pathological. He wrote:

> the phenomenon of dissociation of personality is caused by *breaking up of the complete unitary self into the component selves* of which it is composed, and which respectively correspond to different aspects of social process in which the person is involved, and within which his complete or unitary self has arisen; these aspects being the different social groups to which he belongs within that process.
>
> (ibid., p. 144, our emphasis)

At this point Mead relaxed the idea of 'complete unitary self' and declared that multiple personality was 'in a certain sense normal':

> We carry on a whole series of different relationships to different people. We are one thing to one man, another thing to another. There are parts of the self

which exist only in relationships to itself. We divide ourselves up into all sorts of different selves with reference to our acquaintances. . . . There are all sorts of different selves answering to all sorts of different social reactions.

(Ibid., p. 142)

So for Mead the unity and fragmentation of a person's self reflected the extent of the unity in her social life. Thus an ordinary self could subsume several component selves, each reflecting the unity and structure of the particular 'social process'. To the extent that society is fragmented and one participates in distinct social activities, the self will be fragmented. Mead, however, also argued that some individuals were more prone to fragmentation of self than others. According to him, separate selves were more likely to develop in those who are 'unstable nervously' and 'in whom there is a line of cleavage' (ibid., p. 143) and so he left the door open for categorising multiple personality as partly a matter of individual pathology.

Do Mead's comments on social sectioning of the self help us to understand voices? We could think of voices as 'component selves' but then Mead's account fails us. One problem is an incompleteness of his account – we are concerned with the dialogical engagements between voice hearers and voices, but Mead does not provide an account of how different component selves may interact (and William James did not either, except briefly when he discussed the conflict between different social selves). A more serious problem, however, is that each component self is said to consist of an 'I' and a 'me', so if a voice were a component self it should be demonstrably structured in this way, and have an 'I' and a 'me'. In our discussion of generalised other, we have already pointed out that voices do not seem to be selves in Mead's sense of being a reflexive unity of 'I' and 'generalised other'. Neither is there any evidence to indicate that voices are a dialectic unity of 'I' and 'me'.[7] Voices often reflect the experiences and activities of the voice hearer, but do they also reflect on what they themselves say? Not in our evidence (see Chapter 9). Mead's account was useful to us in a negative sense – in directing our attention to what voices are not: complete persons.

We end this section by briefly summarising some relevant similarities and differences between James' and Mead's accounts of self. James divided the self into material, social and spiritual selves. His social self was in certain respects similar to Mead's socially reflexive self. Both allowed social self to fragment and to be discontinuous, and did not think of these disunities as necessarily pathological – they saw them as socially situated, and a function of social discontinuities. Social reflexivity also characterised self in both accounts. A person's 'I' was an object of judgements by internal tribunals in James' account, censored 'me' in Mead's account. There is, however, one considerable difference between the two accounts. Mead used the I/me dynamic in his analysis of *social* self, but James used it to structure spiritual (i.e. psychological) self. James' autonomous spiritual self, structured into 'I', 'me' and 'not-me', is absent in Mead.

Are voices mutations of self?

The main aim of this chapter has been to decide if the theories of self offered by William James and G.H. Mead afford some insight into the phenomenon of hearing voices. We were particularly interested in the vocabulary they could provide for experiences which a person does not attribute to external sources yet disowns as not parts of herself. We found that in the two accounts a voice could be thought of as either

- a component self;
- a part of self which is a proxy for society – James' tribunal, or Mead's 'generalised other' or 'me', or perhaps fragments of these;
- a 'not me' aspect of James's spiritual self.

We have already seen that simply on empirical grounds many reported voices are difficult to think of as either 'generalised other', 'me', or a 'component self'. So could we think of voices as Jamesian 'not-me'? Perhaps the first step should be to consider the use which James and Mead themselves made of their models of self to understand pathologies of experience. Mead was clearly not interested in mental afflictions, as his comments on Freud and his brief comments on multiple personality attest. William James, on the other hand, was certainly interested in understanding pathological conduct and experience. In the chapter on consciousness of self he divided mutations of self into 'alterations of memory' and 'alterations of the present bodily and spiritual selves', and he categorised the latter into 'insane delusions', 'alternating selves' and 'mediumships or possessions', and discussed these at length. He did not specifically consider hearing voices, aside from the example with which we started this chapter – so he did not explain how hearing a voice of a daemon and answering it is a mutation of self due to a bodily perversion. He did, however, provide a detailed analysis of experiences of a patient reported by Taine (1878). These included the following: 'the world is escaping from me', 'my voice is far away from me', 'my head does not exist', 'my legs do not belong to me', 'I act automatically, by an impulsion foreign to myself' (James, 1891, p. 378). In other words, these included actions and bodily experiences which the patient did not recognise as his own but from the clinicians' perspective should have done. James saw the problem as follows:

> within the objective sphere which formerly lent itself so simply to the judgement of recognition and of egotistic appropriation strange perplexities have arisen. The present and the past both seen therein will not unite. Where is my old me? What is this new one? Are they the same? Or have I two? Such questions, answered by whatever theory the patient is able to conjure up as plausible, form the beginning of his insane life.
>
> (Ibid.)

James made use of his distinction between 'I' and 'me' here, and commented that 'the *I* is unaltered' but 'the me is changed' – it divides into the old 'me' and the 'new' me. The new 'me' gathers into itself pathological experiences; it is strange to the patient and resisted. So how does *James* explain this division of 'me'? He could refer to it by the term 'not-me', which has a well-defined meaning in his account of self, and he could have explained the me/not-me discontinuity in terms of 'bodily perversions'. But James did not do this, and perhaps wisely. His quotation from Taine implies that the experiences were puzzling the patient partly because they could neither be completely rejected as 'not-me' nor accepted as 'me'. So a sharp distinction between 'me' and 'not-me' characteristic of James' model of self might in fact not have been useful to understanding the case in hand. The problem was how that particular patient formulated his new experiences – drawing them to a generalised structure (i.e. the 'not-me') was not necessarily helpful. And in fact most of James' account consists of the patient's and Taine's descriptions of pathological experiences which are not technical but in common-sense vernacular.

So how exactly did James use the model of self which he so laboriously set up to explain 'mutations of self'? The striking point about his discussion of pathologies of self is how little of his foregoing discussion of normal self James utilised. He could have used spiritual self as a resource to formulate and explain the patho-logical experiences. Instead his descriptions of multiple personality and fugues and possessions were in his own and the clinicians' everyday language.

So have we learned nothing about hearing voices in this chapter? Not quite. The exposition of two accounts of self has drawn our attention to two problems. The first arose when we were discussing the social fragmentation of self. Both Mead and James argued that component selves themselves were socially reflexive; so if voices were component selves they should be socially reflexive. But they do not seem to be. The voices which Socrates, Shreber and Marcelle heard were certainly not reflexive and neither were Homer's deities. We must therefore consider whether thinking of voices as persons is confused, but the problem is clearly empirical: To what extent do the voice hearers think of voices as persons, and does this create points of confusion? The second problem arises from James' comments on the continuity of spiritual self and bodily sensibility, and so it concerns the embodiment of voices. Voices are typically regarded as just that – sounds. We have so far paid much attention to the social situatedness of voices but not to the bodily sensibilities which may accompany them. So Mead's and James' accounts of self did decentre our thinking about voices, but the important point is that they did not provide a technical language to substitute for the everyday one. (This may in principle be impossible, as Coulter and Sharrock's work indicates – see Button *et al.*, 1995). In Chapter 9 we will investigate the accounts of voices in their hearers' own words.

6 Verbal hallucinations in contemporary psychiatry

Thus far, our examination of voices has disregarded the most prominent contemporary set of narratives about the phenomenon – that of psychiatry and modern clinical psychology. The significance of these narratives is that they determine what happens to many people who hear voices. Psychiatry interprets these experiences in terms of psychopathology, a word which discloses the medical origins of psychiatry. According to Berrios (1991), the word first appeared in a translation of a German textbook of 1847 by the Austrian physician Feuchtersleben, who set out the principles of medical psychology. The word was slow to catch on in Britain, where medical explanations of mental diseases were subsumed under a number of headings, such as 'mental science', 'mental pathology', 'psychological medicine' or 'mental physiology'. Some authorities (Lanteri-Laura, quoted in Berrios, 1991) have described two approaches to psychopathology at the end of the nineteenth century. Some used the term 'pathological psychology' to refer to that branch of psychology concerned with phenomena which arose from disturbances of normal mental processes in mental diseases. In contrast, psychological pathology, favoured by psychiatrists, regarded psychopathology as the study of abnormal mental phenomena which only occurred in mental disease. Berrios (1984) has used the terms 'continuity' and 'discontinuity' to describe these conflicting models.

Berrios' account is useful because it highlights the extent to which psychiatrists examine the experiences of people suffering from mental illness in a way which sets these experiences apart from normal experience. In pathological psychology the view is that the symptoms of mental illness arise from disturbances of normal psychological functioning. Such a model holds that there is no difference in kind between 'normal' and 'pathological' experience. The latter is inherent in the former. Psychological pathology, on the other hand, presupposes that hallucinations are inherently abnormal, a manifestation of a morbid psychological process. This places these experiences outside the range of the normal and sets them apart as psychotic experiences. We have seen that this was one position in the French medical debate on the nature of hallucinations (Chapter 1). There are two themes in particular that we consider to be important in understanding both the medicalisation of voices and the implications of this for voice hearers. The first deals with the work of the British psychiatrist Henry Maudsley; the second concerns the psychopathological theories of the German psychiatrist Karl Jaspers.

Hearing voices and psychopathology

The medical profession attempted to explain hallucinations even before the formation of the asylum system. As early as 1798 the English physician Crichton talked about hallucinations as 'diseased perceptions', but the most influential figure in the history of British psychiatry was Henry Maudsley. Maudsley was born in 1835 to a humble Yorkshire farming family, but rose to become the most prominent psychiatrist of his day. He lived through a time of great intellectual ferment. Darwin had opened the floodgates of religious scepticism, as evolutionary theory, geological sciences and palaeontology challenged the Christian dogma of the Creation. This threatened established beliefs in the nature of man's spiritual essence and his relationship with God. Maudsley was an agnostic, a devout materialist without religious faith, who believed that mental illness was almost entirely genetically determined. He wrote fluently about a wide variety of subjects, although his later writings became increasingly philosophical. His earlier books included *The Pathology of Mind* (1867) and in 1886 he published the first edition of *Natural Causes and Supernatural Seemings*, in which he developed a rationalist and materialist explanation for a wide variety of supernatural phenomena, including voices.

Maudsley was at pains to point out in the preface to the third edition of his book (1897) that his attack on supernaturalism did not necessarily represent an attack on religion. He regarded the conflict between science and religion as artificial, since the two had quite different spheres of influence. Nevertheless, he argued that so-called supernatural experiences were simply 'malobservations and misinterpretations of nature': '[supernatural] phenomena have not ever been, nor are ever now, events of the external world, but have always been, and are, fables of the imagination' (Maudsley, 1897, p. 305).

Maudsley believed that supernatural experiences could be explained in terms of disorders of the mind. He claimed that the religious experiences of great spiritual leaders, such as Mohammed, St Paul, Ann Lee (founder of the Shakers), Emanuel Swedenborg, Ignatius Loyola, George Fox and John Wesley, could be explained in terms of epilepsy, a condition which for centuries was associated with divine intervention. Hallucinations could also be explained in this way. One reason for this was that their life-styles predisposed these religious leaders to diseases such as consumption and epilepsy, through fasting and self-denial. His work places hallucinations firmly within the domain of mental illness, and is a good example of the 'discontinuous', or psychological pathology model, although in his earlier work Maudsley believed that normal people could experience them:

> No one who has observed himself attentively when suddenly awaking out of sleep but must have noticed that he has had at times hallucinations both visual and auditory. He has heard a voice, which no one else could hear, distinctly say something.
>
> (Maudsley, 1867)

Here, he implies that hallucinations may arise in the normal mind (the 'continuous' view). With this exception, however, he regarded hallucinations as exclusively pathological and indicative of mental illness. This distinction became enshrined within clinical practice, and can be observed today when psychiatrists try to establish whether voices occur in clear consciousness (i.e. abnormal) or in a state of reduced vigilance, such as when falling asleep or waking up.

Maudsley's zeal for rational explanations of what were once regarded as super-natural experiences has a number of features. He assumes that his explanation is not subject to the same criticism as religious or supernatural explanations. While a Christian may regard a natural explanation of a miraculous event as impious, a Muslim 'whose understanding is not overawed by fit faith' could not be expected to respond in the same way: 'The stultification of reason which is truth to one is still nonsense to another religion' (Maudsley, 1897, p. 185).

This principle can also be applied to Maudsley's rationalism, and he assumes that his rational and deterministic account of hallucinations is beyond such criticism. Hallucinations, or for that matter, all aspects of human experience, are secondary to physical processes occurring in the brain. Even though little was known about these processes, Maudsley believed that if we could understand the brain we could understand human experience. If he was unable to explain how brain function determined experience, this did not stop him speculating, and so the preoccupations of late nineteenth-century psychiatry emerge. He asserts that hallucinations are more common in 'savage and barbarous minds, less amply stored with faculties, and these loosely federate, just as they occur more readily in young children than adults' (Maudsley, 1897, p. 199). This reveals Maudsley's belief in the racial superiority of Europeans, which at that time was a prominent theme in scientific thought:

> When the brain, by reason of a natural simplicity of constitution in the low savage and in the animal . . . is without the nervous substrata necessary to subserve new developments of function, then it is impossible to ingraft the finer and more complex associations of ideas.
>
> (Maudsley, 1897, p. 40)

The implication here is that hallucinations are more likely to occur in those whose brains (and thus minds) are less well developed, such as children, primitive peoples or savages. The assumption is that rational European man is less likely to experience hallucinations because he has a more developed brain, the various parts of which function in an integrated manner. Such beliefs represent a primitive attempt to apply Darwinism to human psychology.

Maudsley was a prominent clinician and teacher. His contribution to British psychiatry is recognised by the fact that the main teaching hospital in London for psychiatry bears his name. His work established a scientific framework for the practice of psychiatry as a clinical discipline, which survives to this day. An examination of Maudsley's writing provides no more than a limited view of his influence, for psychiatry is a clinical subject which, like the rest of medicine, is largely taught by precept. The principles underlying the practice of clinical psychiatry outlined by Maudsley and his colleagues have been passed down through generations of teachers and students at the patient's bedside. It is this feature of clinical psychiatry above all else that is responsible for the perpetuation of the pathological view of hearing voices: that these experiences indicate serious mental illness.

The foundations of much contemporary psychiatric thought about the nature of psychosis can be traced back to the work of Karl Jaspers earlier in the twentieth century. Indeed, Berrios (1991) has argued that twentieth-century thought has had little influence on the nineteenth-century ideas which remain pre-eminent in their influence on psychiatric thought about psychosis. Walker (1988) has traced the influence of some of these ideas on Jaspers' psychopathology. At the end of the nineteenth century there was a deep controversy in academic circles concerning the scientific nature of the human sciences. This debate, together with the developing tradition of biological psychiatry under the influence of figures such as Griesinger, Meynert, Kraepelin and Nissl, can be seen to have influenced Jaspers' thought. The essence of the debate about the scientific nature of human sciences can be seen in the work of Dilthey, who distinguished a human scientific (*verstehende*) psychology from a natural scientific (*erklärende*) psychology, a distinction which figures prominently in Jaspers' highly influential work *General Psychopathology* (1963). Jaspers knew the importance of detailed descriptions of personal experiences of psychosis, and was familiar with Schreber's memoir, referring to it at several points in the book.

In Part II of *General Psychopathology*, which bears the subtitle 'Meaningful psychic connections', Jaspers was concerned with the sources of the various psychic phenomena and with what they might be connected. He made two sets of distinctions, first between subjective psychopathology (or phenomenology) and objective psychopathology, and second between understanding and explaining. Natural sciences are concerned with providing explanations of phenomena through establishing causal connections between events, such as can be seen in the laws and rules of physics or chemistry. But in psychopathology it is not possible to formulate such causal equations:

> nor can we ever formulate causal equations in the manner of chemistry and physics. This would presuppose a complete quantification of the events observed and since these are psychic events, which by their very nature have to remain qualitative, such quantification would as a matter of principle remain impossible without losing the actual object of the enquiry.
>
> (Jaspers, 1963, p. 302)

Instead, he argues that psychic events 'emerge' out of each other in a way that can be understood through what he calls *genetic understanding*. Judgements of meaning are based in the self-evident nature of the events concerned, as well as their location as *tangible facts* through language (their verbal content), culture, way of life and so on. The difficulty is that such data, Jaspers argues, are always incomplete, so we still have to resort to interpretation of one sort or another. Understanding (*verstehenden*) is limited, but explanation (*erklärende*) is not.

Jaspers also distinguishes between what he calls *rational* and *empathic* understanding. The former, according to the rules of logic, establishes meaningful connections quite independently of psychology. Indeed, it is even an aid to psychology (this is a particularly perspicacious idea and relevant, given the implicit rationalism of modern cognitive models of mind and thought). Empathic understanding leads directly to the psychic connections themselves; it *is* psychology. Understanding also has to be considered as being embedded within much broader contexts, cultural, existential and metaphysical.

Jaspers describes two functions of understanding. The first is the understanding of 'remote' connections which seem to be incomprehensible. The second is the discovery of universal understandable connections in psychic states governed by abnormal mechanisms such as, for example, hysteria. Within the individual, the total of understandable meaningful connections constitutes the personality. The problem here is that anything that is meaningful has a particular structure which is destroyed by attempts to generalise from it. This particularly applies to scientific approaches to understanding, because of its insistence on systematic approaches to knowledge. Jaspers also draws attention to the role of the investigator. The extent to which we can understand a particular psychic event depends upon the extent to which we are tied to rational schemata or whether we are prepared to approach human experience in its more complex forms.

Psychiatry in the twentieth century is already familiar with the importance that Jaspers attaches to form and content in understanding. These distinctions structure the assessments that all psychiatrists make when examining a patient's mental state. But he also refers to a third element which he considers important in understanding, one which, interestingly, has for too long been neglected by psychiatry. Jaspers here is referring to what he calls *self-reflection* as a basic phenomenon of meaningfulness.

Jaspers argued that for something to be meaningful it has to be part of a 'connected whole'. Meaning arises from the relationship of the part to the whole (the hermeneutic 'round'), and that which is meaningful tends to move in opposites. Any psychic phenomenon gains meaning through its location within a particular context, and it loses its meaning if considered in isolation from this. This leads to a serious difficulty, because the consequence of this is that all psychic phenomena are thus open to endless interpretations and reinterpretations (terminal relativism). Dreams, myths and the content of psychoses are particularly prone to this problem. Indeed, our own interpretation of the meaning of our own lives is open to infinite variations in meaning. Jaspers goes on to offer a scathing attack on Freud and psychoanalysis as a hermeneutic system (1963, pp. 359–360), claiming that it was responsible for a debasement of the cultural value of psychopathology as understood through the work of philosophers such as Kierkegaard and Nietzsche. Jaspers does, however, note that psychoanalysis brought the benefit of directing psychological thought and attention to the problem of meaningful connections and the inner life history (what we would call *narrative*) of the individual.

In relation to psychiatry, Jaspers argues that our ability to understand breaks down altogether in the face of organic disorders and psychosis. Why? So-called reactive psychoses, he claims, have meaning as an escape, a defence or a refuge from an intolerable conflict with reality. But even here, Jaspers would claim that we should not over-emphasise the significance of this understanding, because we do not understand the mechanisms of transformation involved in the generation of psychotic symptoms. Even if trauma is causally responsible for a psychosis, it is difficult to judge the significance of this in relation, for example, to other individual factors, such as the constitution.

As far as the functional psychoses are concerned, Jaspers maintains that it is not possible to discern meaningful content: 'Much has been explained as meaningful which in fact was nothing of the kind' (Jaspers, 1963, p. 408). He disagrees with the Swiss school (Bleuler and Jung) who argue that the content of a delusion is understandable and thus meaningful in terms of dissociated complexes: 'The interpretation of [such] symptoms is doubtful but can be discussed' (ibid., p. 410). The reason why Jaspers doubts the possibility of interpreting delusions seems to be because this is 'translation to schizophrenia of concepts which have been arrived at during the analysis of hysteria' (ibid.).

For Jaspers, there are radical differences between hysterical and schizophrenic processes. There is also the issue of the incorrigibility of delusions (pp. 410–411), which Jaspers argues is quite different from the corrigibility of healthy people's mistaken beliefs, although he is not clear what that difference is. Earlier in *General Psychopathology*, it is clear that he assumes schizophrenia to be a biologically determined disorder, the processes of which ramify through all levels of individual experience, producing profound changes in the individual's personality. For Jaspers, this is the justification for his immensely influential belief that there is no meaning to be found in schizophrenia, including its symptom, auditory verbal hallucinations.

The majority of people who hear voices nowadays are under psychiatric care and on neuroleptic medication. Their experiences have been interpreted within a medical framework which regards voices as a symptom of serious mental illness. This framework precludes any exploration of the content of voices, other than that which the psychiatrist considers necessary to establish those features which she regards as important in establishing a diagnosis. Psychiatrists are only interested in the small number of limited features of voices necessary to make a diagnosis. Some types of voices form part of the group of first-rank symptoms (FRS) described by Schneider (1957). Schneider thought that the presence of one or more of these symptoms, in the absence of organic brain disease, indicated a diagnosis of schizophrenia. FRS include three types of auditory hallucinations: hearing voices speaking your thoughts out loud; hearing two or more voices arguing or having a discussion about you in the third person; hearing one or more voice carrying on a running commentary about your thoughts or actions. These experiences play a prominent role in most modern diagnostic systems, such as ICD-10, which relies heavily on the presence of FRS to establish the diagnosis of

Table 1 Description of verbal hallucinations from SCAN 10

Information on eleven aspects of hallucinations		
17.1	probe for hallucinations	Yes / No
17.3	non-verbal hallucinations	Yes / No
17.4	frequency of verbal auditory hallucinations	Yes / No
17.5	length of utterances	–
17.6	quality of VH	–
17.7	internal hallucinations (inner voices)	Yes / No
17.8	voices commenting on thoughts or actions	Yes / No
17.9	second- and third-person auditory hallucinations	Yes / No
17.12	special features of auditory hallucinations	Yes / No
17.13	insight into auditory hallucinations	Yes / No
17.14	prominence of auditory hallucinations	–

schizophrenia. Table 1 is an extract from section 17 of ICD-10, the standard system of classification used in the UK.

In practice, most psychiatrists would not refer to a list of symptoms but would rely on a series of questions which they ask patients, first to probe for the presence of VH, second to elicit the nature of these experiences. If the content of the voices indicates that they are of the first-rank symptom type, then the diagnosis will almost certainly be schizophrenia. There are two exceptions to this. Schneider pointed out that the presence of FRS indicated schizophrenia only in the absence of organic brain disease, so it is important to ensure that there is no evidence of clouding of consciousness, confusion or other clinical features that would suggest that the subject is organically ill. In addition, the psychiatrist will want to establish whether the subject's voices are understandable in terms of a mood change. Voices can occur in severe depression and hypomania, but under these circumstances it is argued that the content of hallucinatory voices is understandable in terms of the mood change, which is then regarded as the primary problem. For example, a profoundly depressed subject may hear voices saying that she is wicked or evil. A hypomanic subject may hear a voice telling her that she is the new Madonna, and that the songs she has written will top the charts. In each case, the psychiatrist would argue that the content of these voices is consistent with an underlying mood change, and that this is the primary problem, not schizophrenia.

This is usually as far as the experience will be explored. Once these features have been elicited, then no further explication of voices is considered valuable. Indeed, received wisdom in psychiatry requires that the clinician should not discuss her patient's abnormal experiences. Hallucinations, being psychotic symptoms, have no inherent value or meaning. They may have a 'worst fear' quality, but in essence they represent little more than the inevitable consequence of disordered brain function which is primarily responsible for the disease. As Thomas Huxley is reputed to have said of the mind, they are of no more significance than the cloud of steam that hangs over a factory. In psychiatry voices have little or no meaning. They are, like mind itself, an epiphenomenon secondary to what are regarded as more important biological processes. The pharmacological management of schizophrenia then becomes the priority, and the subject's preoccupation with and self-reports of voices becomes little more than an index of the extent to which the underlying illness is controlled by medication.

This model regards any attempt to get the subject to talk about her experiences as meaningless. To do so may actually increase the subject's preoccupation with what are regarded by psychiatrists as potentially dangerous experiences. But why should voices be dangerous if they are just epiphenomena? We have already seen that Bleuler believed voices to be potential sources of delusion, and so did Schreber's psychiatrist Weber. If the subject hears voices telling her to harm herself or another person, the psychiatrist fears that the very act of talking with the subject about the voices may increase her preoccupation with imperative commands, making it more likely that she will act on them. The flames of this fear are fanned by a recent gale of adverse publicity given to a small number of high-profile tragedies (Chapter 8). Such incidents reinforce popular public opinion, and professional attitudes, that anti-psychotic medication is the most important component of treatment for people suffering from schizophrenia, and that attempts to talk with these people about their psychotic experiences are misguided or even dangerous. In Chapter 7 we will present evidence that the contrary is true: that exploration of these experiences can help subjects to cope with them, and conversely, attempts to ignore or suppress them may paradoxically increase the subject's preoccupation with them.

The reluctance of psychiatrists to explore the content of voices can be understood if we see what influential psychiatric texts have to say about the management of psychosis, and hallucinations in particular. Hamilton (1984), the editor of *Fish's Schizophrenia*, says that the clinician is 'not to go along with the patient's delusions and hallucinations; on the contrary, the patient should be encouraged to ignore them' (Hamilton, 1984, p. 145).

It appears that neither doctor nor patient is to be encouraged to explore these experiences, a sentiment shared by Slater and Roth (1969, p. 326): 'it is a waste of time to argue with a paranoid patient about his delusions'. We might be forgiven for believing that this was because the authors were simply concerned with the conviction with which delusional beliefs are held, but we must be aware of a strong undercurrent of opinion that people who suffer from psychoses should not be exposed to psychotherapeutic interventions. Psychotherapy is secondary to medication in the treatment of schizophrenia. This antipathy is clearly seen in Slater and Roth's interpretation of Freud's limited experience of psychoanalysis in psychosis:

> Freud and his successors have done relatively little practical work with psychotic patients; Freud's acquaintance with the psychology of paranoia, for instance, was gained from a book written by Schreber, and from no personal knowledge of the patient. It is not surprising, therefore, that the field of pathological psychology, as shown in the psychotic states, has been left

almost entirely unilluminated by psychoanalytic theory – so much so that many analysts find it difficult to understand that there are differences between the normal and the diseased, between the neurotic and the psychotic, or between reactive and endogenous disorders.

(Slater and Roth, 1969, p. 15)

Slater and Roth may be correct in their observations about the limitations of Freud's experience, but their statement is frankly inaccurate, for nowhere in *Clinical Psychiatry* is there reference to the work of Klein, Segal and other members of the object-relations school who have made significant contributions to understanding the nature of the psychological disturbance in psychosis, especially schizophrenia. Freud (1917/1975) was quite open about the fact that psychoanalysis as he practised it had failed to come to grips with *dementia praecox*:

> sufferers from dementia praecox, remain on the whole unaffected and proof against psychoanalytic therapy. . . . We are faced here by a fact which we do not understand and which therefore leads us to doubt whether we have really understood all the determinants of our possible success with the other neuroses.
>
> (Freud, 1917/1975, p. 490)

Slater and Roth quote Freud again as they argue their case against the psycho-therapeutic treatment of schizophrenia. They refer to comments made to one of his followers, Ludwig Binswanger:

> Prolonged psychotherapy, even in mild cases, can no longer be justified. *Psychoanalysis* is indeed, *contraindicated* in any stage or type of schizophrenia; to apply it is, as Freud himself commented to L. Binswanger, a professional error ('*ein Kunstfehler*').
>
> (Slater and Roth, 1969, p. 325, emphasis in original)

Binswanger worked in Zurich with Bleuler, and in 1907 visited Freud in Vienna with Jung. He fell under the influence of Husserl's phenomenological school, and later was influenced by the work of Heidegger, developing *dasein analysis*, a fusion of psychoanalysis and existential theory, which he used with psychotic subjects. Freud disagreed with Binswanger's application of psychoanalysis to psychotic subjects, and was gently reprimanding him in the (unannotated) reference by Slater and Roth.

Voices can occur in people who are not suffering from schizophrenia, and who have experienced some form of trauma, such as bereavement or sexual abuse. Yet authoritative psychiatric texts used by postgraduate psychiatrists made no reference to the substantial body of evidence that we are about to examine, that voices may occur in a wide variety of circumstances, quite unrelated to psychosis and schizophrenia. Rees (1971) published a detailed survey of almost three hundred widows and widowers, who had been bereaved over the period of his study. All were interviewed by Rees, who had the advantage of knowing most of them personally because he was their GP. They trusted him. He was interested in whether the widowed person had experienced hallucinations, either seeing, hearing or feeling the dead spouse. Nearly 50 per cent of his subjects had experienced hallucinations of one form or another. Over 13 per cent of the sample heard the voice of the deceased partner, and more than 10 per cent had actually spoken to the dead spouse, because they were so convinced of the reality of their experience. There was no evidence that these people were suffering from psychiatric disorders such as depression, which are common following bereavement. The incidence of depression was the same in hallucinating groups (17.5 per cent) and non-hallucinating groups (18.0 per cent). Rees noticed that most people found these experiences helpful; in fact over 80 per cent of those who spoke to the deceased found this comforting. Another interesting point to emerge from this study was that nearly three-quarters of his subjects had not disclosed the fact that they had experienced hallucinations, presumably because they were afraid that if they did so they would be thought of as 'mad', when they knew they were not. This important study suggests that the experience of hearing voices may be much more common than most psychiatrists realise, and not limited to 'abnormal' experience. The study is not without its weaknesses, however. Many psychiatrists would argue that Rees was a GP, not a psychiatrist. The questions he asked when interviewing his subjects were quite limited, so there is no way of knowing whether these experiences were the same as those seen in people who would be diagnosed as schizophrenic by a psychiatrist. This may apply to Rees' study, but Ensink's work in Holland raises extremely difficult questions for those who believe that first-rank symptom voices are specific to schizophrenia.

Ensink (1992, 1993) was interested in the long-term effects of sexual abuse and studied nearly a hundred women recruited from a number of incest survivor organisations in Holland. All subjects were interviewed by trained interviewers to gather information about the subjects' pasts, their experience of abuse, and the consequences of this. These included detailed questions about hallucinations as well as other experiences, such as dissociation. All the women had been sexually abused in childhood, usually by their fathers, or other close male relatives. She found that 43 per cent of her subjects reported hallucinatory experiences, and 28 per cent had auditory hallucinations. Of the subjects who heard voices, 85 per cent of these experiences were identical to FRS auditory hallucinations. She provides some examples:

> she used to be daydreaming alone in her room for long periods of time. During these periods she heard voices. When asked to give some more specific information she said: 'When I hear discussions, it is just like if there are many people in my head and that is disturbing. I can not stop it. They used to say terrible things, that I should be punished and so on.'
>
> (Ensink, 1992, p. 127)

In general, auditory (and visual) hallucinations were more likely to occur in women who had experienced more severe forms of abuse, and in women who had been abused by their fathers. Most of the women who heard voices had done so for many years. Although many of these subjects were in therapy because of the abuse, none was seeing a psychiatrist or had received a diagnosis of schizophrenia or psychotic illness. Support for the idea that voices could occur in non-psychiatric populations came from the work of Marius Romme, also in Holland. He appeared on a Dutch television programme with one of his patients, a woman who heard voices and who had been previously diagnosed as schizophrenic. Following the discussion, over 450 people responded by phone. Romme sent out questionnaires to these people to find out how they coped with voices. Of the people who returned analysable questionnaires, over 40 per cent were not in contact with psychiatric services (Romme *et al.*, 1992). Not surprisingly, people who said they were able to cope with these experiences were much less likely to be in psychiatric care (24 per cent) than those who found difficulty in coping (49 per cent) with the experience.

Ensink's work suggests that hallucinations identical to those seen in schizophrenia are quite common in women who have been sexually abused. Romme's work suggests that voices may occur in people who never get to see psychiatrists and his study indicates that the experience of hearing voices is more common in the general population than most psychiatrists realise. The difficulty is that the study did not compare the experiences of those who heard voices but were not in contact with psychiatric services with those of subjects with a diagnosis of schizophrenia. Another study by the Maastricht group (Pennings and Romme, 1996), however, found no differenes between the voices of non-clinical, and clinical voice hearers with diagnoses of schizophrenia and dissociative disorders. Our own past work has addressed this problem (Leudar *et al.*, 1997). We have compared characteristics of auditory verbal hallucinations in these groups and found them to be basically the same.

Over the years there have been several studies of auditory hallucinations in 'normal' subjects. Johnson (1978, cf. Posey and Losch, 1983) reports a survey in 1897 by Parish in which auditory hallucinations were reported by between 10 and 30 per cent of 'normal' subjects. Sidgewick *et al.* (1894, results reported by Tien, 1991) found that almost 4 per cent of the population admitted hearing voices in a general population survey undertaken for the Society for Psychical Research. The problem was that in 3 per cent of cases these experiences occurred while subjects were falling asleep or waking up. In general, hallucinatory experiences are much more likely to occur in states of lowered vigilance such as when we are drowsy. For example, McKellar (1957) found that over 40 per cent of college students described hearing voices while drifting off to sleep. If these experiences were excluded, 1 per cent of Sidgewick's subjects heard voices while fully awake. This figure is remarkably similar to that obtained in recent work by Tien (1991). This study was undertaken specifically to compare the prevalence of hallucinations in the general population in five American cities (Baltimore, New Haven, Durham, St Louis and Los Angeles) with the prevalence from the Sidgewick study. Tien specifically excluded hallucinations related to sleep. Subjects were interviewed with a diagnostic schedule devised by the National Institute of Mental Health, and widely used in psychiatric research. He found that at least 10–15 per cent of the sample studied admitted to hallucinations of one of the senses, and around 2 per cent of the sample admitted to hearing voices. Both the Sidgewick and Tien studies were of large numbers of subjects. Sidgewick *et al.* interviewed 17,000 adults (largely in Britain) and Tien interviewed over 18,500. We can be reasonably certain that in Tien's study the experiences reported were close to or identical to those experienced by people who would attract a psychiatric diagnosis. He also made strenuous efforts to establish the severity of these experiences, by enquiring how subjects had coped, and whether the level of distress or interference with function was such that they had consulted a professional. He found that the proportion of non-distressing hallucinations (for all senses) was much higher than of those associated with distress or interference with function. This suggests that the majority of his subjects had not seen a psychiatrist, although we cannot be sure about this.

The idea that hallucinations can occur in 'normal' subjects is not particularly new. Forrer (1960) described what he called 'benign hallucinations' occurring in five of his friends. The most important work here though is that of Posey and Losch (1983). Their study was stimulated by Jaynes' (1976) book *The Origins of Consciousness in the Breakdown of the Bicameral Mind*, which we examined critically in Chapter 2. Posey and Losch argued that if Jaynes' theory was correct it would be reasonable to expect to find voices in the general population. They constructed a questionnaire to establish the presence of fourteen different types of voices and gave this to 375 college students, the majority of whom were female. They found that over 70 per cent reported brief verbal hallucinations while fully awake. Almost two-fifths (39 per cent) reported hearing their thoughts spoken out as if aloud (one of Schneider's first-rank symptoms of schizophrenia), and over a third (36 per cent) said they had heard a voice calling their name when they were alone. They interviewed a small sample of voice hearers using a personality inventory to ensure that they were not suffering from psychiatric disorders, but there was no evidence that this was the case.

Voices and therapists

The profound changes in the organisation of mental health services over the second half of the twentieth century have had an impact upon the way we think about mental health problems. The move to community care has resulted in an increased interest in the epidemiology of mental health problems, the realisation that professional mental health services deal only with a small proportion of individuals who develop symptoms of, say, depression and anxiety (Goldberg and Huxley, 1980) in the community. The implication of this is that the majority of mental health problems may be relatively brief, self-limiting events, with which individuals cope themselves without recourse to specialist services. Individuals are only likely to refer themselves for help if, for whatever reasons, they find it difficult to cope with their experiences. In other words, the majority of people who develop anxiety or depression find their own ways of coping, and as long as they do so successfully, they manage to avoid specialist help. There is no reason to suppose that, in principle, the experience of hearing voices is any different from this. So before we consider therapeutic interventions offered by mental health professionals, it is important that we bear in mind the fact that voice hearers themselves have evolved a variety of techniques which help them to cope with the experience. Coping mechanisms are, of course, important for those in contact with mental health services, particularly in view of the evidence that not all subjects' voices respond to neuroleptic medication.

We have seen that the dominant view in psychiatry is that voices are not to be explored psychologically. Most psychiatrists believe that they indicate the presence of psychosis, so medication should provide the main focus of their management. There are two problems here. First, we have already seen that in a significant proportion of cases the presence of voices is unrelated to psychosis, so there is no a priori reason to expect these experiences to respond to anti-psychotic medication. Second, it is far from clear that these drugs are as effective in controlling the symptoms of psychosis as the pharmaceutical industry would have us believe. The evidence here can be difficult to access, but the fact that the industry has invested so much time and money in the development and marketing of new 'atypical' anti-psychotic drugs, such as clozapine and risperidone, indicates that there is a market, and that the market is constituted by people whose psychotic symptoms have not responded to anti-psychotic drugs. Davis and Caspar (1977) found that 25 per cent of people continued to have psychotic symptoms despite taking neuroleptics. Davis *et al.* (1980) reviewed a large database of clinical trial material from the 1960s generated by the National Institute of Mental Health Psychopharmacology Research Branch in the USA. About 30 per cent of subjects in these studies were rated as either minimally improved or clinically worse, following treatment with neuroleptics. Kane *et al.* (1988) suggested that a conservative estimate indicates that the symptoms of one-fifth of all patients suffering from schizophrenia fail to respond to neuroleptic drugs. Curson *et al.* (1988) examined the symptoms of 222 chronically hospitalised patients diagnosed with schizophrenia, using a standard psychiatric rating scale to provide detailed measures of psychiatric symptoms. They found that 46 per cent had persistent delusions, and 32 per cent had persistent voices. The important point here is that this group of people had been exposed to what the authors described as 'energetic pharmacological . . . treatments'. Falloon and Talbot (1981) identified forty subjects living in the community who had heard persistent second-person voices on a daily basis for more than a year. All the subjects had a research diagnosis of schizophrenia and were regular attenders at an out-patient clinic. Ninety-five per cent of the sample were receiving regular anti-psychotic medication. It is not possible to know what proportion of all clinic attenders heard persistent voices, because the study was undertaken specifically to examine coping strategies. We can assume, however, that persistent voices are not at all uncommon in psychiatric out-patient clinics.

The fact that a significant proportion of subjects' voices fail to respond to medication means that it is important to find other ways of helping people to cope with these experiences, and the best way of doing this is to find out what works for the experts; that is, voice hearers themselves. Falloon and Talbot (1981) interviewed their forty subjects, and found that coping mechanisms could be classified into three groups: behaviour change, physiological changes and cognition. The first group included a number of strategies which involved some change in behaviour when the voices appeared. These included changes in posture (such as lying down or getting up to go for a walk), and changes in interpersonal contact. More often than not this involved actively seeking out the company of others. Withdrawal from social contact, which is often how professional staff view subjects' responses to voices, was much less common. Physiological changes involved attempts by subjects to increase or decrease their levels of arousal. These included attempts to relax or go to sleep, or listening to loud, stimulating music. Cognitive changes were represented by two contrasting techniques. Some subjects used self-distraction with the purpose of ignoring voices. About a third of subjects paid attention to their voices and reflected on their content in thought, often accepting the voices' guidance. This appeared to be particularly effective in minimising distress.

In Holland, Marius Romme and Sandra Escher have further illuminated the nature and importance of voice hearers' own coping mechanisms (Romme and Escher, 1989). They (Romme *et al.*, 1992) examined the techniques used by those who could and could not cope. Those who could not were twice as likely to be in psychiatric care (49 per cent) as those who could (24 per cent). Coping strategies included distraction, ignoring, selective listening and setting limits. Of these, distraction was the only strategy more likely to be used by non-copers than copers, whereas setting limits (telling the voices to come back at a more convenient time) was more likely to occur in copers. The most important outcome of this work was the formation of Resonance, a self-help group for voice hearers in Holland. This work has now spread throughout Europe and has made an impact in the USA. In Britain the Hearing Voices Network started in 1989 in Manchester following a visit to Britain by Romme and Escher. The Network now offers national self-help and support groups for people who hear voices.

These studies constitute a starting point for the social intervention of empowerment for people who hear voices, but we will consider psychological interventions in detail. There have been hundreds of such studies and the following account is not intended as a comprehensive review, but rather to provide exemplars of the techniques used. We will consider these interventions under the following headings: behavioural, information processing (including 'language therapy'), cognitive, focusing and dialogical. It is important to bear in mind that these headings are artificial, in that they have many features in common.

Behavioural interventions

Behavioural interventions were frequently used in chronic psychoses to help shape more appropriate behaviours in institutionalised patients who had so-called negative symptoms, especially social withdrawal, poverty of speech and avolition. Token economy systems were a feature of rehabilitation wards, which used operant conditioning techniques to reward appropriate behaviours. Patients would earn 'tokens' which could be exchanged for 'privileges' such as sweets or cigarettes, in reward for the performance of particular tasks. A number of studies suggested that both reinforcing and punishment strategies could decrease the frequency of expression of delusional ideas and hallucinations. The issue here is whether delusions and hallucinations had actually diminished, or whether the patients simply learned not to talk about them. These techniques raised a number of problems. First, there are serious ethical questions about the use of punishment strategies in people whose ability to give valid consent may be impaired. Second, there are potential difficulties about the use of techniques which encourage patients not to report their symptoms. Subjects' ability to monitor and report their experiences may play an important part in bringing distressing hallucinations under control. Third, behavioural approaches pay little or no attention to the phenomenological aspects of experience. Voices are simply regarded as problem behaviours and there is no attempt to engage the self as the subject of the experience. Subjects who hallucinate may remain frightened by experiences that they are struggling to make sense of. The exception to this is systematic desensitisation, which was shown by Slade (1972) to be effective in reducing both the frequency of hallucinations and the amount of distress and anxiety they cause. The important point about this technique, which involved the subject keeping a detailed diary of voices and mood state, is that it constitutes an important component of many psychological interventions, including cognitive strategies and focusing. Another important feature of this study was the importance attached to the identification of environmental cues which appeared to trigger voices. Many behavioural interventions appear to work well in clinic or ward situations, but it can be extremely difficult to generalise this to more natural settings in subjects' day-to-day lives. This problem emerged in a single case study by Allen *et al.* (1985), who used removal and distraction techniques for voices, on the basis that such interventions had proved useful for subjects who experienced intrusive obsessional thoughts. Distraction techniques (such as getting up and making a cup of tea when the voices start) are widely used by voice hearers themselves (see Romme *et al.*, 1992).

Information processing interventions

A number of simple and effective techniques for the control of voices have been evolved on the basis of information processing theory. There are several strands of information which support this view, and there is insufficient room here to deal with them all (Bentall (1990) has written an excellent and comprehensive review of the area). Slade (1974) suggested that variations in auditory input might be beneficial for some people who hear voices. For example, one patient reported that reduced auditory input (wearing sound excluders) increased his voices, whereas listening to others talk, or 'white' noise, reduced the intensity. Other subjects reported that their voices were less troublesome if they were involved in some activity which required a high level of concentration. Another said she never heard voices if she was involved in a conversation herself. In his study, Slade found that as the amount of information the subject had to process increased, the frequency of voices diminished. Margo *et al.* (1981) investigated the effect of ten different types of auditory input on the intensity of voice hearing (VH). Again, white noise increased the loudness and duration of VH, but the one experimental condition which produced the greatest reduction in voices was that in which subjects were required to produce an overt response through monitoring. In this task, subjects were requested to read aloud a passage of prose, at the end of which they had to summarise the content. The most widely used intervention based on information processing is Walkman therapy. Many people who hear voices find that wearing a Walkman, or portable audiotape, on which they can listen to music helps to damp down voices. In one study (McInnis and Marks, 1990) a man who had experienced persistent imperative voices telling him to commit suicide found that the duration (but not frequency) of the voice was reduced considerably if he listened to a tape he had recorded himself, in which he recalled pleasant childhood memories.

Hoffman and Satel (1993) have described what they call language therapy for persistent voices. The rationale for this comes from Hoffman's (1986) theory of hallucinations, in which it is hypothesised that voices arise from disrupted fragments of discourse plans which are regarded as alien because they are experienced as 'non-intended'. Theoretically, attempts to improve subjects' ability to plan discourse should reduce the frequency and intensity of voices, so therapy takes the form of a series of tasks which encourage the subject to produce increasingly complex forms of utterance. There are close similarities here with the tasks found to be effective by Margo *et al.* (1981), including exercises such as 'discovering' the story in a film or television programme. In Hoffman and Satel's study, three out of four patients who were given these exercises increased their ability to complete the language therapy, and these patients also reported significant reductions in the severity of their voices.

The difficulty with these studies is that, like the behavioural interventions, the benefits only appear to last as long as the subjects are engaged in the experimental condition. In the Hoffman and Satel study, all three subjects experienced a recrudescence of voices within three months of the end of therapy. It is also difficult to be sure what the effective component of therapy is in these studies. The tasks in language therapy are very similar to those in the Margo *et al.* study. Both involve the subject as an active participant in a complex language task involving comprehension, interpretation and self-monitoring. Most interesting of all here is an observation made by Hoffman and Satel. Treatment with language therapy appeared to progress most rapidly when subjects started to recognise their own speech incoherence. As in the Margo *et al.* study, situations in which participants in therapy are encouraged to develop greater *self-awareness*, through the process of self-monitoring, appear to be particularly valuable.

Cognitive therapy for voices

A feature common to behavioural and information processing interventions is that they pay no attention to the content of the voices, or the subject's belief systems concerning the voices. The main objective of these interventions is to reduce the frequency and intensity of VH. Bentall's detailed theoretical review (1990) reaches a number of important conclusions in relation to the cognitive processes that underpin hallucinatory experiences. He suggests that there is considerable evidence that, in psychiatric patients, hallucinations may arise from an impairment in the skills involved in discriminating between real and imaginary events. People who hallucinate may make faulty judgements about the origins of their perceptions; that is, whether they come from an internal or external source. He also makes an important point concerning the *content* of hallucinations:

> Hallucinators do not hallucinate random events. Auditory hallucinators often experience threatening voices, and visual hallucinators see visions of dead ancestors or other persons of psychological significance to them. *Presumably the contents of patients' hallucinations are related in important ways to their personalities and to the stresses that precipitate their psychoses.*
>
> (Bentall, 1990, p. 91, our emphasis)

Bentall's position here challenges the therapeutic nihilism implicit in the Jaspersian psychopathological account of voices, that these experiences are meaningless. The problem is how to develop the therapeutic implications of this. As Bentall observes, attempts to get hallucinators to reattribute their experiences to themselves may cause considerable anxiety. The medicalisation of halluci-nations within the field of psychiatry has proscribed any discussion of the content of voices, but intuitively it is difficult to contest Bentall's point about the psychological significance of the content of many verbal hallucinations. Our own work on the pragmatic features of voices in Chapter 9 indicates clearly that voices have psychological significance and meaning. It is here that we can see the potential of cognitive therapy and other approaches which explore voices in detail. Many years before he introduced cognitive therapy as a psychological therapy for depression, Beck described the use of an early form of the intervention for delusions in schizophrenia (Beck, 1952). He described the therapy of a man who believed he was being followed by members of the FBI, in which he identified the antecedents of this belief, before moving on to a reality-testing technique which helped modify it. Although the potential value of cognitive interventions for people experiencing psychoses has been recognised for some time (see, for example, Kingdon and Turkington, 1991a, 1991b), it is only recently that such interventions have been used to help people who hear voices.

One reason for the slow uptake of cognitive interventions for people who hear voices is the widely held belief that it is inappropriate to discuss in detail the content of hallucinations (or delusions). This is reinforced by the view that voices are discontinuous from 'normal' experience, that they are a pathological phenomenon associated with psychosis. But it is difficult to sustain such a view. Voices constitute a range of experiences, some of which are associated with mental states in psychosis, some not. We have argued that voices are a variety of 'inner' speech, which constitutes an integral part of our conscious and reflexive activity. In this model, inner speech is an important regulating process which helps us to plan and organise our activities, solve problems, and mould and re-create our social identity. This model allows us to consider the psychological and cognitive significance of voices, and is consistent with a variety of cognitive and other psychological interventions.

Cognitive interventions can offer subjects the opportunity to develop alternative explanatory models. This point has been made by Kingdon *et al.* (1994), who have used these techniques with over sixty people suffering from schizophrenia (Kingdon and Turkington, 1991a). They used a number of interventions, including the identification of 'faulty' cognitions associated with the formation of delusional beliefs, and the modification of these through the processes of reattribution, analysis of the evidence for the beliefs, and the generation of alternative explanations. They were probably the first to point out the importance of reattributing the origin of voices to the self, a technique which is central to focusing. This idea is not without its dangers, however. We have seen in Chapter 5 that the human self cannot be considered to be a homogeneous structure. Mead and James both recognised that such self is socially reflexive, and Mead, for example, argued that self consists of an 'I' and '(generalised) other'. So when we ask a client to reattribute voices to self, we have to be clear about what exactly we are asking her to accept. Are we saying that the voices are really parts of her 'I'? If so, we are bound to confuse her because this is simply not so. Or are the voices to be reattributed to the part of self which makes it socially reflexive? We have to be clear that we explain the sense in which voices are to be a part of her self. It is not at all clear to us that there is one general and theoretical answer to this question. Voice hearers' own particular accounts of how they relate to voices may be helpful (see Chapter 9).

Subjects in Kingdon and Turkington (1991a) were also asked to consider the idea that if their voices were generated externally other people should be able to hear them, and then to test this hypothesis. We shall see in Chapter 9 that this is indeed one of voice hearers' mundane reality-testing procedures. Kingdon *et al.* (1994) have described cognitive therapy as a normalising approach, in which subjects were told that hearing voices is not necessarily a sign of madness. Much work also took place within the context of families and carers. These interventions appeared to be safe, and widely acceptable to patients and carers. It appears that everyone benefits from discovering that it is safe to talk about the content of voices. An additional benefit was a reduced need for neuroleptic medication in those subjects who received cognitive interventions.

Perhaps the most thorough account of cognitive therapy for voices has been provided by Chadwick and Birchwood (1994). Their work is firmly rooted in Beck's cognitive model in which the behavioural and affective changes of depression are seen as a consequence of negative beliefs. In hallucinations they argue that subjects' beliefs about the nature and origins of voices have an important effect on how they respond to the voices. First, they tested the hypothesis that the amount of distress caused by voices was related to the subjects' beliefs about the voices, and not to voice content. They interviewed twenty-six voice hearers to establish voice content and beliefs about voices, and undertook a cognitive analysis of each individual's experiences. All the subjects regarded their voices as omnipotent and extraordinarily powerful. In over 70 per cent of subjects these beliefs were supported by additional experiences (such as visual hallucinations) which contributed to this sense of omnipotence. In 46 per cent of subjects voices were regarded as malevolent, and 23 per cent believed that their voices were benevolent. There was a clear connection between voice content and the subject's belief about the voices. For example, people whose voices gave them evil commands cited this in evidence that the voices were evil, although in over 30 per cent of subjects beliefs about the nature of the voices appeared to conflict with the voices' content. There was a very clear link between the subjects' beliefs about the nature of the voices and responses to voices. Engagement between subject and voice invariably occurred if the subject considered the voices to be benevolent, and in situations where the voices were considered malevolent the voice was resisted (we will see the importance of this in our own intervention). It appears, then, that subjects' beliefs about the identity, omnipotence and purpose of voices determine whether the voices are regarded as malevolent or benevolent, which in turn influences subjects' behaviour towards the voices.

In the second part of the study Chadwick and Birchwood developed the therapeutic implications of these findings through cognitive therapy, as they attempted to reduce the distress associated with voices by systematically changing ('undermining') the subjects' central beliefs about voices. They defined these beliefs, and asked each subject to consider the advantages and disadvantages that these beliefs might be wrong. The next step involved disputing these beliefs, a task which was achieved in three stages. First, they established the extent to which subjects were prepared to consider that a hypothetical situation would alter their beliefs. Second, subjects were given a *verbal challenge*, in which they were asked to question the basis of their beliefs, and to generate alternative interpretations. Finally, subjects' beliefs were questioned directly and alternative explanations developed. At this point, subjects were encouraged to test their beliefs empirically. For example, statements such as 'I cannot control my voices' were reframed as 'I cannot turn my voices on and off'. Therapy then engineered situations in which it was possible to test the reframed beliefs so that subjects could prove that they could turn their voices on and off, and thus that they could indeed control their voices. Chadwick and Birchwood describe the use of these techniques in four subjects, all of whom reported reduced frequency and duration of voice activity.

Although this is an important piece of work which opens up new therapeutic possibilities for voice hearers, attempts to 'undermine' subjects' beliefs about voices pay scant respect to 'folk' psychology. While Chadwick and Birchwood's cognitive therapy takes the meaning of voices seriously, in doing so it privileges the psychologist's account, which is used to challenge the voice hearer's explanatory system. This reveals a degree of insensitivity to the potential complexity of human experience. For many voice hearers, their explanatory frameworks are deeply rooted in past experiences and life histories. We will demonstrate this in Chapter 7. To challenge the person's explanatory framework means demanding that the person rewrites this narrative using the psychologist's script, thus denying personal truths.

Focusing interventions

Arguably, focusing should be included with cognitive therapy. It shares some features with this, as it does with behavioural interventions, particularly progressive desensitisation. But focusing is set within a different theoretical and research perspective set out by Bentall *et al.* (1994). This argues that voices arise from a failure to attribute internal events to the self. There are several strands of evidence in support of this. Hallucinations are related to psychophysiological states of arousal, such as anxiety and stress, or conditions of sensory deprivation. In addition, in some subjects, voices are associated with 'sub-vocal' speech; that is, barely perceptible activity of the speech musculature. This activity may be blocked by tasks such as reading or humming, which inhibit sub-vocalisation. (See Chapter 9 for a more detailed exposition of this evidence.) Bentall *et al.* argue that distinguishing between internally and externally generated events is a metacognitive skill which is a function of the events to be distinguished, and the individual's beliefs and expectations. Some aspects of this theory are consistent with those of Frith (1992) and Hoffman (1986). Bentall points out that there is experimental evidence in support of this. Hallucinating patients appear more likely to detect speech in white noise than non-hallucinating patients. Beliefs and expectations, however, are shaped by social and cultural factors. For example, an individual's beliefs about the type of event that is, or is not, likely to occur in public or private domains is likely to be influenced by cultural assumptions about the nature of causal agencies, such as telepathy, spirits, or belief in the existence of cognitive psychology. In essence, Bentall *et al.*'s hypothesis is that people who experience voices fail to attribute self-generated events to self, and furthermore, attributions about the origin of these events are determined by the subject's expectations and belief systems.

Richard Bentall's hypothesis about the origins of voices is attractive in that it recognises the complexity of their nature, and encourages us to think of them as an emergent property of an exceedingly complex system. Cognitive and neuropsychological factors are important, as are social and cultural factors which provide an explanatory system for the experience. It is this aspect in particular which is important in focusing. The aim of focusing is to reduce the frequency and distress caused by voices, by encouraging the reattribution of the experience to the self. If this proves difficult because of the fixity of the individual's explanatory system, attempts are made to encourage reattribution by restructuring these beliefs using a cognitive model similar to that of Chadwick and Birchwood. In practical terms, focusing consists of a number of interventions. Self-monitoring plays an important role in the early stages. Subjects keep a weekly record of the intensity and severity of the voices, as well as a daily diary of duration, loudness, distress and hostility of the voices. As therapy progresses, the subject is encouraged to focus in greater detail on the voices, using the self-monitoring data to do so, and also to compare the experiences with inner speech, and other self-generated subjective experiences, such as thoughts and feelings. Particular attention is paid to the physical characteristics of the voices, voice content, and associated thoughts and assumptions about the voices. By this stage it should be clear whether or not the subject feels comfortable reattributing the voices to self, and the final stages of therapy encourage the subject to reformulate the experience. A particularly interesting feature is the extent to which focusing encourages subjects to recognise specific problem areas in their lives from the *content* of the voices:

> In such cases, *patients are encouraged to use the content of the voices to help them to recognise specific problem areas.* For example, one patient . . . recognised that her voices tended to become worse following family arguments. She became aware that the content of her voices reflected the things that she was feeling and thinking about her family but that she was unable to express.
>
> (Bentall *et al.*, 1994, p. 58, our emphasis)

The therapist then uses this content to help the subject with problem-solving techniques.

A detailed account of focusing in two subjects has been provided by Haddock *et al.* (1993). Both received twenty sessions in which they were gradually encouraged to explore the content and meaning of their voices. One subject appeared to gain considerable benefit from the approach, the other had an equivocal response. This work highlights the importance of obtaining clear descriptions (from the subject) of the nature of these experiences, through daily records and diaries. The voices of the first subject fell into three distinct types. First, there were exclusively external voices which, as therapy progressed, became mostly pleasant or neutral. Second, there were voices which arose only in the presence of people, television or machinery. Once the subject accepted that these experiences were misinterpretations of auditory events, their troublesomeness diminished. The third set of experiences were not voices at all, but intrusive thoughts. Another point relates to the extent to which reattribution of voices to self is a prerequisite for therapeutic change. The subject who benefited from focusing appears to have been able to accept that his experiences were self-generated, whereas the second subject found it difficult to do so. His voices appeared to be distorted fragments of real conversations which he heard, usually at night, in the hostel in which he lived, and to which he attributed hostile intentions.

The problem here, as the authors comment, is that this subject's voices are understandable in terms of the depressing social and material circumstances in which he was living at the time. Attempts to intervene psychologically without attending to the person's social reality are likely to be unsuccessful.

7 Working with voices

In our culture voices represent something that is to be feared. For ordinary people the experience has become inextricably bound up with unpredictability, being out of control and the general issue of danger. The reasons for this are complex, but in Chapter 8 we will see that the media play a significant part in generating this message. Society regards psychiatry as being the appropriate technology for dealing with the problems posed by the experience of voice hearing, and in Chapter 6 we examined the response of psychiatry and clinical psychology. Psychiatry talks about voices as verbal and auditory hallucinations, a symptom of psychosis to be controlled and dissipated with medication. Yet significant numbers of people appear to gain little or no benefit from medication. Besides, the very act of giving and taking medication implies that the participants in the exchange share a common perspective on the significance of voices: that the experience is understood in terms of mental illness. In reality the extent to which this perspective is shared is debatable, because psychiatrists are ultimately empowered to coerce their patients into accepting medical interpretations of their experiences. Those who doubt this should remember that at the time of writing, the British government has set up a review body to make recommendations about changes to the Mental Health Act. It seems highly likely that this will result in the introduction of even more coercive legislation, in the form of community treatment orders, to ensure that people who stop taking their medication when out of hospital can be given medication against their wishes in the community.

In press releases heralding changes in mental health policy in the summer of 1998, the then Health Secretary, Frank Dobson, repeatedly stressed the importance of security, such as assertive outreach services – 'to keep tabs on people who have been discharged and make contact with people who shy away from getting help', and changes in the law to cover measures such as 'compliance orders' and 'community treatment orders' to ensure that patients take their medication. Health Minister Tessa Jowell repeatedly stressed the word 'safety' in her speech at MIND's Annual Conference in November 1998. The government, in allowing its mental health policy to be partly determined by newspaper headlines (see Chapter 8), is covertly reinforcing a less obvious role of psychiatry – that of risk assessment. The 'therapeutic' credentials of psychiatry are being eroded.

We also have to accept an inescapable fact about the experience of voice hearing; that is, the responses of those around the voice hearer – her friends, family and the wider society in which she lives – play a central role in influencing how she understands and deals with the experience. There are several sources of evidence to support this view. In Maastricht, Sandra Escher has recently completed a study of eighty children who hear voices, half of whom were drawn from child psychiatry clinics, the rest being non-clinical voice hearers identified through the press. Children whose parents interpreted the experience within a medical framework, regarding it as a symptom to be got rid of or treated, were more likely to show higher levels of distress, and to find it more difficult to cope with the experience (Escher, 1998, personal communication). This brings to mind Sodi's (1995) account of voices given from within the Xhosa culture of the Northern Transvaal of South Africa, where, in contrast to our culture, a young person who begins to hear voices is found a valued role as a traditional hearer. The response of those around the voice hearer, whether the experience is something valued or, conversely, feared and to be erased, is of great significance. This emerged in one of our own interviews with a voice hearer (KL) as part of our work (see Chapter 9). KL's voices started a few months after she was abused at the age of 5, but it took a while before she realised that something unusual was going on. She asked a friend at school if she could hear things in her head. Her friend said no, at which point KL realised that she was the only person who had these experiences. She found this upsetting, because originally her voices had made her feel special, and she did not regard them as a bad thing. But finding out that other people regarded voice hearing as a bad thing upset her, with the result that she felt unable to discuss the experience with other people for many years.

These are the contexts in which this chapter should be read. The traditional way in which psychiatrists respond to people who hear voices (i.e. 'It's dangerous to get them to talk about these experiences') has been reinforced by popular culture and political life. Both participants in the events we are about to narrate were exposed to this context, for many of the newspaper reports which will be described in Chapter 8 were published contemporaneously with the work described here. In addition, given the nature of Peg's voices, particularly the things they told her to do, this context becomes even more significant. Another context which must be remembered is the setting in which this work took place. The work described did not result in a new 'therapy' or 'intervention' for people who hear voices. We are sceptical of the value that our society attaches to therapy and the political implications of this (see, for example, Rose, 1989; Leudar and Antaki, 1997). This work emerged out of a fusion of the day-to-day clinical work of Philip Thomas (PT), with our joint study of the pragmatics of experiences of hearing voices (Leudar *et al.*, 1997; and see Chapter 9). There was nothing extraordinary about the clinical work, which initially took place in out-patient clinics which PT held as part of his clinical work in a rural part of North Wales. What emerged, though, was that the very process of talking about voices, systematically and in detail, in a sympathetic, non-judgemental way, helped Peg to understand her voices and to be much less distressed by them.

Again, we must stress that this was not therapy. The only assumption we had was that voices are a form of private speech, and that this perspective makes it possible for voice hearers to provide a detailed account of the properties of their voices to themselves and to others. Both participants (Peg and PT) were keen to explore the meaning of voices, and as it turned out our pragmatic interview (Leudar and Thomas, 1995) played an important role in this. We must also make it clear that we are not making any specific therapeutic claims for the pragmatic interview. One of us (PT) is widely experienced in the use of both the pragmatic interview, and the Maastricht interview devised by Marius Romme and Sandra Escher. In recent work with the Maastricht interview, similar outcomes were obtained. Nevertheless, the work described here raises the possibility that a dialogical model of human experience may be useful in helping someone who is distressed by their voices.

In particular, it became possible for Peg to introduce moral responses to distressing and potentially dangerous imperative verbal hallucinations, through the mediation of the new voice. Her engagement with this voice enabled her to deal effectively with the troublesome voices, and was a powerful source of self-esteem. There are some similarities in the processes described here and focusing. In Chapter 6 we saw that the main difference between focusing and other cognitive behavioural interventions was that one of the main objectives of cognitive behavioural therapy (CBT) (as described by Chadwick and Birchwood, 1994) was to change the voice hearer's explanatory framework in order to reduce the distress caused by voices. Like focusing, we worked within the voice hearer's explanatory framework, but no attempt was made to challenge it, because we believe that the explanatory framework is in itself related to, or symbolic of, the voice hearer's life.

The participants

PT is a 49-year-old psychiatrist who has been a consultant since 1983. Since his training he has gradually come to adopt a highly critical position in relation to his chosen profession, because of the extent to which it is dominated by the medical model and clinical neuroscience. This interprets human distress in terms of 'symptoms' of mental illness, and locates the origins of distress within the individual. This serves two functions that are important politically. First, it plays down the importance of social, cultural, economic and political factors in understanding human distress (Thomas *et al.*, 1996). Second, because the distress is constructed in terms of disordered brain function, it means that both the person and the social contexts in which the person exists have no control or influence on what happens to the person in distress. This is the process by which society remains isolated from involvement in, or culpability for, distress, but it is also the process by which the individual is seen not to be responsible for her actions when distressed.

Peg is a 59-year-old single retired woman who was referred to PT by her GP in 1993. She was originally admitted to a hospital in the English Midlands over twenty years earlier, but had remained under the care of her original consultant because she got to know him and trusted him, travelling a round trip of over 150 miles once every two months to keep her out-patient appointments with him. He was responsible for the diagnosis of schizophrenia, and Peg had taken depot neuroleptic medication more or less ever since. He retired a few months before Peg first saw PT, and this was the reason for the referral. She was seen by PT in the company of her companion, Sheila. This must have been a difficult change for Peg, for over the years she had grown to trust her previous psychiatrist, and had come to feel comfortable with a medical approach to her problems. The idea that she was ill was appealing in that it meant that she personally did not have to accept responsibility for the way she had acted in response to the voices' commands in the past. The way she had acted was to do with her 'illness' (her voices), and was nothing to do with Peg. This was clear from her reaction in one of her early meetings with PT, when he raised doubts about the diagnosis of schizophrenia.[1] She became angry at this suggestion, and especially when PT expressed the view that, illness or no illness, he found it difficult to accept the idea that hearing imperative voices exonerated a person from responsibility for their actions.[2] Besides, there were other reasons for wanting to reformulate the nature of Peg's experiences. Peg had been on neuroleptic medication for many years, and like many people in her situation, she was unaware of the risk of long-term neuro-logical side-effects of these drugs, particularly tardive dyskinesia. It was important that she was made aware of these risks so that she could make an informed decision about the risks and benefits of continuing on this medication. The first six months of out-patient contact between Peg and PT dealt more or less exclusively with these issues: the problem of responsibility for Peg's actions in response to her voices, and the problems of long-term neuroleptic medication. Peg reported that her voices were profoundly disturbing and difficult to resist (see below). The medication had not got rid of the voices, and Peg continued to hear them from time to time. True, the medication damped down the voices, making it easier for Peg to ignore them, but, as we will see, there were still occasions when she heard them and acted on their commands. This indicated that medication was at best only a partial answer to her problems.

At the end of this initial period, Peg's attitude to her experiences began to change. She wanted to start reducing her medication, but was rightly concerned about the possibility that she might find it more difficult to cope with her voices. Because of this it became important for her to find other ways of coping with her experiences, and to do this we agreed that it would be necessary to achieve a greater understanding of the meaning of her voices. The approach used in this task was much influenced by the work of Romme and Escher (1989, 1991, 1994), who were using the Maastricht interview to clarify the meaning of a subject's voices, in the context of the person's life narrative. So Peg chose to produce her own narrative by writing out her life story in longhand. She gave the following account of her life.

She was adopted at the age of 12 months, after her biological mother had abandoned her, and she has never met her since. Her adoptive parents were well-to-do, professional people in their forties when she was adopted. She described herself as a 'difficult child', disobedient and naughty. She completed normal schooling and attended teacher training college, before starting work as a teacher in a school for physically handicapped children. She did well and was eventually promoted to headmistress of a residential school for maladjusted children. She described herself as gifted in this work, having a particular empathy with the children, a fact confirmed by Sheila, who had got to know Peg through working with her. In the mid-1970s Peg started to suffer from considerable stress. Work was very busy and emotionally demanding, and she also had to deal with the impending loss of her elderly adoptive mother, who was terminally ill. It was at this time that she had her first psychiatric admission, in 1977, after she had tried to give her mother an overdose of tablets and suffocate her. She said her actions were in response to voices which told her to place a pillow over her mother's face, having first given her the sleeping tablets. She had not considered herself responsible for these actions. Peg could easily have become one of the cases of violent mentally ill voice hearers reported in the British national newspapers (see Chapter 8).

Little is known about Peg's voices at this time, as their characteristics were not investigated in detail. Their presence as hallucinations was of diagnostic significance only. After this admission Peg returned to work, but was re-admitted two years later. She had broken into the local Catholic church and stolen the Host from the Tabernacle, again in response to imperative voices. Her medication was increased and this appeared to resolve the problem. On discharge, she took early retirement and moved to Wales with Sheila. For this reason she relied heavily on Sheila, going nowhere without her.

In her narrative, Peg produced a detailed account of her history from her earliest memories to the present, including all events that she considered significant. In her writing she used the first-person singular, the 'I', placing herself at the centre of action. She selected the following points as being of particular significance. Her adoptive parents were extremely strict, and found it difficult to deal with emotional intimacy. Peg remembers wanting to be hugged by her mother, but these requests were not responded to. They also never allowed Peg to forget that they had saved her by adoption, but she was puzzled as to what it was they had saved her from. As a result she felt in debt to them, a debt she could never repay. She felt compelled to be the perfect daughter so as to feel worthy of their love. She believed that she had always had to keep herself 'in check'; that is, to monitor her behaviour and edit out impulses to do things that she thought would be unacceptable to her parents. There are uneasy parallels between her position at home and that of 'guests' at Tuke's York Retreat – see Foucault (1991 and 1967, Ch. 9). She never felt, however, that she could be a good enough daughter for her adoptive parents. In early adulthood she traced her biological mother, and discovered that she had had to give up caring for Peg while having to look after her own mother who was dying of cancer. Peg expressed the view that the part of her self that she held in check was in some way related to her biological mother.

Dialogical properties of Peg's voices

Peg's voices were investigated in 1995 over a period of two weeks, immediately after she had completed her narrative. We obtained a detailed description of her voices using the interview which is described in detail in Leudar and Thomas (1995). The purpose of this was to identify her voices and to describe their interactions with Peg. The interview categories are not technical terms, but simple words which are used in reporting ordinary conversations such as, for instance, 'ask', refuse', 'order', 'ignore'. We used the questionnaire to help Peg to structure the information about the voices. What this means is that Peg talked to us about her voices without having them rendered 'meaningful' (and meaningless) in psychiatric interpretations.

Peg first heard voices after the Aberfan disaster of 1966, in which over a hundred children were killed when a slag-heap engulfed their school. She recalled 'seeing the suffering in their eyes, hearing their [the victims'] screams and being powerless to help'. This was a one-off chorus voice – it was composed of many individuals and she heard it once only (cf. Leudar *et al.*, 1997). But since 1977, Peg had experienced two recurrent voices with stable and well-defined identities. The following descriptions of these voices emerged.

Voice 1 – 'The Guardian Angel' (GA)

This voice first spoke to Peg when her mother was dying. She felt powerless to help her mother, but the voice suggested she should suffocate her and give her an overdose. It had no gender features, but sounded adult. It sounded like no one she knew, but she immediately said that it reminded her of her father because, like him, it had an opinion about everything. For example, it directed her and instructed her what to do. It occurred when she was under stress, such as in the company of old people who 'invaded' her space. She had always thought of it as her friend, but she was now beginning to doubt this because it told her to do 'wicked' things which she found impossible to resist. The voice continued to be very troublesome for her, despite medication. For example, she had heard it some months before while visiting a friend in hospital. Once again Peg had felt helpless to relieve her suffering, and the voice told her to smother the old lady, who was very ill. She would have reacted to the voice automatically by embarking on the course of action it suggested, had it not been for Sheila's presence. Over the years Peg and Sheila had recognised the circumstances in which this voice was likely to appear, and one way they had dealt with it was to make sure that Peg was never left alone with elderly people who were either ill or otherwise demanding. Fortunately even if this failed, Peg's unconsidered actions in response to voices would not inevitably come to fruition, since acting on ordinary intentions, and on voice directives, are not just mechanical behaviours but situated activities which require effort and intelligence (cf. Leudar and Costall, 1996).

More recently Peg had tried to cope by avoiding situations which precipitated the voice. This voice was pragmatically restricted to issuing instructions and providing information relevant to carrying them out. Other than tell the voice to go away, Peg would not question the instructions it gave her. Her main problem with regard to this voice was automatically reacting to its instructions.

Voice 2 – My 'Little Devil'

This voice had no gender or accent, but sounded younger than the GA. She named it her 'Little Devil' (LD) because she could see it sitting on her shoulder – 'it is a total experience'. It came on when she had 'destructive' thoughts, such as those which heralded the appearance of the GA. She regarded this voice as helpful, because it told her to do things like take the Host, which she believed would help her to resist the GA's suggestions. She never questioned the LD, and acted in response without consideration. Like the GA, this voice was pragmatically restricted: for instance, it never gave her permission or forbade her from doing things, but it granted her information to resource the actions it suggested. It might say 'the key [to the Tabernacle] is there – there is no one there', information indicating that she could take the Host without being discovered.

Both voices addressed Peg directly as 'you'. They always spoke individually and were never present together. They never spoke to each other, nor did they address other people through Peg. The GA commented on things that PT had said. For example, it told her to ignore his opinion that despite its commands, Peg was responsible for her actions. Peg was confused about the conflict between PT's views and those of the GA. She could distinguish between her voices and her inner dialogues, because talking to herself was quite different from being addressed by the voices – 'I am doing the talking – that is me. The voices are outside me, the voices are directional' – meaning they told her what to do and their intentions were not her intentions. She had frequent internal dialogues with herself which did not involve the voices, so hearing voices did not substitute for inner speech.

We have seen that Peg's reactions to both voices were impulsive rather than mediated. When, later, she considered what she had done in response to the voices' instructions, she was horrified. The difficulty was that this consideration came too late to modify her immediate response to the voices. Interestingly, she relied on other people (Sheila, PT) to stop her acting as the voices commanded. Peg was in a difficult situation: a part of her mental life was alienated from her and she recruited others to help regulate her activities. They did so, but as a result her personal autonomy was compromised. The problem of how voice hearers respond to their voices' injunctions to commit dangerous acts is complex, and in need of much more detailed consideration (see Chapters 8 and 9). In the course of our work together, however, it became clear that there was no particular reason why voices should be compulsive. PT's strategy was to help Peg to introduce moral considerations to mediate the voices' commands and her actions. This placed the onus on Peg to consider potential actions as her own. Psychiatrists often function to take away responsibility from patients, but here the purpose was to work with Peg (and Sheila) as allies, to help her assume more responsibility. The purpose here was to enable Peg to comment on the voices' instructions. The difficulty was that the voices usually appeared in specific contexts, making it difficult to introduce these comments during the course of the limited time we were able to spend working together. To overcome this, she was asked to rehearse in memory situations in which the GA and LD appeared. Any intervention with her voices was achieved through Peg, Peg's 'I', which follows from our theoretical approach which regards voices as regulating the subject's actions. Unlike psychotherapeutic interventions in dissociative states, where the therapist may interact directly with subpersonalities, there were no interactions between PT and the voices. The intention was that she should write out in longhand (as part of a journal that Peg had decided to start herself, after having written out her life story) a typical sequence of statements made by each voice, and for her to insert her considered reply to the voices, which she could rehearse, like learning the lines of a play. This proved unnecessary. After the interview in which she explored her voices, she felt very stressed, and she awoke in the early hours, hearing a new voice telling her that the GA would not destroy her. The following is Peg's own account of developments, taken verbatim from her journal (text in square brackets is our own editorial comment).

Peg's Journal: excerpt 1

I was a bit stressed out in the night but I was awake so I know I did not do anything untoward except that a new voice has joined the happy band reassuring me that I would be all right. Telling me that my Guardian Angel will not destroy me. I have called it my Holy Angel, but I think it is the voice of Peg.

Does that make sense? I told it eventually to go away I must sleep and it did.

Voice of my Holy Angel

'You are going to be all right. You will come through this. Your Guardian Angel is not going to destroy you. Don't be afraid of me. I am your friend'.

It was like Peg speaking.

~~You are~~ I am going to leave behind now my GA and my LD and have my new voice. (My response).

I call it my Holy Angel. But it is Peg. Constantly reassuring me positive comments you are going to win through this time. When it first came a couple of days ago I thought I must be imagining things but I am not. I told it to let me go to sleep – now 4 a.m. it is a kind warm voice not cold and clinical.

Peg also made the following notes about the things this new voice said to her.

Peg's Journal: excerpt 2

Peg: My Holy Angel loves me.
HA: I love you I won't let any harm come to you.
It comes after I have been stressed out.
It brings me peace.
I felt lonely and it came to me.

Monday night – Tuesday morning
It comes when I have been stressed out – need reassurance [Peg found the interview stressful with me on the Monday because of the presence of another doctor whom she does not know.]
HA: You won't go to prison.
HA: You are not to blame for what you did.
Response: What if (her adoptive brother's name) found out I tried to kill his mother.
HA: You are not to blame I love you as you are.

Tuesday
HA: You see Peg there is nothing wrong in hearing voices. You are not evil. Don't hide me away.
After my voice HA, comes peace and relaxation.

Wednesday morning 3 a.m.
HA: There is no need to try me out. I am here for you.
Response: You know me well.
HA: Yes I know you.
Response: Will you stay with me always.
HA: Yes I will stay with you.
(My Holy Angel likes the dark)
HA: I am your friend. Your GA was not your friend although you thought he was. You did bad things with him. You must not listen to him. he is wicked.
Accept my love as it is free. Sheila loves you. You know Sheila?
Yes I know Sheila yes I love Sheila.
They loved you.
Response: I hated and loved them at the same time.

The Holy Angel told her that she would be all right and that the other voices would not destroy her. This new voice was 'like Peg speaking', and although she called it her Holy Angel, it was Peg's voice. We are not using a metaphor here: Peg heard a new voice, sounding like her own, but she was not speaking to herself. It may have sounded like Peg but it shared pragmatic qualities with Sheila and PT – like them, it reassured and supported her, and enhanced her self-esteem.

Subsequently, she provided a detailed journal of her interactions with this new voice, which indicated that complex new dialogues took place between the

HA and Peg. For example, it reassured her spontaneously with positive and encouraging comments, and also did this in response to her requests. We can see from the above extract that one set of dialogues concerned Peg's quest for reassurance about her biological mother, especially that she had loved Peg. The new voice also told her that she should not 'punish' that part of herself which represented her biological mother. This part of her needed love and acceptance, and it was important that Peg was able to do this for herself.

Traditionally, the appearance of a new voice might be viewed as a negative sign indicating yet further fragmentation of self. It is clear, however, that HA worked constructively on Peg's behalf. The voice mediated between Peg and the other voices by commenting to her that what they told her to do was wrong. The HA, though autonomous from Peg's 'I' (that is, Peg referring to herself as 'I'), was aligned with her and faced the other voices with her. It reassured her directly in response to her questions about itself and the other voices.

Peg engaged in dialogue with the Holy Angel about many troublesome aspects of her life. In the following sequence, she discusses the difficulties she encounters in going to church. She had avoided doing this because of the fear that the Little Devil would suggest to her that she could take a piece of the Host. In fact, Peg confesses to the HA that she still has a piece of the Host in a drawer at home, of which Sheila is unaware. She suggests to the voice that she should ask Sheila to eat it, but the voice disagrees, saying that the disposal of the Host is Peg's responsibility. Peg finds this difficult to accept. The presence of the Host at home is clearly a great moral support for her, and it is clear that she does not yet feel that she is ready to face life without it.

Peg's Journal: excerpt 3

Thursday night–Fri 3 a.m.

Peg.   Why do you come in the ~~dark~~ night when it is dark
HA.   Because it is quiet. Just you & me. Like you I don't like a noise.

Peg.   I don't want to break into a church again
HA.   You are not going to. There is no need I am with you.
Peg.   It upsets so many people
      Did I do it
      Why you did it
HA.   You were afraid
      You are not frightened now I am with you
Peg.   I have got a Benediction host at home.
      I will ask Sheila to eat it.
HA.   No. You must do it yourself. You must face up to it yourself.
Resp.   I turned my back on my H.A.
      It is asking too much of me.
      Always I keep one hidden at home
      If I let it go, I will have nothing

HA.   You don't need it now. You have me
      You will not be afraid. I am here now.
      Go to sleep now.

      I was too troubled to sleep so I put the
      world service on the radio & did my knitting
      waiting for the Temazopan to work. I did sleep eventually.

Peg regards the voice as her conscience, but the following extract reveals that this is Sheila's account of the new voice speaking through Peg:

Peg's Journal: excerpt 4

Your Guardian Angel may come again.

HA.   Your Guardian Angel may come again
      But I will be with you as well.
      Good and evil you can choose.
Peg. Please help me H.A.
      Sheila tells me you are my conscience
HA.   Does it matter.
Peg. No.

Two days later, Peg is still grappling with whether she feels able to attend Mass the following day. She wants to be able to do so, but is still afraid that the LD will appear. The Holy Angel initiates this exchange, suggesting that Peg can indeed go to church the next day. It reassures her, telling her she will be safe and that it will accompany her. Peg then explicitly deals with her fear, that she will be unable to trust herself if the LD suggests she takes the Host. Again the HA reassures her, telling her that she is no longer alone. It also points out that Christ is in the Host for everyone, thus implying that it is wrong for Peg to take the Host away for her own use. The Host is for sharing. The HA reassures her again, and then, like a loving parent talking to a fretful child, it orders her to go to sleep. This time the voice's support seems to have been effective, because Peg decides that she can go to church the following day, and that she is now excited at the prospect of doing so, as much for her friend Sheila's sake as her own. At last she feels confident about being able to go to church.

Peg's Journal: excerpt 5

Sat–Sunday 3 a.m.

HA.   You can go to church tomorrow
Peg. Will my L.D. be there to tempt me. I don't
      need the host now you are with me.
HA.   You can just go and enjoy the Mass.

Peg.   I'm afraid to walk down there alone.
HA.   You will be quite safe. I am with you.
       You are not alone.
Peg.   I don't want to take anything. Food for the
       week ahead. I don't trust myself. The LD
       will come & tempt me, once the host is in my
       hand.
HA.   You do not have it in your hand. I trust you.
       Now trust yourself.
       I will be with you. You are quite safe
       You can do it. You are not alone now.
Peg.   Please H.A. help me to achieve this. The LD
       hasn't come this week when I've been upset.
HA.   No you don't need him now I am here
       Go & spare time for God. Pray to Jesus that
       you will not hurt him anymore. He is in the
       host for everyone. You must not take him
       away.
Peg.   If the LD comes, he will spoil everything again.
HA.   No he won't come. I shall be with you.
       Go to sleep now.

Response. I would be really happy to go. I am too
         excited to sleep. Sheila would be pleased (?)
         I made it.
Peg.   If the little D. comes I will tell him to get
       lost. I don't need him anymore. He will only
       cause trouble.
       I love you H.A. You really are my friend.
HA.   He is wicked and your L.D. only causes
       upset to other people & makes Sheila sad.

       This conversation went on the holy Angel
       re assuring me that he was my friend.
       Not to trust the G.A, or the L.D. they are wicked.

Peg attended Mass uneventfully the next day with Sheila. She was able to attend regularly following this.

There were two other themes in Peg's conversations in the fortnight after the appearance of the HA. The first helped her to resolve conflicts concerning her biological mother and adoptive parents. The second concerned the issue of responsibility for her actions in the face of the commands the first two voices gave her. In the following sequence we see a conversation in which the HA raises the issue of Peg's relationship with her biological mother, whose name is Roseanne. Here, the initials JCM refer to Peg's name before she was adopted. In response to the initiation of this sequence, Peg wonders why her mother gave her up. The HA goes on to say that she (Peg) must learn to love and accept JCM, that part of herself which Peg identifies strongly with her biological mother.[3] Peg then identifies the confusion that she had experienced throughout her life on account of having been renamed at adoption. The issue is raised again the following evening, but this time it is Peg who initiates it, as she addresses the HA by name, and then asks it whether it loves both Peg and JCM. She also seeks reassurance that the two are not different people. The voice confirms that the two are one, and that they always loved each other. It then goes on to describe how Peg had driven a wedge between the two in order to cope with her confusion over the adoption. The identity Peg (well behaved and self-controlled) was acceptable to her adoptive parents, whereas JCM (identified with Peg's biological mother) was unacceptable to both her adoptive parents and her biological mother who rejected her through adoption. Peg's emerging ability to accept and love JCM as a frightened, vulnerable part of herself is reinforced and supported by the voice. This sequence is interesting, because some of the issues raised in it had been dealt with by Peg and PT during their discussion of Peg's life story some weeks earlier. It appears, therefore, that the voice is to some extent aligned with PT in this sequence.

Peg's Journal: excerpt 6

Saturday 3 a.m.

HA: You've resurrected J.C.M.
You took the blame for her existence.
You were not to blame for being born.

Peg: I wonder if Roseanne wanted me or whether
she was afraid.
She kept me for 6 months. why did she give me up.

HA: You will never know. But she did love you.
She loved you enough to give you away.

Peg: I tried to find her. She was only 19.

HA: Don't punish yourself. Love her.
J.C.M is not evil. JCM wants to be loved.
She is part of you. Love her.
J.C.M is very quiet She likes to be alone
with you.

Peg: They shouldn't have changed my name.
I didn't need a new identity
I was already in existence.

HA: Leave it alone now.
J.C.M wanted to be loved & acknowledged
Don't hide her away anymore.
Go to sleep now.

. . .

Sunday a.m.

Peg to HA. Are you there

HA.　Yes I am here

Peg.　Do you love J.C.M and Peg.
　　　They are not two people are they.

HA.　No they make one now called Peg.

Peg.　And they love each other.

HA.　They always did. – They were one whole person
　　　only you separated them into good and bad.
　　　It was the way you survived. You were confused.
　　　You had two identities. Peg was acceptable and
　　　J.C.M was not wanted.
　　　Roseanne didn't want her & the Davies' did not want her.

Peg.　But she existed and must have been very
　　　unhappy

HA.　She is is happy now you have accepted her as a
　　　living part of your life. Acknowledge her and
　　　love her. She was weak and vulnerable and
　　　afraid and very insecure. Love her she is
　　　part of you.
　　　Go to sleep now.

(*next page*)

HA.　We are all good and evil in part.
　　　You can go to Church today.
　　　You'll be alright, You have not been obsessive
　　　Your L.D. will not tempt you

　　　I did go to Mass. Phyllis came with me.
　　　I was alright. No problems.

In the next sequence the voice addresses Peg on the issue of trust in human relationships. It seems reasonable to assume that Peg had problems with trusting others. Her biological mother had rejected her, and she was made to feel that love and acceptance by her adoptive parents was contingent and not unconditional. The voice comments on the fragility and preciousness of trust for children, but it reassures Peg that she can trust the voice, as she can her friend Sheila. Peg points out that people who find it difficult to trust others are afraid of getting hurt, and the voice's response is complex and interesting. Until this point in the sequence its responses were pragmatically similar to those of PT (as in the previous sequence). The voice repeatedly stresses to Peg that it is not prone to the same human frailties – 'Human beings are frail. I am strong'; 'I am not frail like you'; 'I am not vulnerable like a human being'. The implication here is that Peg can trust the voice because it is an angel and thus beyond human weaknesses. At this point we can understand the importance of Peg's religious faith, and the role this played in helping her to come terms with her problems.

Peg's Journal: excerpt 7

Monday 4 a.m.

Trust me was the underlying theme. My
HA just talked to me

HA.	Trust in a child is something beautiful
	But you are vulnerable. Life deals its blows.
	JCM was hurt & you are a result of that
	damage. But do not worry. I am with you.
	You can trust me. I am your friend. A real
	Friend like Sheila.
Peg.	Sheila hasn't been with me this time.
HA.	No. You needed my help. Sheila is human,
	I am not. Human beings are frail.
	I am strong. You can trust me. I am
	strong as your G.A. Think of me when things
	get rough. I will be here for you
	Trust me, trust me, trust me.
	Do not take the benediction host it is for
	everyone. You are not on your own I am
	with you.
Peg.	Trust means getting hurt
HA.	Not trust in me. I am not frail like you.
	You can trust me. Trust like a child.

Mon. cont'd.

HA.	Trust me, trust me, trust me.
	I am not vulnerable like a human being
	I will not let you down
	You loved your children. They had been hurt.
	You cared and they knew. They knew they
	were wanted. Like an animal knows who it
	can trust. They trusted you. Now you
	trust me. You will not be hurt this time.

My H.A. went on reassuring me & then told me to go to sleep.

Peg's religious faith is an important aspect of the final sequence, which the voice initiates by telling Peg that although she is not schizophrenic, and thus responsible for her actions, God forgives her for her actions. Again, the voice's pragmatic alignment is with PT initially (recall earlier that PT had upset Peg by expressing the firm view that schizophrenic or not, she remained responsible for her actions), but it is not clear where its reference to Peg's God came from. Peg and PT did not discuss Peg's religious faith to any great extent, although PT openly acknowledged the importance of this for Peg. The voice then absolves Peg of her guilt, perhaps in a manner similar to that of a compassionate priest. Peg then makes the comment that she remains troubled by PT's assertion that the GA is wicked. She goes on to say that this means that she (Peg) too must be wicked because the voice must have been a part of her. This is interesting because previously Peg had found it difficult to identify the GA and its imperatives as having anything to do with her. It now seems that this is starting to change. The voice switches back into an alignment with PT, pointing out that Peg will always be sad whenever she witnesses pain and suffering (remember that Peg's voices first started when she heard about the Aberfan tragedy). The implication is that humans must accept the inevitability of pain and suffering, because only God has the power to give and take life, at which point the voice's alignment shifts back to Peg's religious faith.

Tuesday 4 a.m.

HA.   Is your God big enough. Your God is great and all powerful. He can and does forgive you. You are not schizophrenic. Yes you are responsible for what you have done and you are responsible for the future. But you are not to blame.

Peg.   I should feel guilty.

HA.   No you are not guilty. That would be self destroying. You have destroyed too many things in your life. Don't destroy yourself now. You are not to blame for your childhood.

Peg.   But I was not a child when my GA came to me I thought he was my friend.

HA.   We will fight him together. With me you will be strong enough.

Peg.   Dr Phil said my GA was wicked. So I am wicked because he must have been a part of me.

HA.   No he was not the controllable part of you you were not to blame.

Peg.   I tried to kill my mother. She loved me. She was so unhappy.

HA.   We are all unhappy some time. Without it we don't know what it is to be happy. You know that. You will be sad when you see pain and suffering now. You will not destroy yourself. Only God can give and take life. Your GA was wicked.

Peg.   But I believed him he was all powerful and my friend.

HA.   To a child every one is more powerful but you are not a child now. You must do as I say. I will not harm you. I love you. Have me, I am your friend. Your GA was not your friend. The LD was not your friend. They only destroyed you inside.

Follow-up

After this quite intensive period of work, Peg maintained a detailed written diary. This indicated that her self-confidence increased and she started driving for the first time in two years. Four weeks after discharge she requested a reduction in her depixol. She heard neither the GA nor the LD after she was discharged, and she heard the HA less frequently, about once a week. The appearance of this new voice was associated with a subjective decrease in voice frequency. Eight weeks later, she found herself in difficult situations in which her old voices usually appeared. They visited Sheila's ageing mother, who was physically ill. During the visit the GA spoke to Peg, suggesting that she could ease the old lady's suffering, but the HA appeared immediately, telling the other voice to leave Peg alone, which it did. This was immensely reassuring for Peg, who felt sure that had the new voice not intervened she would have acted on the GA's suggestion. Then, on Christmas Day, she accepted the role of sacristan at church, which meant having access to the Host. She was able to do this without any problems and without the appearance of the LD.

Then, in March 1996, fifteen children and a teacher were shot dead in the Dunblane massacre. At some point that day she heard the children's voices crying out in her head. She was also distressed by vivid visual images of the carnage in the gymnasium. 'It was like Aberfan again.' This chorus voice took over despite her attempts at distraction by knitting and watching television. She phoned PT that evening to ask for advice, and she also talked through her response with the HA (she had heard no voices for three weeks before Dunblane). The children's cries were very distressing but the HA comforted her, saying that although the tragedy was terrible, the children were out of this world, so there was no more pain or suffering for them. The injured children had Holy Angels to care for them, because doctors and nurses would relieve their suffering. Gradually the cries abated and she fell asleep. She awoke feeling 'sad and desolate' but free of voices until that evening, when they reappeared as she tried to sleep. The HA appeared again and reassured her, so that she was able to sleep. Over the next week the cries recurred in response to reminders of the tragedy, such as the funerals, but each time the HA reassured her, so that her distress did not get out of hand.

Peg's religious faith relates to voice identities and even to the way she sets out her journal. Note the way Peg laid out her account in the journal, with 'Holy Angel' and 'Response', resembling a church ceremony. The voice was reflecting back key problems to Peg – dealing with rejection by both biological and adoptive parents. Did Peg cope with the rejection by dividing self into subpersonalities represented by the voices? Did they represent the parts of her she thought were unacceptable to others? The new voice was helping her to re-integrate the alienated parts of herself, and to start to accept responsibility for her actions. Psychiatry absolved her from responsibility – as do confessions (go on, admit you're schizophrenic, take the tablets – like the Host! Say three Hail Marys, go home and don't do it again).

Peg's voices are not exceptional (Nayani and David, 1996; cf. Leudar *et al.*, 1997). Overall, she had five voices. Two were chorus voices (Aberfan and Dunblane children), and the three remaining ones had stable identities. The identities were supernatural and yet the voices were not attributed supernatural powers. Close examination by Peg and PT revealed that even though the voices had supernatural names (angels or devils) we could discern pragmatic elements of people known to Peg (the GA resembled her father, the LD resembled Peg, the HA resembled Peg, Sheila and PT). Why disguise these characters? We speculate that this relates to differences in the process of socialisation in childhood. The representation of the internalised other depends on the nature of her parental relationships, which in her case were authoritarian. Romme and Escher (1991) have noted that voices have metaphoric properties, and that clarification of this may allow the meaning of the voices to become more apparent. In addition, religious faith and spirituality formed an important feature of Peg's explanatory framework, and this may have influenced voice personification. It must be stressed, however, that this is speculation, although we argue that a dialogical approach has hermeneutic potential capable of generating meaningful individual accounts of voice-hearing experiences.

The dialogical arrangement of Peg's voices is not unusual. The voices LD and GA were focused on Peg and regulating her activities. They addressed her, not each other or anyone else. The HA intervened on Peg's behalf when the GA appeared, but there was no dialogue between the two. Peg's dialogical relationship with her voices was that of a small child in relation to strict, authoritarian parents. Her relationship with the HA was quite different. This was a dialogically rich interaction, in which she sought and was granted reassurance. The origin of this voice is puzzling. It started several hours after the interview with PT about her other voices, and after she was asked to write a 'script' of her own responses to the other voices. This opened up the possibility of engagement with voices, which she did through the mediation of the HA. This new voice shared pragmatic features with Peg's own voice, as well as Sheila and PT, suggesting that Peg internalised aspects of these figures, making their reactions to the voices her own. The increase in the number of voices does not imply a deterioration in her clinical state, or increased ego fragmentation. The new voice had an integrative function and was associated with a gradual improvement in her self-esteem and social function, observed by her close friend of many years. The pragmatic features of the new voice were not unusual. In our earlier study, we found similar voices quite frequently in non-clinical voice hearers. We argued that this is consistent with the dialogical organisation of human experience, and the mediational use of language as inner speech. Vygotsky (1978) proposed that in the socialisation of the child, language plays a central role as a self-regulating device in interpersonal action (cf. Leiman, 1994; Ryle, 1994). Peg, of course, is not a child.

There are similarities and differences between cognitive techniques and our approach. Unlike the dialogical approach, cognitive therapy disputes and challenges the subject's explanatory framework to make the voices more benign. On the other hand, cognitive therapy, like the dialogical approach, draws out the structure and meaning that lies at the heart of the subjective experience of psychosis. Focusing also brings out the significance of personal meaning in voices, especially the importance of understanding the functions that voices have for the subject. Another similarity between the three approaches is the role ascribed to the wider social world and its influence on voice content. The voices of case 3 in Chadwick and Birchwood's study became worse after the dramatic economic changes of 1992. Likewise, Peg's voices intensified following the Dunblane massacre. All three techniques draw attention to the meaning of voices. There is evidence that attempts to help people cope with intrusive thoughts by ignoring them may, paradoxically, make the thoughts more intrusive (Wegner *et al.*, 1987; Lavy and van den Hout, 1990). The outcome of our study suggests that, contrary to perceived wisdom, attending to the content and meaning of hallucinatory voices may be beneficial.

8 The frenzy of Anthony Smith

Hearing voices in British national newspapers

Patrick Alesworth, Sara Benyon, Caroline Beale, Milton Brown, Horrett Campbell, Darren Carr, Sharon Dalson, Regina Fasuyi, Glen Grant, Wayne Hutchinson, Brendan O'Donnell, John du Pont, Robert Sartin and Anthony Smith. These fourteen names should evoke uneasy feelings in readers of British national newspapers, but perhaps not many will remember that each of the named had committed a terrible deed. Alesworth, for instance, 'killed his daughter' (*Guardian*, 28 September 1995), Brown 'stabbed his 16-month-old son, leaving the child brain damaged and blind' (*Guardian*, 10 May 1994), Campbell 'ran amok with a machete at a Wolverhampton infants school' (*Guardian*, 7 December 1996). The killings were reported in British national newspapers, analysed, put into context, explained and the blame for them shared out. According to the journalists each of these people was mentally ill, a voice hearer, and moreover the hearing of voices and the violent deed were connected.

The main theme of this chapter will be to analyse these fourteen cases in order to consider how the topic of 'hearing voices' is presented in British national newspapers. Do the journalists explain it as a personal experience to those of us who do not 'hear voices' – what is it like to hear voices and to live with them? Or are the voices of newspaper articles somehow beyond common sense, a symptom of insanity which can be understood by the psychiatrists but which is best left to them as a technical matter? Are the 'voices' given as causes of violence, and if so, how direct and powerful is their influence on the actions said to be? And if the voices are bound to violence, what sort of violence is it – a measured violence meant to secure some advantage for the aggressor, or, for instance, a blind frenzy?

It is, of course, not the case that 'hearing voices' is only ever presented in conjunction with insanity and violence. We start with a brief survey of articles published during the period 1993 to 1996 in the *Guardian*, *Observer*, *The Times*, *Daily Telegraph* and *Independent*[1] which mentioned the experience, as well as the articles in this period which in any way concerned the fourteen individuals. The two sets of articles are not the same – for one thing not every article mentioned 'hearing voices'. Here we present a brief summary of reporting trends in the *Guardian* and *Observer* to put our subsequent qualitative analysis into context.

Voices in British national newspapers

In 1993 'hearing voices' was mentioned seven times in the *Guardian* – it was not a daily topic. In three of the articles ordinary individuals took the experience to indicate mental problems; for instance: 'I used to be a hairdresser but I started hearing voices telling me what to do and I got a bit worried' (*Guardian*, 23 June 1993), and one article gave it as a psychiatric symptom. Only once was it offered in court to mitigate the killing and this account was rejected ('Yorkshire Ripper' Sutcliffe was said to have claimed to hear voices 'from God' telling him to kill prostitutes). Finally, only twice in this year were 'voices' *not* tied to a mental instability – hearing voices in these articles was a 'religious experience', but the journalists presented this with a certain irony:

(1) *Guardian*, 30 August 1993

Apparitions lure Ireland's fervid faithful
[. . .] It was at this Catholic shrine two weeks ago that Fiona Bowen, aged 18, from Cork, claimed she saw a vision of 'Our Lady'. She was, according to local reports, overcome with joy, and *heard voices telling her to bring others to the next vigil* [our emphasis].

In 1994 'hearing voices' was by coincidence again mentioned in seven *Guardian* articles. This time, however, four journalists in four different articles tied voices to extreme violence against others, by 'mentally ill' individuals. Another article mentioned voices simply as a symptom of mental illness and once, 'hearing voices' was presented as a worrying experience, indicating mental problems in everyday life. The exception to linking 'voices' to mental problems was a piece on G.B. Shaw's play *Joan of Arc* – the leading actress seemed to have accepted hearing voices as a valid religious experience. This was the only instance in which the experience was set out as being positive. Overall in 1994, then, the tie of hearing voices to mental problems was strengthened in journalists' writing, as was their link to violence.

In 1995 the references to voices by journalists increased and their nature became less taken for granted and more subject to debate. Hearing voices was mentioned in eleven *Guardian* articles, three of which were actually dedicated to the experience (the pieces in the 1993 and 1994 newspapers mentioned hearing voices as if by the way). Two of the articles presented a research perspective on hallucinatory voices (one was on what Freud had to say on the matter, the other was on voices in lucid dreaming). One provided some evidence that hearing voices might happen to ordinary people or, perhaps one should say, to otherwise ordinary people (*Guardian*, 25 April 1995). In fact, one substantial article gave two Hearing Voices Network activists a platform to contrast various perspectives on the experience aiming to normalise it (*Guardian*, 22 April 1995). A review of William Burroughs' (then) newly published book (*My Education: A Book of Dreams*) presented 'hearing voices' in his own voice as an uncommon experience not necessarily bound by reason.

(2) *Guardian*, 11 August 1995

Those who have heard voices from the nondominant brain hemisphere remark on the absolute authority of the voice. They know they are hearing the Truth. The fact that no evidence is adduced and that the voice may be talking utter nonsense is irrelevant. That is what Truth is.

The final article in our 1995 sample set up 'hearing voices' as a cult experience claim, rejecting its genuineness.

(3) *Observer*, 14 May 1995

Cults psychology
Dr. John Collee
[. . .] Chronic schizophrenics become withdrawn and neglectful of their appearance, whereas gurus like Jones, Koresh and Jouret are described as well groomed, 'plausible', 'arresting'. The diagnosis of schizophrenia simply doesn't fit. Let's look again at the symptoms these men manifest. *Any claims of seeing visions and hearing voices can perhaps be discounted. After all, we only have their word for it, and as self-styled messiahs these phenomena are more or less expected of them* [our emphasis].

So according to (3), hearing voices is properly seen as a psychiatric symptom which nevertheless can be faked in order to mystify. (3) is noticeable for contrasting two perspectives on hearing voices with one of them being dominant – we shall return to this below. (It is not clear, however, why one should believe psychiatric patients but not cult leaders when they say they hear voices.) Indeed, as in 1994, a large proportion of articles – almost half – tied the experience to mental pathology and to violence as its cause or its result. 'Voices' were used four times as evidence to support attributions of mental illness – and in three of these articles the 'insane' individuals had killed. The final article presented hearing voices as an experience indicating mental problems due to stress, and in one the experience was a result of sexual abuse (in a young woman who had been abused by the killer Rosemary West).

Finally in 1996 hearing voices was mentioned in twenty *Guardian* and *Observer* articles. The majority – fourteen pieces – related the experience to a psychiatric diagnosis, and nine of these associated it with extreme violence to others. One article presented the experience as a cause of self-harm in a person with a psychiatric diagnosis. Still, in six cases no connection was made between voices and mental pathology. Two of these were pieces which defy classification, and two related voices to the supernatural. Two articles mentioned voices as experiences avowed by artists. The sculptress Rachel Whiteread told the journalist about hearing voices in childhood but was sceptical that voices were the spring of her art.

(4) *Observer*, 1 September 1996

The Observer Interview: In a private world of interiors
'Not that it was an incredibly unhappy time, but quite disturbing. I used to hear voices. A lot of the time I didn't really understand what they were saying, but they were like a communication. And it was a male voice, I remember, quite a deep voice. This is going to sound incredibly strange if you write this. . . . But often you hear of children hearing voices and a lot of people think it's a spiritual thing . . . I don't know. I was a sensitive child. I just thought it was normal. But when I told my mum she was worried. It's a difficult thing to talk about now because it was such a long time ago, but I think it affected me quite a lot, and I do remember it and often think about it.' Has she ever felt a glimmer of it coming back? 'Very occasionally, yes. You know, sometimes you just feel incredibly lonely and it's almost like you're rattling round inside yourself and there's nobody that can be a part of you? There have been moments like that when maybe I start hearing a little voice, but it's not something I worry about.' *Does she believe these voices might have anything to do with her becoming an artist?* The shutters come down again: '*I've no idea. It's a good soundbite*' [our emphasis].

So between 1993 and 1996 the experience of hearing voices was not in the news every day and it rarely figured in articles dedicated to it. Hearing voices was presented in a few set ways:

• as a psychiatric symptom;
• as a concomitant of violence committed by people with mental illness;
• as an experience of ordinary people which they take as worrying;
• as a religious or spiritual experience – historical or contemporary;
• as something which happens to creative artists;
• as a downright fraud.

Only in (4) was there any attempt to give an account of what 'hearing voices' is like.

It is clear even from this brief summary that the tie between 'hearing voices', mental illness and violence was a major recurrent theme in British newspapers between 1993 and 1996. It is this tie which we will analyse in this chapter. Our concern will be with how journalists align 'hearing voices' with psychiatric symptoms, with how they relate it to violence and with the kind of violence involved.

So far in our analysis we have extracted some general themes but ignored how the articles are situated in the wider context – we did not say what sorts of articles presented voices in a particular way – say as a symptom; nor did we look at what the articles did in a wider social context – at their pragmatics. But these two things are crucial if we want to understand why voices are presented as they are on a particular occasion. It is not our aim to extract decontextualised mundane epistemes concerning voices.

We will proceed by analysing in detail the 'mass media career' of one voice hearer, Anthony Smith, and use his case as a backbone to present the materials on the remaining thirteen. We must stress that we are not using newspapers as a source of evidence about the nature of voices and their relationship to violence; rather it is the actual reporting of voices which concerns us. We will not go 'beyond' what is given in the newspapers, except to consider how the articles are situated in wider social controversies, and how they might be used by their readers – not necessarily as a source of knowledge but as a concrete argumentative resource; one does not learn from a hammer, one uses it. Newspapers may be the only source of information about 'voices' to many people but this does not mean that they use them as a textbook. Our position on how newspapers influence 'the public' is methodological – the best research move is to investigate empirically how newspaper articles are structured as texts and how they can be used by people as resources in their social activities. We would certainly not start with the assumption that the influence of newspapers on mundane activities is mediated through effects on readers' beliefs.

The frenzy of Anthony Smith

Anthony Smith's name first appeared in national papers in the *Daily Telegraph, Guardian, Independent* and *The Times*. This was on 7 March 1996, and each of the four articles was dedicated to his case. The *Guardian* mentioned him again on 30 July, but this time as one of three cases indicating the dangers of caring for people with mental illness in the community. Then on 25 October two articles (in the *Guardian* and *Daily Telegraph*) reported the results of an inquiry into his case as well as the reactions of those involved. On 26 October a letter to the *Guardian* used him as an epitome of infamy. Finally, on 30 October the *Daily Telegraph* mentioned his case, together with that of Christopher Clunis, as tragedies motivating deliberations by the Royal College of Psychiatrists.

So, who is Anthony Smith? We shall consider no information about him except what national newspapers tell us, in other words his public persona. Let us begin with a complete text of the article which appeared in the *Guardian* on 7 March 1996, complementing it subsequently with what the other three papers said on the same day.

(5) *Guardian*, 7 March 1996

Schizophrenic freed to kill mother and brother
MARTIN WAINWRIGHT
Judge sends man to Rampton and calls for community care inquiry
A PARANOID schizophrenic who discharged himself from hospital and then stabbed his mother and younger half-brother to death was yesterday sent to Rampton secure hospital for an indefinite period.
    Anthony Smith, aged 24, denied murder but pleaded guilty to manslaughter by reason of diminished responsibility at Nottingham Crown Court, not far

from the Derbyshire village of Sandiacre where the tragedy took place last August.

Mr. Justice Latham asked for a painstaking investigation into the case, in spite of an internal review by Southern Derbyshire mental health NHS Trust which found no evidence of major breakdowns in care.

An independent panel headed by John Wood, former Professor of Law at Sheffield University, is about to start work and will focus on medical treatment and the level of support offered to Smith's worried family before the killings.

The hearing was told that Smith had volunteered to be admitted to hospital after being diagnosed as a paranoid schizophrenic. After a month he discharged himself, with the approval of a consultant, and at home had refused to take medication shortly before using a Bowie knife and an iron bar to kill and mutilate his victims.

His mother, Gwendoline, aged 48, and his father, Peter, an accountant aged 47, had expressed concern at looking after him when his condition appeared to be worsening.

The judge said the case presented 'in startling nature the nightmare those who care for people with schizophrenia must fear'. He said: 'This is a case where the circumstances of this young man's release into the community, and perhaps more importantly, the circumstances of the care he was given in the community, will have to be looked at with great care.'

John Warren QC, prosecuting, said that Smith had bickered with his mother on the morning of August 8, and had become increasingly paranoid after she told him that he ought to be undergoing treatment in hospital. He told police that he felt 'possessed by demons and voices telling him to kill his mother. He felt she was conspiring against him to make him leave the house. He just went berserk, stabbing his mother and his 11-year-old half-brother, David, who unfortunately came upon the scene when the defendant was attacking his mother,' said Mr. Warren.

The court heard Smith then went to the local medical centre, telling the receptionist: 'I have killed my mother and my brother.'

Peter Joyce, QC, defending, said: 'It is quite clear from reports that Anthony was a very sick young man before he went into hospital and a very sick young man when he was discharged.'

Mr. Smith said after the hearing that he had known that his son was a 'ticking time bomb'. He and his daughter, Hayley, aged 20, are considering legal action against Derby City general hospital and medical staff.

Andy Clayton, medical director for the trust, said that its review had found no major breakdowns in care, but it had strengthened its risk assessment system and would be 'very ready to learn' from the results of the independent inquiry.

The article is clearly not a straightforward report of a crime or of a court case. The theme is sketched out in the headline ('Schizophrenic freed to kill mother and brother') and the sub-headline ('Judge sends man to Rampton and calls for community care inquiry' – Rampton being a high-security hospital for the 'criminally insane'). The category 'schizophrenic' and the activity 'killing' are joined from the start, but that is just one building brick – the gist is that the 'care in the community' for a person with a psychosis has failed yet again, resulting in a tragedy. The information subsequently introduced into the article develops this theme in concrete detail. The first paragraph introduces the culprit ('a paranoid schizophrenic'), his two actions – the first one (he 'discharged himself from hospital') making the second one (the killing) possible, and then comes the part-resolution (Smith is sent to 'Rampton secure hospital'). But of course being sent to a hospital – even a secure one – is meant not as a punishment, but rather to cure the individual and to protect society against the consequences of the illness. In fact, Smith pleads not guilty to murder on the grounds of 'diminished responsibility' (paragraph 2). The journalist writes all of this in a narrator voice, telling the reader 'the facts of the matter'. He does, however, use other voices besides his own. In paragraph 3 he quotes the judge's call for an independent inquiry into community care – and the power of such a call depends on its coming from the judge. And indeed such an inquiry is imminent (paragraph 4). The *Guardian* article is situated in the continuing controversy on the merits and shortcomings of the care in the community, as are the *Times*, *Daily Telegraph* and *Independent* pieces. In fact the article in the *Independent* almost entirely focuses on the implication of Smith's case for the government policy.

We would argue that this wider positioning of the stories about Smith underpins how his 'hearing voices' is presented. First, notice that the logic of the story which the article narrates requires a violent madman who is not responsible for his violence, and from whom the community should be protected. Indeed, the characters in the article accept that Anthony Smith was not responsible for the killings: the defence counsel says, 'He was "a very sick young man when he was discharged".' Anthony Smith himself pleads 'diminished responsibility' (and he is quoted in *The Times* as having said, 'I've just killed my mother and brother', adding 'It was inevitable'). Even the counsel for the prosecution characterises him as becoming 'increasingly paranoid' prior to the killings. The court's final decision was to accept that Smith was guilty of 'manslaughter by reason of diminished responsibility', but not of murder.

The story so far fits very well with Thomas Szasz's analysis of the medical conception of insanity (Szasz, 1997). Insanity is associated with violence for which, however, the mentally ill person is not responsible, hence the need to control the insane: in mental hospitals or with medication in the community. It is usually a psychiatrist who testifies whether the accused is insane or responsible for his actions but the psychiatrist in this role is a figure missing from the *Guardian* article. The point is of course that the people whose professional duty it is to control the insane – the psychiatrists – have failed in Smith's case. The psychiatrists involved in the case are in the article represented by the 'Medical Director for the Trust' and he denies any 'major breakdown in the care'. (In the *Daily Telegraph* he further specifically defends the clinical judgement of the psychiatrist in charge of Smith.)

But everybody else, in the *Guardian* article that is, *knows* that Smith should not have been at large. The counsel for the defence says he was clearly ill when he left the hospital. His parents are reported to have 'expressed concern at looking after him when his condition appeared to be worsening'. The hospital's denial of failure of care is not accepted either by Smith's remaining family (who are reported to be considering legal action against the hospital and the medical staff) or by the judge (who asked 'for a painstaking investigation into the case'). The *Times* article demands that individuals are blamed – it implies that Anthony Smith's psychiatrist was seriously out of touch and should shoulder some responsibility.

(6) *The Times*, 7 June 1996

The day before the killings his doctor, Sarah Barrett, had sent him a card detailing his next hospital appointment as an outpatient. Dr. Barrett, who is on maternity leave from Derby City Hospital, has not faced any disciplinary proceedings.

The four articles are best seen not as objective representations of events, but as accounts aligned in a controversy concerning the place in the community for people with a mental illness.

So Smith is not responsible for the killing – he pleaded 'diminished responsibility', which the court accepted. The responsibility for his conduct is partly vested in psychiatrists who in his case failed to anticipate and prevent the tragedy. But of course the *Guardian* article does not say that psychiatrists caused Smith to behave as he did, rather that they did not prevent him. This being so, and if Smith's intent did not *directly* cause the violence, then what did? Or do the journalists treat the killing as a random act defying an explanation? (Terrible events need an explanation.) To answer these questions, we have to pay some attention to how Anthony Smith's social identity develops in the *Guardian* article and how his deed is characterised and tied to that identity.

The point is that Smith is not named in the headline; instead he is presented as a 'schizophrenic' (and as a 'paranoid schizophrenic' at that – the sub-headline). So to begin with the article is not really about him personally – it is a generality about a schizophrenic who 'discharged himself from hospital', 'killed his mother and a (half-)brother', and was 'sent to Rampton secure hospital for an indefinite period'. This schizophrenic becomes Anthony Smith in the second paragraph, where he is said to have pleaded guilty to manslaughter (rather than to murder) 'by reason of diminished responsibility'. The article then talks about a schizophrenic who is Smith, not about a person called Smith who happens to have schizophrenia.

The articles in the other three newspapers are the same in this respect. In the *Daily Telegraph* Smith starts as a 'schizophrenic' and then becomes a 'paranoid schizophrenic'; in the *Independent* he starts and continues as a paranoid schizophrenic, and in *The Times* he is a '"possessed" patient' and then 'a man suffering from paranoid schizophrenia'. In all four articles Smith is first categorised as a schizophrenic and only then becomes a person with a name, gender and age who can deny or admit and plead (in court).

Smith, however, does not figure in the *Guardian* article as just a schizophrenic. He is also a 'man', 'son' and 'brother' and 'a very sick young man'. The interplay between Smith's incumbency of these different categories is of some interest. The headline and the first paragraph categorise Smith as a 'son' and 'brother' *indirectly* – he must be a son of his mother whom he killed, and he must be a brother of the brother he killed. But, as the words go, he does the killing *as a schizophrenic*, not as a brother or a son – his agency in killing is presented as that of a schizophrenic. (Moreover, we shall see that this is consistent with his violence being construed as being of a sort specific to schizophrenia.) Being schizophrenic elbows into the background Smith's other social identities – being a brother and a son. We could borrow an expression from Hughes (1971) and say that so far in this article, being schizophrenic is Smith's *major status*. Why? Murderous attacks are not in general expected from one's brother or son, but this is precisely what Smith did to his family. This raises a possibility that categorising somebody as 'schizophrenic' implies that he or she is in general likely to act in a manner which is inconsistent with his or her incumbency of other category collections. This of course does not mean that a schizophrenic cannot *be* a husband, son, brother or sister. Anthony Smith's father still accepts him as 'his son' but he is reported to have said that he had known that his son was a 'ticking time bomb'. Anthony is not a regular sort of a son – as 'a ticking time bomb' he is a danger, not a joy or a comfort in the parents' old age. So even though Anthony Smith is biologically and historically a son and a brother, his psychiatric diagnosis and his conduct make this status problematic. In the fifth paragraph of the *Guardian* article the 'paranoid schizophrenic' Smith does not 'kill and mutilate' his mother and brother, but his 'victims', and his situation is strangely Oedipal. He is an 'aggressor' rather than a family member, and his violent conduct is bound to schizophrenia. Note also that the journalist does the binding of violence to schizophrenia and the categorisation of Smith as a schizophrenic in the narrator voice.

One important aspect of membership category analysis (Jayyusi, 1984; Sacks, 1992; Hester and Eglin, 1997) is that activities can be normatively bound to categories. Schizophrenia seems to operate on this connection and, so to speak, it may dissolve the binding. This is just to say in a technical way that an insane person is in some respects outside of moral order.

We have seen that the journalist started the article by binding violent conduct to the membership category 'schizophrenic'. Now it seems that not just any violence is bound to schizophrenia. Smith acted with terminal violence not just to anybody but to his family, and contrary to normative expectations. This is obviously a core fact of the tragedy and it is reported in all four articles.

Are there any other features distinguishing Smith's violence? The *Guardian* article narrates an interaction between Smith and his mother which culminated in the killing. To begin with, the journalist reports in the voice of the counsel for the prosecution that the killings were preceded by an argument.

(7) *Guardian*, 7 March 1996

John Warren QC, prosecuting, said that Smith had bickered with his mother on the morning of August 8, and had become increasingly paranoid after she told him that he ought to be undergoing treatment in hospital. He told police that he felt 'possessed by demons and voices telling him to kill his mother. He felt she was conspiring against him to make him leave the house. He just went berserk, stabbing his mother and his 11-year-old half-brother, David, who unfortunately came upon the scene when the defendant was attacking his mother,' said Mr. Warren.

The verb 'bicker' presents the argument between Smith and his mother as an ordinary everyday matter. We all bicker but we do not end up killing our families, yet this is just what Anthony Smith did. Just how does this article account for the escalation of the conflict from bickering to berserk killing? We are told that at some time during the argument Smith's mother suggested to him that he should be in mental hospital. Bearing in mind that Smith had recently discharged himself from such a hospital, this comment might seem a provocation. But consider how an ordinary person might react – leave the room and slam the door, burst into tears or swear. Smith's reaction reported in the article is none of these and certainly far from ordinary – he becomes deranged and kills his mother and his brother. So the *Guardian* article uses the transition from 'bickering' to 'going berserk' to present schizophrenic violence as inappropriate in extent and situationally unpredictable. Did anything happen between the argument and the killings or were the two continuous? Not in the *Guardian*, but the *Daily Telegraph* journalist fills the gap:

(8) *Daily Telegraph*, 7 March 1996

[. . .] On Aug 8 Smith began to argue with his mother and she told him he should still be in hospital.

Mr. Warren said: 'He went upstairs and began to feel increasingly paranoid. He heard voices telling him to kill her, to get rid of her.

'He said that he felt she was conspiring against him to make him leave the house, something he didn't want to do because he was afraid he would degenerate into a tramp-like condition and would be tormented forever.

'Then the voices told him what to do. He took a Bowie knife he had downstairs with him and effectively just went berserk, stabbing his mother and then his 12-year-old brother, David, who unfortunately came upon the scene.

'It is clear he was driven by delusions and hallucinations and the over-powering urging of voices.'

The mother–son argument and the killing are not presented here as temporally contingent. Smith actually leaves the place of argument, suffers an attack of schizophrenia (feeling increasingly paranoid) and then goes berserk. And the article clearly implicates the 'voices' in the killing. *The Times* does not refer to the argument between Smith and his mother but it achieves the same effect – it presents a transition from frenzy of killing to calm, rational action, which in this context is odd – he washed his hands, informed the health centre of the killing, and calmly (the journalist writes) disclaimed responsibility ('It was inevitable'). So putting the four articles together, we have a presentation of Smith's violence as unpredictable – calm, orderly action and compulsive violence can change into each other without warning – and as we shall see, these transitions are explained as due to attacks of insanity.

These killings are reported as a dramatic affair. Smith's violence is presented in all four articles in some detail and always as excessive. He is 'berserk' and 'mutilates' his victims in the *Guardian*, he 'bludgeons' his mother and 'stabs' his brother in *The Times*, and we are given the exact number of times the victims had been stabbed (though this number differs in different papers). All the articles specify the instruments of killing ('11-inch knife' – *The Times*; 'twelve inch knife' – the *Independent*; 'Bowie knife' – the *Daily Telegraph* and 'an iron bar' – the *Guardian*). This degree of detail puts the violence into focus. And why did Smith stab his mother and brother so many times? Clearly not just to kill them, so did he do it in the delirium of mental illness? His violence seems excessive and unstoppable; it is narrated to us as being out of control. So much so that his brother who, as the *Guardian* puts it, 'unfortunately came upon a scene', gets caught in this maelstrom of violence.

The account of how the bickering escalated into killing is presented in the eigth paragraph of the *Guardian* article and it is multi-voiced – that is, presented in several embedded voices. The dominant voice is that of the prosecuting QC Warren – the whole paragraph is bounded by two verbs of communication marking that the journalist is reporting what the QC had said. Warren narrates what has happened on the morning of the tragedy – he says, without specifying how he knows, that Smith and his mother had bickered and that he 'had become increasingly paranoid', but he also reports what Smith had said about it. First, he reports what Anthony Smith had said to the police that he 'felt possessed by demons and voices telling him to kill his mother' and second, that his mother 'was conspiring against him to make him leave the house'. So the journalist provides us with two versions of events – the QC's and Smith's, even though both are narrated in the QC's voice.

One question we asked at the beginning of this chapter was: How does the writer present the experience of 'hearing voices'? The interesting thing is that here the journalist actually presents two perspectives on 'hearing voices' – a supernatural one, used by Anthony Smith, and a psychiatric one, used by the prosecuting barrister to explain Smith's conduct. The two perspectives are contrasted but neither is developed in any detail: in the former, hearing voices is conjoined with 'possession by demons'; the latter perspective characterises both of these as being paranoid. And the perspectives are not equal in the article – the psychiatric one is dominant. This is partly a matter of formulation – Smith *was* paranoid but he *felt* possessed – and partly a matter of who proffers them – the rational figure of the prosecutor and the insane accused. Are two such perspectives on voices presented in the other three articles? First, the *Independent* does not mention voices at all. *The Times* article, however, does, and it presents the two perspectives perhaps even more clearly than the *Guardian* piece. In the headline Smith's abnormality is specified as a possession: '"Possessed" patient killed relatives after release' (*The Times*, 7 March 1996). The word 'possessed' is in quotes, however, and who is being quoted? It becomes clear that 'possession' is Smith's formulation of his problem. In the second paragraph it becomes clear that it was he who claimed to be 'possessed by demons' – clearly a supernatural formulation of his experience. The article contains another formulation of Smith's problem, this time by his own QC, who characterises him as a 'sick young man', documenting this by referring to 'delusions and hallucinations' and 'overpowering voices'. This formulation is written in technical psychiatric terms and it is significant that the journalist has the QC to specify that the formulation is 'clear from reports'. The QC is a proxy for the absent psychiatrist. In other words, we again have two versions of hearing voices and the psychiatric one is dominant. The *Daily Telegraph* article is not different in this respect – the prosecuting QC reports Smith's version of his experiences and follows this with his assessment.

So the dominant presentation of Smith's exceptional experiences is in the language of psychiatry – they are 'paranoia', and according to the barrister, his mother's comment in an ordinary argument put Smith into this abnormal state. Minor conflict triggered Smith's schizophrenia, and 'he just went berserk', says the prosecuting barrister. So we are told – in the barrister's voice – that Smith's abnormal reaction to the argument with his mother is mediated by his becoming acutely schizophrenic with hearing voices being a ground for this attribution. The account develops the presentation of Smith and the violence earlier in the article – voices are just one symptom.

Smith's version highlights the role of 'voices' in the killings – the voices told him to do so. It is not clear from the article whether the voices are presented as an overbearing and compulsive influence – he may have killed his mother for his own reasons, irrespective of what the voices had said. The article is at this point either loosely written or strategically ambiguous. It is not clear whether Smith said he was possessed only by demons or also by the voices. On the latter reading, the implication would be that Smith could not resist the voices. In fact, this is the version of the power of voices proffered in both *The Times* and the *Daily Telegraph* by Smith's barrister – who explains Smith's conduct thus: 'He was driven by delusions and hallucinations and by overpowering voices to commit these offences. He is shocked by the horror of what he did.' The defending barrister removes the responsibility for the killings from Smith – he is sorry now – and he attributes it to his voices.

To summarise: the *Guardian*'s prosecuting QC gives Smith's attack of 'paranoia' as the antecedent of him going berserk. Smith ties voices to the killings as a direction in language, and finally the defending QC presents the influence of voices as compulsive. So the relationship between voices and the violence presented in the article varies, and the versions are indexed to the characters voicing it. The prosecuting QC in the *Daily Telegraph* actually gives voices a twofold role in the killings. First, as in the *Guardian*, they motivate Smith ('He heard voices telling him to kill her, to get rid of her'). But Smith would now have to decide himself exactly how to carry out the voices' suggestion. In the *Daily Telegraph* version of the events he does not have to – the voices instruct him just how to kill: 'Then the voices told him what to do' and he follows the instruction: 'He took a Bowie knife he had downstairs with him and effectively just went berserk.' So the voices both motivate the killing and instruct Smith what to do. Now of course carrying out any instruction is never just mechanical movement, it always involves situated intentionality (Leudar, 1991; Leudar and Costall, 1996). So is Smith after all seen as partly responsible for the killings? No – it is significant that, according to the *Daily Telegraph*, having been instructed by the voices what to do, Smith 'just went berserk'. So he acts as an irrational agent and the formulation absolves him from the possible vestige of responsibility.

So this was how Smith's career in British national newspapers began. The next time he was mentioned was almost four months later in the *Guardian* (30 July 1996). The article was not dedicated to him or to any other particular individual. The journalist (C. Dyer) discussed the relationship between violence and mental illness, and Anthony Smith was one of her examples. He was grouped with two other schizophrenics who have killed – Martin Mursell (a schizophrenic who was reported to have 'stabbed his stepfather to death in a frenzied knife attack and left his mother barely alive') and with Wayne Hutchinson (who was released from hospital, following a 'mistake' by a locum doctor, to 'embark on a six-day Christmas orgy of violence that left two dead and three wounded') (Mursell was never reported to be a voice hearer, whereas Hutchinson was). Thus the journalist herself actually created a collection of schizophrenics who engage in violence and Smith was displayed in this collection and his story was thereby contextualised. The three individuals were of course already schizophrenics by virtue of their psychiatric diagnosis and each one was reported to be violent. The point is that in the journalist's collection violence becomes typical of schizophrenics, normatively bound to it, even though the journalist modifies the connection, saying that schizophrenics are only more likely to commit acts of gross violence if they use drugs (those not usually obtained on prescription) and do not take their medication. How did the journalist summarise Smith's case and can we say where her information comes from?

(9) *Guardian*, 30 July 1996

[. . .] When *24-year-old Anthony Smith stabbed his mother and 11-year-old half brother to death in 1995 a month after discharging himself from hospital with his consultant's agreement* a hospital spokesman said the acts he committed were 'totally unexpected'. Unlikely as it may seem, that statement is probably literally true. Research over the last 20 years shows that the accuracy of doctors' risk assessments on psychiatric patients is little better than chance [our emphasis].

What is mentioned is Smith's violent deed and the collusion between him, the patient and the psychiatrists in the release. This recapitulates the theme of the four articles we analysed above. Moreover, the words C. Dyer uses are almost exactly those used by M. Wainwright: '24-year-old Anthony Smith', 'stabbed his mother and 11-year-old half brother to death' are almost verbatim quotes, and 'with his consultant's agreement' closely paraphrases 'with the approval of the consultant'. So Dyer uses previous articles as a resource to present Anthony Smith. Note also that voices have disappeared from the account – they are not thematically needed.

Anthony Smith was next mentioned in the *Guardian* in October. This followed the results of the inquiry 'announced' in the Guardian article with which we began.

(10) *Guardian*, 25 October 1996

Anger at inquiry into sick killer
MARTIN WAINWRIGHT
Martin Wainwright on care-in-the-community deaths
A FATHER is considering legal action following the exoneration of medical staff by an official inquiry into the care-in-the-community treatment of a schizophrenic who murdered his mother and young stepbrother in a frenzied attack with a knife and spiked baseball bat.

This article is a continuation of the first one by Wainwright. The inquiry the judge had ordered has taken place – it had found some faults with the system of care but it did not attribute individual blame. The medical trust would see the matter as closed but the family is not satisfied. The matter of Anthony is put into general context as follows:

(11) *Guardian*, 25 October 1996

Marjorie Wallace, chief executive of the mental health charity Sane, said: 'This report is one of the most inadequate I have ever read. In Anthony's case the warning signs were absolutely clear; you couldn't want a more classic picture of a tragedy waiting to happen.

'How can a patient who believes he is possessed by demons and his soul has been taken away be left to decide if he is fit enough to be discharged?'

Sane is a pressure organisation campaigning for care in mental institutions rather than in the community. The article does contain two references to 'hearing voices'. It indicates that Anthony Smith experienced voices for some time and was troubled by them (12) and it ties the voices to violence (13).

(12) *Guardian*, 25 October 1996

The report said Smith had an 'unstable relationship' with his mother during adolescence, spent a lot of time in his own room and told his friends he was 'troubled by voices'.

(13) *Guardian*, 25 October 1996

Smith was apparently driven to a frenzy by the 'voices' in his head and his step-father said he still failed to understand why officials, particularly Dr. Clayton, had failed to react to his warnings.

Smith's penultimate appearance was in a letter to the *Guardian* the following day.

(14) *Guardian*, 26 October 1996

Letter: A family stalked by injustice asks if we really are colour blind
Y MORRIS, V MORRIS, D MORRIS
The offence committed by Clarence does not deserve such a drastic measure as indefinite detention in Rampton. He is fine in the medium-secure unit where he resides at present. His condition can easily be treated. The fact that he was not on his medication at the time of the offence is the fault of this government's mental-health policies.
   Anthony Smith was sentenced to indefinite detention in Rampton recently for murdering his mother and stepbrother in an horrific attack. Clarence scared Perry out of her wits; but where is the comparison? [our emphasis]

The letter writers compare the 'crime' of their son to what Anthony Smith had done. We assume that the only information the writers had about Smith was what they had read in the newspapers. They summarise it as follows: 'Anthony Smith was sentenced to indefinite detention in Rampton recently for murdering his mother and stepbrother in an horrific attack.' Their summary is not simply an echo. None of the previous newspaper articles presented the killing as a murder – it was in their logic that Smith was not culpable. In the Morris family account Smith is not explicitly a schizophrenic and the killing is 'murdering'. So what was written in the newspapers is adapted and used to mitigate the conduct of their son – what is stalking when compared to a horrific attack to warrant incarceration in a high-security hospital? We come again to our point about the effects of newspapers on the public: the research problem is to see how the articles and their parts are subsequently used by others. With regard to his 'career', Anthony Smith has effectively become an inverse saint – an epitome of infamy.
   The final article in Smith's career which we shall consider mentioned him alongside Christopher Clunis, who is perhaps an even more often used illustration of a violent schizophrenic. Smith has obviously become an important precedent – his case is posed as an antecedent of a change in the policy on medical confidentiality. The *Daily Telegraph* headline of 30 October 1996 reads, *'Doctors end privacy rule over violent patients'* and 'The guidelines [of the Royal College of Psychiatrists] follow last week's report by Derbyshire Health Authority into the case of Anthony Smith'. His final public persona in the period we investigated is 'violent patient' and a 'a schizophrenic who stabbed his mother and half-brother to death after being discharged from hospital'.

Let us summarise how Anthony Smith's experiences of hearing voices were presented in English national newspapers. They were presented from two perspectives, a psychiatric one and a supernatural one, but neither was ever explained in any detail. The former was dominant, and this reflects the specific grounds on which the two versions of hearing voices met – the court, where the psychiatric version was used by the barristers and psychiatrists, and the supernatural one by the accused Smith – a violent schizophrenic lacking in reason.

The account of the tie between voices and violence was not unanimous. Some connection between voices and violence was always made but its nature varied – the voices were sometimes said to be overpowering but at other times only a weaker relationship was asserted. Smith's violence itself, as the journalists saw it, was not really his own but that of a schizophrenic. In character it was situationally unpredictable, inappropriate and delirious. It cannot be predicted on a specific occasion – Smith's mother could not and nor could his brother. This, however, does not mean that Smith's violence was presented as incomprehensible or without order – it was bound to Smith's mental illness and to its symptoms. And who understands 'mental illness' (or should understand it)? Psychiatrists. In a way, Smith's violence was beyond common sense and his voices were a part of it.

Is the presentation of Anthony Smith and the events unique, or something more general? Remember that the journalists wrote about Smith the schizophrenic, that their accounts of the events were part of a wider social debate and that they were conditioned by this, so probably the latter. In the remainder of this chapter we shall use the other thirteen cases to appraise the generality of how Smith's voices were narrated and we shall show that it was not idiosyncratic.

First, the portrayal of Smith's violence in the newspapers was not unique. The violence in the thirteen remaining cases had similar targets. Children were involved in five cases. Campbell attacked children in an 'infants school' (*Guardian*, 7 December 1996); Carr killed a 'mother and her two daughters' (*Guardian*, 30 April 1996); Dalson 'strangled one of her children and suffocated the other' (*Guardian*, 5 January 1994); Fasuyi 'repeatedly slashed her daughter with a kitchen knife' (*Guardian*, 3 May 1996); 'Beale suffocated her baby' (*The Times*, 9 March 1996). Other targets included close friends (du Pont) or complete strangers (Sartin, Hutchinson). Descriptions of violence were again sometimes vivid – Campbell 'ran amok', Hutchinson brought a 'crescendo' of 'mindless and horrifying violence' to Brixton – but not all of them. Some were more subdued (cf. Alesworth, Carr, Brown). Finally, Smith's violence was presented as situationally unpredictable but tied to psychiatric diagnosis and this again was not unique to his case. The *Observer*, for instance, presented even the schizophrenics with 'no history of violence' as a danger.

(15) *Observer*, 1 September 1996

A FEW DAYS ago, Martin took a hammer to the head of a fellow resident in their Bristol hostel. Martin suffers from schizophrenia, and until the attack was looked after under the 'care in the community' programme. No one saw the attack coming. In fact, only three hours earlier *Martin had been seen by a social worker who found no cause for concern – sometimes 'difficult', he had no history of violence* [our emphasis].

'Martin' is named in a familiar manner, but is used as an instance of a schizophrenic who attacked a 'fellow resident' violently and without warning. The journalist's point seems to be that the category 'schizophrenic' by itself invokes the danger of violence despite personal evidence to the contrary.

So the presentation of schizophrenic violence in Smith's case was by no means unique, but what about his experiences of 'hearing voices'? First, not all the presentations of 'hearing voices' were polyphonic. Sometimes only the voice hearer's version and sometimes only the psychiatric version is given. The voice hearer's version was often in quotes. It could be supernatural, as when McDonnell 'claimed the Devil told him to shoot his victims' (*Independent*, 3 April 1996) or when Dalson is said to have had written in her diary: 'It came and saw me, the evil beast, and told me to do it – kill, kill, kill' (*Guardian*, 5 January 1994), but it could also be ordinary, with the relatively neutral term 'hearing voices' used. Fasuyi, for instance, 'told police afterwards she had heard voices ordering her to kill her daughter'; the brief item on the sentencing of Carr was headlined 'Killer "heard voices in the head"' (with the only other mention of voices in the piece being 'Carr told police he started the fire after hearing voices in his head'). The same phrase 'hearing voices' was also used to present the psychiatric version, however, with hearing voices being one evidence of insanity: 'bizarre thoughts, hearing voices, paranoia, delusion – that characterise schizophrenia, manic depression or psychosis' (*Observer*, 1 September 1996, said in the voice of a psychiatrist).

Even so, the polyphonic presentations of Smith's voices were not rare. Sometimes the polyphony was striking. The journalist reporting the Horrett Campbell case had him report hearing children abusing him in unpleasant but very ordinary terms.

(16) *Guardian*, 07 December 1996

Campbell, diagnosed as a paranoid schizophrenic, said that as he walked past St Luke's school in Blakenhall "the kids would run to the fence and say abusive remarks such as "nigger".'

In the very next paragraph, however, hearing children abusing him was re-presented in psychiatric terms as 'auditory hallucinations', which are a 'classic symptom of his mental illness'.

(17)

But psychiatrists said the 'auditory hallucinations' and conspiracy theories were classic symptoms of his mental illness, undiagnosed before the attack on July 8.

Campbell was presented here and elsewhere as not having an insight that the voices of children were not real but hallucinations, and here is an interesting variant of the polyphony. What is involved is not simply a translation from the language of the supernatural to the language of psychiatry, but a transformation of type of experience – perception in the patient's version becomes hallucination in the psychiatrist's version. (This translation is not innocent – who can say now whether some of the children really abused him or whether he only ever heard hallucinatory voices?)

Another example of clear polyphony was in the only article on Caroline Beale which presented her as a voice hearer. The headline in *The Times* said '"Devil voices" may have led Beale to kill the baby' and the third paragraph continued, 'Caroline Beale may have believed she was possessed by the Devil when she killed her baby in New York' (*The Times*, 9 March 1996). One paragraph later, this was retold by a psychiatrist who 'said that Beale might have heard voices in her head instructing her to kill the baby as a result of the post-partum psychosis she developed'. It is not clear whether she thought these 'devil voices' were real and, if so, in what sense she did so.

The polyphony of versions can be subtle, and it can be condensed into one sentence, as in a *Guardian* article on Wayne Hutchinson: 'He was suffering delusions, complained that his mother was trying to poison him and said he was hearing voices' (*Guardian*, 6 January 1996, reported in a narrator voice). The first part is a psychiatric assessment, the second part is Hutchinson's version of his experiences.

So as in Smith's case, the newspapers presented both the psychiatric and the voice hearer's versions of the experience. The two were sometimes joined together in polyphonic texts, not as equals but with the psychiatric versions always being dominant and the voice hearer's version usually as evidence of the diagnosis.

Finally, what about the connection between hearing voices and violence? In Smith's case, hearing voices was presented as the psychiatric symptom which specifically connected his violence to his insanity – his voices told him to kill his mother and they also told him how. The former role given to voices is not unique to his case. As we have already seen, Sharon Dalson was said to have written in her diary: 'It . . . told me to do it – kill, kill, kill', and Regina Fasuyi 'heard voices *ordering* her to kill her daughter' (*Guardian*, 3 May 1996, our emphasis). Patrick Alesworth killed his daughter 'after hearing voices telling him to destroy himself and his family' (*Guardian*, 28 September 1995).

Sometimes, however, the directive function of voices is omitted and not mentioned explicitly: Milton Brown 'stabbed the baby *after* hearing voices' (*Guardian*, 10 May 1994, our emphasis), and Carr 'started the fire *after* hearing voices in his head' (*Guardian*, 30 April 1996). So the same phrase – 'after hearing voices' – is used to join voices and violence and so voices are somehow implicated in the subsequent violence, but the manner of influence is not specified. Indeed, what is involved is not just ellipsis – voices in newspapers are not necessarily orders, requests or instructions. Horrett Campbell reportedly attacked the schoolchildren not because voices told him to do so, but after he heard voices abusing him: 'Campbell, who spoke in little more than a hoarse whisper, described the voices that constantly abused him. They were always there, he said, murmuring words like "nigger, celibate and masturbator"' (*Daily Telegraph*, 7 December 1996). According to the *Guardian* the defending QC explained Campbell's conduct to the jury as follows: 'He was not in his right mind. He did not know, and still does not, that he was genuinely ill and was hearing voices – voices he believed were real. . . . He desperately wanted to stop the tide of abuse' (*Guardian*, 7 December 1996). So voices are usually presented as telling the voice hearers what to do, or perhaps even how to do it, but not always. Campbell reacted to the abuse of voices. Similarly, Regina Fasuyi was said to have 'stabbed her daughter after hearing "abusive voices in her head"' (*Independent*, 3 May 1996).

So in general, 'voices' in British national newspapers are tied to violence, but journalists are hesitant about how strong the connection is between the two. Sometimes they write that voices are compulsive, as in Ms Dalson's case. But even then it is not usually the journalist who asserts this in his or her own voice – instead such claims are presented in either the voices of the accused insane person or the defence counsel. Usually, however, the journalists stop short of presenting voices as irresistible and the genre indicates several degrees of influence. The connection can be presented as simply temporal – the journalist writes that the voice hearer acts violently *after* he or she heard voices, without specifying what the voices had said. The connection becomes stronger when the journalist writes that the voices told the person to injure or kill the victim and the voice hearer did so. Even then, of course, it is possible to argue, as did Pierre Janet, that the perpetrator may not have attacked the victim *just* because of the voices but also because of their own desire (see Chapter 4). We can resist suggestions, requests and even commands of other people in everyday life, so why should voices be different?

Voices in the House of Commons

We are interested not only in how journalists present hearing voices in newspapers, but also in the influence their writing may have on readers. Hearing voices is not a mundane phenomenon, and for many people newspapers might be the main incidental source of information about it. Yet it is unlikely that many readers read newspapers as textbooks. Some may, but the influence of newspapers on readers is best approached without prejudice as an empirical problem concerning how readers use newspapers in their everyday activities. Rather than investigate how the media instil beliefs in people (or change them) we are interested in how people use what has been written in newspapers in their arguments (see Leudar and Nekvapil, 1998). We have already seen that journalists quote each other, and construct between them a 'library' of infamous cases of violent 'madmen'. Another context in which newspaper writing is used in arguments is the British House of Commons. Like the rest of us, Members of Parliament read newspapers but, unlike the rest of us, they have the power to influence our lives through the legislation they enact. What concerns us here is how they use newspaper texts as resources in parliamentary debates.

(18) *Hansard*, 13 January 1997, col. 49

1. Mr. Michael: The new clauses and amendment deal with an important issue, which is
2. the way in which we deal with mentally ill offenders. Hon. Members will be familiar with recent horrific headlines, such as the question posed by the Daily Express:
3. 'Why Was Machete Man Free?'
4. 'Zito's killer wins right to sue over "inadequate" care.'
5. The House must answer such proper questions. In the case of Christopher Clunis, who killed Jonathan Zito, there are questions about the efficacy of community care and about the system's failure to act on problems known long before the tragic offence that led to Clunis's court appearance. The introductory paragraph of the Daily Express story on Horrett Campbell states:
6. 'A court knew machete maniac Horrett Campbell had mental health problems before he attacked children at a teddy bear's picnic.'
7. Such facts demonstrate why we have introduced the new clauses.
8. We believe that courts must have powers and systems in place to ensure that mental illness is identified and dealt with, before sentence, by the courts and, after sentence, by prison staff or by means of the disposal chosen by the courts.

The speaker, Alun Michael, does not mention hearing voices but he does use the case of Horrett Campbell, a man who, as we have already seen, attacked schoolchildren reportedly because his voices told him to do so. Mr Michael – at the time an opposition Labour MP and the spokesperson on law and order – started by setting up the problem before Parliament as being how to 'deal with mentally ill offenders'. He 'reminded' the other MPs of two 'horrific headlines' – one from the *Daily Express* and another from *The Times*. He clearly did not mean that the headlines were horrific as pieces of writing, but used them to demonstrate the mentally ill offenders he had in mind: 'Machete Man' (line 3) and 'Zito's killer' (line 5). So he adopted the newspaper headline presentation of the two men, and used them to establish the problem which concerned him as (1) involving the danger to the public from such individuals, and (2) the lack of care they them-selves receive in the community, and so in both cases the care in the community was the problem. In fact, in line 6 Mr Michael characterised the headlines as the 'proper questions' which the House 'must answer'. The two newspapers have in effect partly set up the agenda for the parliamentary debate and this is not unusual. (This mode of communication is not unique and elsewhere we have referred to it as 'distributed dialogical network' – see Leudar, 1998.) What is more, however, Mr Michael, one of the leading participants in that parliamentary debate, imported the newspaper formulations of the problem into Parliament and used them in his argumentation. He elaborated the headlines: one headline question he quoted was 'Why Was Machete Man Free?' In line 7 Mr Michael continued it by adding (again quoting from *The Times*) that Horrett Campbell's problems were known to the court. His legislative proposals (lines 7–8) were built on these grounds. In effect the newspaper reports of incidents and individuals were presented by him as 'facts', and used to justify the need for courts to have powers to ensure that mental illness is identified and dealt with.

Remember the point we made earlier in this chapter. The newspaper articles are not factual accounts, and in some cases they are one-sided arguments aligned with particular positions in social controversies. The controversy relevant here was over the place of people who experience mental health problems in the community. We have seen that Campbell, Smith, Clunis and others were first categorised in newspaper reports as 'schizophrenics' and only subsequently emerged as individuals. Their violence was construed as impulsive, irrational and linked to schizophrenia and voices, ignoring sound statistical evidence against such a link in general. We pointed out that this categorisation excuses the person from the normal moral constraints under which the rest of us act, and militates against caring for mentally ill people *in the community*. By quoting the partisan newspaper accounts as he did, and by presenting their formulations as facts, Mr Michael aligned himself with one side of the ongoing social debate concerning care in the community.

But newspaper articles are not used just by the opposition MPs to ground their arguments. Labour is now in government, and it has set out its own agenda for the reform of mental health services and for changes in mental health legislation. A focal theme in most of the proposals remains that of safety and the protection of the public. In December 1998 the Department of Health (DoH) issued the following press release concerning the government's proposals to change mental health services in the UK.

(19) Department of Health, December 1998[2]

FRANK DOBSON OUTLINES THIRD WAY FOR MENTAL HEALTH
Reforms designed to deliver safe and comprehensive mental health services are set out today by Health Secretary Frank Dobson.
   'Care in the community has failed. Discharging people from institutions has brought benefits to some. But it has left many vulnerable patients to try to cope on their own. Others have been left to become a danger to themselves and a nuisance to others. Too many confused and sick people have been left wandering the streets and sleeping rough. A small but significant minority have become a danger to the public as well as themselves. . . . In place of this I want to see a system in which both patients and public are safe and sound – a system which provides both security and support to all who need it.'

Despite the use of quotation marks, the press release is actually a selected and edited summary of Frank Dobson's speech to the House of Commons. There he admitted that 'most people who suffer mental illness are vulnerable people who pose no threat to anyone but themselves'. But then he continued: 'the whole system is in crisis, because it is not coping with the small minority of mentally ill people who are a nuisance or a danger both to themselves and to others' (*Hansard*, 12 August 1998, col. 145). In this argument he partitioned the category of mentally ill individuals into a harmless majority and a dangerous minority, thereby acknowledging statistical evidence showing that the relationship between insanity and violence is weak. Subsequently however, his proposals were motivated solely by reference to the dangerous minority which came to represent all the people with mental illness. So both Dobson's original speech and the Civil Service version of it highlighted the issue of public safety as a motive for the changes.

Dobson's speech in the House of Commons was also picked up in the national newspapers on the next day. The *Daily Telegraph*, for instance, had two cross-referenced pieces. One, on page 11, was simply a list of thirteen individuals with mental illness who had committed violent deeds, and we will not reproduce it here. The other article was on the front page and it reported the part of Dobson's speech which the civil servants used in the press release.

(20) *Daily Telegraph*, 9 December 1998

02. *Dobson to overhaul mental health care*
03. By Philip Johnston, Home Affairs Editor
. . .
08. But crucial legal changes that would allow potentially dangerous
09. individuals – like the double murderer Michael Stone – to be locked away
10. indefinitely and that would give doctors the power to order compulsory
11. treatment of schizophrenics could take at least 18 months to enact.
. . .
16. He told MPs yesterday that caring for the mentally ill in the
17. community had failed to deal effectively with the most severe cases.
18. 'Discharging people from hospitals brought benefits for some. But it
19. has left many vulnerable people who find it difficult to cope,' Mr
20. Dobson said. 'Others have become a danger to themselves and a
21. nuisance to others. Too many have been left wandering the streets and
22. sleeping rough. A small but significant minority have become a danger to
23. the public.'
. . .
56. The proposals caused deep division among mental health professionals
57. and campaign groups. Marjorie Wallace, of Sane, said: 'Now we have a
58. chance to reverse a policy that has led to hundreds of unnecessary deaths
59. and incalculable suffering for patients.'
. . .
69. However, other campaigners attacked the measures. Cliff Prior, of the
70. National Schizophrenia Fellowship, said: 'This is a package with glossy
71. wrapping but when you look inside it is half empty.
72. The government has concentrated on public relations spin that has

73. left people with severe mental illness feeling further stigmatised by an
74. association with a relatively tiny number of violent incidents.'
75. The human rights implications of compulsory treatment orders and
76. forced incarceration also caused concern. Rabbi Julia Neuberger, of the
77. King's Fund, said: 'We must have a balance between securing public
78. safety and honouring the rights of individuals.'

This article demonstrates that it is not just Members of Parliament who use newspaper material in their arguments and in doing so tacitly take sides in the social controversies. The journalists in turn report their parliamentary arguments (lines 16–23) and situate what has been said in those social controversies. In this case the situating was accomplished by reporting reactions of campaigners for and against community care (lines 69–74 and 56–59 respectively), as well as human rights campaigners (lines 75–78). In other contexts we have characterised this function of newspapers as establishing dialogical networks (Nekvapil and Leudar, 1998).

So the government's arguments concerning the dangerousness of people with mental illness and the risk they pose to the public are in debt to newspaper headlines, rather than to statistical evidence. A recent paper in the *British Journal of Psychiatry*, however, challenged the assumptions that are driving government policy, by producing evidence that there was no increased risk of homicide from people with mental illness, and, if anything, the risk had fallen over the forty-year period which had seen the growth of community care. The article by Taylor and Gunn (1999) (entitled 'Homicides by people with mental illness: myth and reality') presented a detailed trend analysis of data drawn from Home Office statistics between 1957 and 1995. The authors found little fluctuation in the numbers of people with mental illness committing criminal homicide over the period studied, and an annual 3 per cent decline in their contribution to official statistics, this being over the period which witnessed the growth and expansion of community care with the closure of the Victorian asylums. The paper concluded: 'there is no evidence that it is anything but stigmatising to claim that their [people with mental disorder] living in the community is a dangerous experiment that should be reversed' (Taylor and Gunn, 1999, p. 9).

Psychiatric evidence thus challenges the assumptions about the relationship between mental illness and dangerousness, which forms a central plank of the case against community care. Taylor and Gunn's article has two intriguing features which make it into more than just a routine report in a scientific journal. First, it was accompanied by a press release from the Royal College of Psychiatrists (1999), summarising the findings and conclusions, which explicitly referred to the role of the mass media in fuelling what it described as the 'entrenched popular belief that people with mental disorders are dangerous'. Second, the authors acknowledged the support of Robert Kendell, the then President of the Royal College of Psychiatrists, for 'urging' them to carry out this work. The paper is thus the public response of a professional body to public perceptions of those with mental health problems, and in particular the destructive influence of the type of newspaper reporting analysed earlier in this chapter. How did the politicians respond? Sixteen days later the Department of Health issued another press release in which Health Minister John Hutton rejected the argument fronted by Taylor and Gunn:

(21) Department of Health, January 1999[3]

Ministers . . . make no apologies for their emphasis on safety, Health Minister John Hutton said today. [He] responded to recent claims that care in the community had not failed. He also argued for a change in mental health law to allow compulsory treatment in the community. He said:
    'I know some organisations have expressed concern about the emphasis which we have placed on safety. A recent article in the British Journal of Psychiatry is being used by some to argue that this emphasis is misplaced. . . . But I make no apologies about our stance on safety both for service users, carers and the wider public.'
    . . .
    'I know that there has been a fair degree of speculation about compulsory treatment in community settings. . . . The introduction of some form of compulsion which is not necessarily coupled to detention is an important step in providing safe, sound and supportive services.'

It is important to note that the Taylor and Gunn article did not claim that there were no problems with community care but their introduction did draw attention to the influence of 'highly selected information in the mass media' (Taylor and Gunn, 1999, p. 9) on the public and the politicians. In other words, it criticised the government for changing policy in response to inaccurate media accounts, rather than basing its changes in more objective sources of evidence.

There is a final irony concerning the type of legislation which the government proposes to introduce. Newspaper presentations we analysed earlier implied that voice hearers cannot be held morally responsible for their actions when influenced by voices, and this deficit in moral responsibility was further emphasised by the categories into which voice hearers are assigned. As Bauman (1989) has suggested, categories such as 'schizophrenic' or 'mentally ill person' develop according to a logic which liberates conduct from ethical constraints:

Definition sets the victimised group apart (all definitions mean splitting the totality into two parts – the marked and the unmarked), as a different category, so that whatever applies to it does not apply to the rest. By the very act of being defined, the group has been targeted for special treatment; what is proper in relation to 'ordinary' people must not necessarily be proper in relation to it. Individual members of the group become now in addition exemplars of a type; something of the nature of the type cannot but seep into their individualised images.

(Bauman, 1989, p. 191)

The result is an ironic twist in moral accountability. The special treatment for the category 'schizophrenic' (or voice hearer) is compulsory treatment in the community. This means that even though they may have done nothing wrong, and even though they may show no evidence of being unwell, 'schizophrenics' may be given medication against their wishes if they decide to stop taking it. The usual ethical principles process of autonomy and consent to treatment do not apply to this group of people, who do not enjoy the same range of human rights as the rest of us.

It may seem that we have drifted from our topic, the conceptualisation of hearing voices in British national newspapers – after all, hearing voices was not mentioned once in any of the material we have analysed in the last section. This is not so, however. We have seen how Members of Parliament used cases of people with mental illness who committed violent deeds to justify their arguments and the need for legislative change, and these cases were composed by journalists using the phenomenon of hearing voices. In journalists' writing, hearing voices was typically (but not exclusively) presented as a symptom of mental illness and a concomitant of unreasoned violence. When other versions of the experience were presented, it was as versions of the experience belonging to individuals who are either mentally ill or defending them. The last section in this chapter showed that these presentations are not just journalists' images. They were subsequently used in public argumentation of some consequence and affected it to some extent.[4] The final chapter in this book will show that journalists' presentations of hearing voices are not so much false as selective and partial and so not representative.

9 Voice-talk

Hearing voices by definition involves language, whatever a voice hearer, a psychiatrist or a researcher decide that voices really are: messages from supernatural beings, re-experiences of traumatic events, or psychological errors. But what kinds of speech are voices? We have already presented the arguments of Seglas and Janet (Chapter 4), who saw verbal hallucinations as voice hearers' own automatic inner speech. More recently, Gould (1949) reported that she amplified sub-vocal speech in individuals hearing voices, and found that the reported content of verbal hallucinations corresponded closely to that of sub-vocalisations. Green and Preston (1981) recorded the electrical activity from lips (of which voice hearers are not aware and which they cannot control directly), related it to the reports of verbal hallucinations, and found a reasonable correspondence between the two (cf. Cacioppo and Petty, 1981). Recent positron emission tomography studies indicate that during verbal hallucinations the areas of brain usually involved in processing speech are active (Cleghorn *et al.*, 1992; McGuire *et al.*, 1993). Suzuki *et al.* (1993) reported that during verbal hallucinations, a left superior temporal cortex – a speech perception area – is activated. McGuire *et al.* (1995, 1996) reported that when voice hearers imagine other people speaking, the same areas of the brain are activated as when they hear voices. But since verbal hallucinations are not experienced as one's own inner speech they have in addition been construed to be *impaired* inner speech. Hoffman (1986) and Frith (1992, 1995), for instance, explained them as inner speech which is wrongly attributed to external sources. In Hoffman's account such misattributions were a function of pre-conscious perceptual inferences, and Frith explained them by reference to lesions of the neuro-cognitive internal monitoring device.[1] Looking inside the brains of individuals hearing voices, McGuire *et al.* (1995) reported a reduced activity in the areas of cortex thought to be 'concerned with the generation and monitoring of inner speech' ('the left middle temporal gyrus' and 'the rostral supplementary motor area'). Experimental neurophysiological studies therefore also suggest that inner speech and hearing voices are related.

We now need to ask: What sorts of inner speech are voices? Clinical reports and surveys show that voices may have stable identities and engage in structured dialogues with voice hearers (Putnam, 1989; Romme and Escher, 1994, Ch. 6; Nayani and David, 1996; Leudar *et al.*, 1997). These dialogical properties are not taken into account in the cognitive models we have just introduced. The problem is that the cognitive conception of 'inner speech' is restricted, both as a conception of speech and as a conception of what the word 'inner' can mean.

First, neuro-cognitive approaches focus on representational properties of inner speech, but as we pointed out elsewhere, inner speech has pragmatics (Leudar *et al.*, 1997). It is a means of regulating and evaluating activities (cf. Pavlov, 1928; Vygotsky, 1934/1962; Luria, 1961) and the medium of mental problem solving (Diaz and Berk, 1992). Sentences articulated to oneself can scold, commend, advise – they have pragmatic functions – and textually they can be parts of dia- logues one has with oneself (Wertsch, 1991). It is now a well-established position in developmental psychology to argue that mental skills are internalised social practices (e.g. Vygotsky, 1934/1962; Wertsch, 1985; Rogoff, 1990), and that human experience is, at least at some level, dialogically organised (e.g. Bakhtin, 1981, 1988). We take it for granted that inner speech is not just a representation, but that it also has pragmatic properties. It is of course possible that specific voice hearers experience their voices as just sounds and words without a communicative purpose. One empirical problem we shall discuss below is to determine whether voices are experienced as just speech sounds or as endowed with other aspects of communicative agency.

The second problem is what the 'inner' in 'inner speech' means. The word 'inner' has a reasonably clear meaning in cognitive psychology and psychiatry – since cognitions are said to coincide with brain processes, 'inner' means 'in the brain' and 'in the head', and so one individual's cognitions are hidden from others, like sweets in paper bags. Wittgenstein commented on this conception of 'inner' and found it to be incoherent, since it combines two incommensurable uses of the word 'inner'. The meanings of 'inner' in physical and mental domains differ – the mental uses, for instance, lack the transitivity of physical uses, and the possession of mental states is not alienable, while physical objects can be moved from container to container (see Baker and Hacker, 1983; Hacker, 1996, pp. 130–132). We will not diverge into this argument but just assert that the words 'inner' and 'outer' can have various contingent meanings, and that we need to be sensitive to which of them operates on a particular occasion. Cognitive psychology and psychiatry use a simple contrast between 'inner' and 'outer' to underpin 'reality-testing' procedures. Hallucinations are said to arise from failures of these procedures, resulting in confusion between inner and outer realities (e.g. Bentall, 1990). But we have seen that Schreber's reality did not simply divide into 'inner' and 'outer' domains – he had two outer worlds: one supernatural, which was his only, and one which he shared with others. Events could thus be external to himself in more than one way, and so 'inner' meant for him something different from what it means to experimental psychologists. Schreber had no problems assigning his experiences to the three domains, and so it is easier to accuse him of being ontologically deluded than of having problems with reality monitoring.

Not all psychologists use the word 'inner' to mean literally 'in the head' and 'outer' to mean 'beyond the body'. Developmental psychologist Barbara Rogoff, for instance, argued cogently that the inner/outer distinction separates children

too sharply from their learning environments, and she suggested that internalisation should be treated not as the movement of objects from the social realm into
mental space – which is how Vygotsky (1934/1962) used the term – but instead
as an appropriation of skills by a child. Nevertheless, most psychologists do use
the word 'inner' to mean in the head, and 'outer' to mean outside the body, and
would say, together with Freud (1911/1972), Niederland (1974) and Sass (1992),
that Schreber was simply wrong, and that the supernatural was in no way external
to him but really his mind which he disowned. This argument is plausible partly
because Schreber was diagnosed to be insane, but do we want to say the same
about Socrates, whose 'reality' was also threefold – social, personal and divine?
The daemon was a part of Socrates' soul but also a messenger of the gods and
so independent of him, and the polar distinctions between inner and outer
(and subjective and objective) make it difficult to understand Socrates (see Chapter
1). What could 'reality monitoring' mean for Schreber, or for Socrates? Do they
display its failures or are they, to their own satisfaction, assigning phenomena into
subjective, social and supernatural/divine domains? The sensible conclusion
is that whatever our own ontology we also need to understand the conduct and
experience of voice hearers in terms of their own categories. For other people the
'inner' does not need to mean 'in the mind' or 'in the brain'. We take it that what
Rogoff did was to make the meaning of 'inner' relative to the activity of learning,
and indeed 'inner' can have several meanings which are indexical to activities in
which the word is used. Rather than impose an a priori inner/outer or subjective/
objective distinction we shall pay attention to how the voice hearers themselves
construe the status of voices. It is certainly not a part of our project to determine
for anybody the true meaning of 'inner' as it may apply to voice-talk.

We reiterate that our operational assumption is that verbal hallucinations –
or hearing voices, if that is the preferred term – are talk, 'voice-talk'. This simply
means that we approach verbal hallucinations as matters of language. Our aim
here is to establish what pragmatic properties voice-talk has in comparison to
ordinary conversations while paying attention to how well words describing
ordinary talk fit the experiences of hearing voices. Our second aim is to establish
how voice hearers themselves categorise voices ontologically in their narratives.

On what voices do with words

If only one could record conversations between voices and their hearers, transcribe
and analyse them, but despite what Gould (1949) reported, this is impossible. So one
has to work with references to voice-talk in conversations and other activities. These
make the experience public and accountable and so they are precisely the kind of
materials needed to assess pragmatics of voice-talk. Some time ago, Coulter (1973)
analysed an interaction between a social worker and a man who was possibly
experiencing bereavement hallucinations, showing how both participants oriented
at a psychiatric conception of hearing voices, using it as a resource to invoke and
forestall a psychiatric diagnosis. Unfortunately for us, in ordinary talk hearing voices
is rarely publicly avowed or invoked as an interpretative resource, and when it is,

the context is rarely accessible to researchers. Most of the material we shall use in this chapter was therefore obtained through interviewing voice hearers (see Leudar and Thomas, 1995; Leudar *et al.*, 1997).

All our informants have heard voices for over four years, some of them for much longer. Some of our informants could report the first time they heard voices (see (1) below). Those with bereavement voices usually noticed them several weeks after the death of the voice-analogue. Most of our informants, however, could not pin-point the first onset of their voices. Some even said that they had always had voices and only eventually discovered that this was unusual.

Some of our informants had a psychiatric diagnosis (not always of schizo-phrenia) but as many did not. We have elsewhere compared the hearing of voices by people with schizophrenia and by individuals without psychiatric problems (Leudar *et al.*, 1997). Here we shall not indicate whether the informant had a psychiatric diagnosis or not. We do not claim that our sample of voice hearers is representative of all those who hear voices, but it is sufficient to demonstrate the range of experiences that count as hearing voices.

Voices as speech

Voice hearers can usually report voice-talk word for word, but do their experiences necessarily have an auditory aspect? Janet (1891) did not think so, and argued that hearing-like qualities were optional to verbal hallucinations. Bleuler (1911/1966, p. 110) also allowed for silent verbal hallucinations. Schreber (1903/1955) heard voices in silent nerve language (Ch. 4); Socrates, on the other hand, *experienced* his daemon as an audition, and his contemporaries were puzzled how he could hear in absence of sound. The phrase *hearing* voices used by mental health activists does imply that these experiences are like hearing other people speaking, and so the verbs used to report speech, such as 'say', 'shout' and 'whisper', should be conditionally relevant. So perhaps all voice-talk should be describable as language, and some of it (or perhaps much of it) as speech.

Most of our informants had in fact no problems reporting their voices to us as speech. We provide one example here and others *passim*. The informant UN used the verb of communication 'say' and quoted the voice verbatim, including the repetition ((1), line 38).[2]

(1) PT and UN[3]

33. PT: So when did the voices start in relation to the drinking did they start while you were drinking or after you stopped drinking?=

34. UN: =Well no I've I'd been there about (0.63) five years and they started just like that ((finger snap)) | just

35. PT: | Right

36. UN: (0.43) started like that, I was sat (0.20) behind the bar. (0.42) honest I can remember it (0.55) as plain as day. | Yeah.

37. PT: | Just tell me ehm try (0.36) and re-create it for me | would you

38. UN: | Well I just sat there an' (0.36) somebody said 'What do you *want?* What do you *want?*' (0.84) and I thought 'well there's bloody no one there' 'who were that?' you know=
39. PT: =Ri:ght. (0.53) Ri:ght
40. UN: It was like that.

...

73. PT: What was the question about?
74. UN: Oh no: no: that that was that was it you know 'What do you want?'
75. PT: Was it like somebody in a bar might ask you what you want?
76. UN: Yeah Yeah.

Despite what Janet believed, only two of our informants reported voices in terms indicating that, like Schreber, they may have experienced them as silent language. One of them was RO:

(2) AG and RO

163. AG. And how do you hear these voices? Do you hear them as other people through your ears or do you hear them in your head?
164. RO. No. It's the same sort of um (. . .) perception which you make when you speak to yourself.

RO rejects the disjunction the interviewer offered him (and so the predicate 'hear') and he characterises the experience as a 'sort of perception', as when one speaks to oneself, presumably sub-vocally. The other informant was UN whom we have introduced already ((3), lines 124 and 128).

(3) PT and UN

123. PT: (0.54) and em could you tell a little bit about what the voice sounds like to you. Is it er=
124. UN: =Well I couldn't tell you whether it's male or female.
125. PT: R:ight (0.46) | you you couldn't (0.31)
126. UN: | eh
       No=
127. PT: =make a distinction | ((unclear))
128. UN: | No it's definitely in my mind you know what I mean it's (0.41) I'm not 'earing it with me ears, you know what I mean =
129. PT: ri:ght
130. UN: it's it's definitely | in in my head
131. PT: | It's definitely in your head. You don't hear hear it.
132. UN: Oh yeah.

There is no contradiction between how UN presented his experiences on the two occasions – in (1) he was speaking about the past, and in (3) about the present. (1) and (3) could be jointly taken to imply that his verbal hallucinations lost their auditory concreteness over time, perhaps because, as we shall see, he changed his conception of what it was he was experiencing from 'hearing a voice' to 'neuro-logical symptom'. But it could be that some of UN's voice-talk around the time of the report was speech-like and some was not – remember that Schreber reported some voices which were silent and others which were voiced, so the two are not mutually exclusive. The difference between the two presentations could also be a matter of rhetorical face-saving strategy – we observed that our informants tended to narrate some of their more disturbing and bizarre experiences as having taken place in the past.

But there are certain respects in which even the voice-talk with clear auditory qualities is unlike hearing other people speaking. Barring ventriloquists and head-phones, voices of other people come from their mouths, or from some artefact reproducing sound. This is typically not so for voice-talk. Only one of our informants, EF, aligned her voices with an external object – the television set – even though her hesitancy ('I think' in line 39) implies that this may be a explanation of something which puzzles her rather than an unambiguous experience (4).

(4) PT and EF

37.   PT: it frightens you? Do you feel that the voice is part of you, or it's, or it's coming from the outside?
38.   EF: I think it's coming from the television | that
39.   PT: | from the television
40.   EF: mm
41.   PT: it ah i |
42.   EF: | it tells me where I am and everything
43.   PT: ri:ght, does it?
44.   EF: mm
45.   PT: does it ss, does it come even when the television isn't even, isn't on?
46.   EF: no, no no no. Once the television is off, the voice goes.

Many of our informants, however, heard voices 'in their heads' and some, like TK, even claimed they could localise different voices to left and right sides ((5), lines 59–60) and in this he did almost as well as the state-of-the-art PET scanners.

(5) DM and TK

59.   DM: | yeah. (0.7) so: do they um (1.28) kind of (0.65) <u>where do you</u> hear them? (0.35)
60.   TK: In me left-hand side of me head. (0.52)
61.   DM: ri:ght=
62.   TK: =the left-hand side (0.78) and, it's funny, 'cos sometimes God speaks to me right-hand side. I don't <u>know</u> whether it's <u>God</u> or just meself, y'know. (0.99) I've not sorted that one out yet. I've not come to terms with that yet.

Finally, there were some informants who said they heard voices through their ears, but significantly from fixed spatial positions *relative to their bodies*; for instance, always from behind on the left. This means that voice-talk moves with the body of the voice hearer, whether it is experienced in the head or through the ears. So voices may sound like other people speaking, but they are typically tied to their hearers' bodies, and in this respect voice-talk is unlike ordinary speech. This property of auditory experience could be used as a sign that one is 'hearing a voice' rather than hearing another person, and some informants indeed reported doing this. They judged voices not to be real hearing because they 'hear' them in their heads (see, for example, (2) and (33)). We shall return to this point later in this chapter, but the implication is interesting. 'Hallucination' is a cognitive conception, with a strong element of functionalism and methodological solipsism. It claims that two experiences – for instance, hearing and hallucinating – can be phenomenally exactly the same, even though one has an object and the other does not. But we can see that the phenomenon of hearing voices is evidence to the contrary – the absence of a speaker is itself a constituent part of the experience: UN was not puzzled by what he 'heard' – that was quite ordinary – but by hearing it in the absence of an obvious speaker ((1), line 38).

This is where ecological accounts of auditory perception based on Gibson's work may allow us to understand hearing voices better than cognitive accounts because they consider perceptions as being inalienably situated in the environment and with respect to one's body (cf. Gaver, 1993). So we need to pay attention not only to formal pragmatic properties of voices but also to how the voice hearers relate them to their bodies and to the objects in their environment. The manner in which voice-talk is embodied and situated is clearly the feature which distinguishes it from ordinary speech. In fact some (but not all) of our informants hesitated when applying the verbs of speech to voice-talk for precisely this reason. UN, for instance, had problems saying that he hears his voice ((2), lines 131–132) because he 'hears' it in his head.

With this proviso voices are in most cases describable as speech, but are they *only* speech? Are they not sometimes accompanied by experiences in other sensory modalities? Homer's gods were not just voices, but the daemon of Socrates was. Schreber not only heard birds but he also smelled them – they carried 'the putrefaction of corpses' (Schreber, 1903/1955, p. 167). None of our informants reported coordinated multi-modal hallucinations, such as a voice with a visually defined body. But hearing a voice could still be accompanied by experiences in other sensory modalities. NJ experienced her deceased husband not just as a voice but also physically.

(6) PT and NJ

180. NJ: and erm I would almost feel that kind of comfort and almost feel him
     there (0.44) almost feel his breathing on my face, | comforting me.
181. PT: | ri:ght ri:ght

182. NJ: So even though he never said anything, I could (0.25) feel (0.53) like a comfort, like like a (0.83) feeling OK. (0.28)
183. PT: ri:ght.
184. IV: it wasn't words? (0.45)
185. NJ: no, no it was a feeling but it's not something I could do to myself. (0.34)
186. IV: right

Thus NJ could initially experience her voice as being present even when it did not speak ((6), line 182). This is unusual because ordinarily voices are assumed to be present only when they speak. What indicated to NJ that the voice was present when it did not speak? Her bodily sentiments, the feelings of comfort, his breath on her face (line 180). The bodily aspect of her voice cannot be set aside – NJ uses it to differentiate the voice from herself; the bodily sentiments are her own but they are not caused by herself (line 185). NJ did not feel the voice *only* when it was silent – she also felt it when it spoke. In fact the bodily sentiments helped her to identify the experience as the voice.

(7) PT and NJ

301. IV: how | do you know
302. NJ: | yeh
303. IV: that you're hearing a voice rather than somebody (0.73) talking? (0.56)
304. NJ: because I can like feel him as well.
305. IV: right (0.68)
306. NJ: It's like I can feel him and it's his (0.36)
307. IV: yeh
308. NJ: I can like feel him.
309. PT: Sensing a physical pre|sence?
310. NJ: |Yes

NJ's voice is no longer comforting but clearly she does not just hear it. She can also feel it, and the two sensory aspects of the experience are tied together by common pronominal references to her dead husband: she feels 'him' ((6), line 180, (7) 306), 'his breathing' ((6), line 180), 'he never said anything' (line 182). This is a matter of language and does not imply that NJ actually believes in spirits – she never presented the voice to us in supernatural terms. (In fact it is surprising how few voice hearers embrace supernatural or paranormal accounts of their experiences.)

Another informant, TK, reported that he did not only hear God comforting him, he also felt 'fire' and 'love inside'.

(8) DM and TK

67. DM: Is it the, for instance, does it eve:r↑=
68. TK: =It's funny 'cos I'm a Christian, you know an er and the: (0.56) God does (0.84) I lie on me bed sometimes and I can feel fire feel love inside (0.70) and God'll just say you'r (ho:ur?) 's not very good, for this, sort of stuff

but (0.80), he says like, 'I love you' or 'you're alright, (name)', jus:t, and he *talks* to me, you kno:w.

69. DM: Do you ever talk ba:ck?
70. TK: I do I talk back yeh
71. DM: mhm↑
72. TK: We have conversations in me head.

The only other informant who reported bodily feelings accompanying voices was ND (see (10) below), even though some others mentioned that voice-talk can be accompanied by urges, but these will be discussed below. This absence of reports does not necessarily mean that such bodily sentiments are usually missing – the problem is that the concepts 'hearing voices' and 'auditory hallucinations' direct the attention of both informants and researchers to the auditory aspects of the experience, and the accompaniments in the other sensory modalities are neglected.

Not all speech is clear, and an important characteristic of voice-talk is whether the voice hearer can make out what a voice is saying. All but one of our informants reported hearing some voices which could be clearly understood, but several also reported voice-talk which was either completely unclear or contained just odd clear words. NC reported a group of voices whispering without being able to make out the words ((9), line 12).

(9) PT and NC

5. PT: First of all if you could just tell me how many voices you hear?
6. NC: So far I have heard two, and
7. PT: Right
8. NC: And that is not counting the whispering
9. PT: And whispers
10. NC: Yeah
11. PT: Now is that the same voice as the whispers or is it different voices you hear whisper
12. NC: I can't tell, it's it's, um the whispering, it just sounds like a group of people, you can hear the whispering the talking but you can't grasp at what it is, it's not loud enough to know what's been said
13. PT: You can't make out what's being said?
14. NC: No
15. PT: You can't hear words
16. NC: No, but it's a group of people, quite a lot of people, whispering,

Another informant, ND, reported a voice which was vaguely male, but had no name or social identity. As in NC's case, the voice was possibly not one individual at all, but many voices heard all at the same time – a chorus – and ND could not understand it at all. She reported vividly that this rushing voice 'flooded her mind', and was difficult to ignore ((10), line 38).

(10) AG and ND

35.   AG: Right. What sort of things would you tell the voice?
36.   ND: Er (..) er (..) I don't know just normal (..) as if we were having a conversation.
37.   AG: OK. And what do the voices do when you tell them things?
38.   ND: Just respond as if it was a conversation. The last set of voices, the sort of rushing voices I can't (..) there's no sort of conversation with that, it sort of floods into my mind. It's just like er (..) as if when my heart beats start beating faster so it's if, like in an exam or something like that (. . .) it's not a conversation

One informant, TY, could not say how many voices he hears or make out what the voices are saying. He explains in (11).

(11) AG and TY

17.   AG: Do they appear together?
18.   TY: Yeah it comes really quickly in really sort of rapid succession and like I'll be trying to think (. . .) this is it (. . .) it's just the ends of sentences. While I'm trying to think what one was, the other one comes along.

TY could, however, say that some voices were old, others young, some male, others female.

All informants but one reported that they had no feeling of being addressed when hearing this kind of unclear voice-talk, and they did not attempt to address the unclear voices either. These voices were relatively rare in our informants, and indeed only one such voice has been reported by Nayani and David (1996) in their sample of 100 schizophrenics. We started this section expecting that all voice-talk would be describable as language and some of it also as speech. It is now clear that some voice-talk is experienced as speech, but not as language with a determinable meaning or purpose.

Individuation and personification in voice-talk

Some voices are encountered only once, but more often they recur – the majority of our informants experienced such voices, on average between two and three of them. One of our empirical concerns has been to establish exactly how voice hearers identify particular voices as being those which they had experienced in the past. It turns out that the identity of a voice is indicated by a variety of phenomenological characteristics, such as the experienced voice quality, gender, accent, but also the knowledge it displays, and by its typical verbal behaviour. Most of our informants reported that their voices were gendered and with an approximately determinate age – they were 'youngish', 'old', 'my own age'. Using these terms, a voice could be spoken of as, for example, 'an unknown old woman', or 'a man with a deep voice'. The recurrence of voices is formulated in terms of those qualities which remain the same on different occasions. Some voice hearers, however, could not assign their voices into these categories – UN experienced a 'silent' voice and could not tell its gender ((3), lines 124 and 128).

Some voices do not have names and they do not resemble anyone known to the informants. PB presented her voices to us as 'anonymous' and said that they only ever swear at her. DS said she hears a deep male voice calling her name in warning when she walks at night through dangerous parts of the city. Some informants reported having only such 'anonymous' voices, but most had voices which were aligned with individuals in their social world. Such alignments were accomplished in terms of any of the above phenomenal qualities. This is obvious in (12).

(12) PT and NJ

5. PT: right (0.55) and (0.36) how (1.28) what I'd like to know now is is what the sort of how you identify the voices (0.41) erm is it a male voice?=
6. NJ: =a male voice | yeah
7. PT: |a male voice, young or old?
8. NJ: older (0.39)
9. PT: right and does it is it a person that you know?
10. NJ: yes it is=
11. PT: right right and (0.40) erm (0.67) wd'ye would you mind me asking | who it is?
12. NJ: | It's my husband who died (0.39) suddenly he's (0.23) five and a half years ago.
13. PT: ri:ght. | right right
14. NJ: | mhm
15. PT: (0.25) right (0.37) a:nd (0.45) does th (0.34) is the voice just exactly like his voice?
16. NJ: exactly=
17. PT: =yeh | yeh OK right
. . .
26. NJ: (cough) because it's his (1.38) I I'd I I interpret well whenever ye he's talking or if he's talking to me (0.90) it's his mannerisms it's it's his speech, it's the way he raises his voice at the end (0.24) even the anger in his voice sometimes.

NJ aligns the voice she hears with her deceased husband ((12), line 12). But the alignment is not simply a matter of the voice sounding like her husband used to. NJ also warrants the connection by reference to her dead husband's speech mannerisms and the anger in the voice (line 26), both of which are shared by the voice and her dead husband ((13), line 56). The voice has memories of their life together, that the husband might have had ('it never was like that'), but, since it moved with the family, it is also ascribed new experiences of its own ('you are being stupid' – line 56).

(13) PT and NJ

54. PT: So what what sort of things would would he say to you (1.34) | in those circumstances?

55. NJ: | ((cough))
     erm

56. I've got to think of an instance (0.40) uhm I can remember (0.26) there was quite some occasion I wasn't sleeping very well (0.46) and I would start (0.25) *missing* him and thinking of him (0.56) a:nd (0.52) remembering occasions where we were happy together (0.30) looking for comfort from him (0.38). But he would come and he would say 'you're being stupid, it never was like that' (0.53) 'you're being' erm (0.33) 'you're not being a proper mother' (0.28) 'you're neglecting things' (0.35) e:rm 'you're a mess'. It would be *very* derogatory to me.

So NJ's voice is clearly not just an echo – it is endowed by a communicative agency and it has dispositions and knowledge. Not all voice hearers endow voices with a communicative agency, or recognise it, however. RO, for instance, does not ((14), line 105), even though he perceives what the voices tell him, and though he could attribute to the voices a communicative intent and a knowledge of himself, he does not do this – the voices are just voices.

(14) AG and RO

102. AG. Do they say nice things to you?
103. RO. They do say, I suppose they do, yeah.
104. AG. Do you know what sort of things?
105. RO. Maybe the sort of things a close friend would say. Somebody who knew you very well. But that's not to say that they know me or anything like that, because they're just (. . .) it's voices.

There were two other common ways of individuating voices. One was to distinguish them from each other in terms of what they typically 'do with words' – some, for example, may criticise, others may encourage or warn. UN experienced the silent voice as being the same on different occasions because it said similar sorts of things. The other way was to identify a voice in terms of situations in which it typically appears (for example, in a dangerous situation, or when the hearer is depressed). The perceptual, social, pragmatic, situational bases of voice individuation are of course not exclusive. BN, for example, reported hearing a voice which 'sounds very much like' her mother, and which typically criticises her (see (15) below).

On the whole, the socially aligned voices usually sound like individuals who are known to voice hearers: family members, public figures, friends, or even like themselves. We have already mentioned NJ, who hears a spouse who had died; another of our informants, TL, heard the voice of his dead father. In most cases, however, the relatives and other voice analogues were still alive. This distribution of alignments is partly consistent with Mead's conception of self outlined in

Chapter 5 – the voices frequently correspond to individuals who are significant to voice hearers. They are not, however, integrated into one voice which could be said was the 'generalised other'. It is also significant that not all voices were aligned with *other* individuals – several informants reported voices which sounded just like their own. BN, for instance, heard three voices: her mother, father and a voice like her own. She nevertheless perceived the latter as a voice, not as herself ((15), line 102) (cf. Price-Williams, 1989).

(15) RA and BN

94. BN: erm er but, it's difficult because th the erm the critical voice is u is a kind of I don't know if it is my mother, I just know it sounds like her, it's
95. RA: mm (inaudible)
96. BN: got her intonations, but it's very much often putting down what I've done
97. RA: (inaudible)
98. BN: or s or criticising me or saying erm y you're doing it for the wrong reasons it's a ve a negative voice
99. RA: yeah
100. BN: erm and the er but very loud and clear and often drowning out the other two
101. RA: right
102. BN: and then erm the me voice is again slightly like my voice is and rather squeaky and just trying to maintain something but not n altogether certain and. . . .

After Schreber's supernature these personifications are surprisingly mundane. Some of our informants, however, did align voices with supernatural characters as did NC in (9) and KT in (16), or with public figures as did EX in (17).

(16) AN and KT

28. AN: yeh yeh so is it like same voice every time that tells you to?
29. KT: I have about four voices. I get a mankof (0.67) ji:sod (0.84) harg and dart which is all to do with the cabalistic tree of life which is to do with tarot card (0.54)
30. AN: ye:h
31. KT: which is interesting the: eh colten tarot cards (0.60) the night there is such thing as the cabalistic tree of life which integrates appliance of the solar system (0.34).

(17) DM and EX

7. DM: Oh, did you know who they were, did you recognise the voices?
8. EX: Yeah, I recognised the voices. Frank Shinatra, Johnny Cash (1.45), Clint (0.49), Clint Walker, that's not Clint Eastwood, that's that big bloke that's (0.35) part Indian, used to play Chianne years ago on TV.

According to Chadwick and Birchwood (1994), most personifications in voice hearers with schizophrenia are supernatural and hence, the authors claimed, 'delusional'. But giving the voice a supernatural identity does not mean that one has to believe that one is communicating with the supernatural ((18), line 62).

(18) DM and TK

58.   TK: and it's put me in a psychosis, I've walked around (0.62) I'd used to think it was God, you know what I mean, I was really ill (1.3), I've walked around hospital (1.0) fearing people can hear me me voices, you know what I mean, I've I've been in a pychosis, you know what I mean | Debs?

59.   DM: | Yeah. (0.71) So: do they um (1.28) kind of (0.65) <u>where do you</u> hear them? (0.35)

60.   TK: In me left-hand side of me head. (0.52)

61.   DM: Ri:ght.=

62.   TK: =The left-hand side (0.78) and, it's funny, 'cos sometimes God speaks to me right-hand side. I don't <u>know</u> whether it's <u>God</u> or just meself, y'know. (99) I've not sorted that one out yet. I've not come to terms with that yet.

63.   DM: So, right, is the voice you, there's a voice that you sometimes think is God?

64.   TK: Yeah.

TK asserts that God speaks to him on the 'right-hand side' of his head (18, line 62) but this clearly does not mean that he is certain against all possible evidence that the voice is actually the God one does not meet in churches (line 62). He did not explain to DM precisely why he thinks the voice is God – but he did attribute the belief that it is God to his psychosis.

There is therefore one important point to bear in mind about the social alignments of voices. When talking about them, most of our informants reported that the voices were like someone, not that they were that someone. BN did not believe that the voice which sounded like her mother was actually her mother speaking to her telepathically from their home in L. NJ did not claim that her dead husband was somehow speaking to her from beyond the grave; she heard a voice which sounded like her husband when he was alive and she spoke to it. NJ did not volunteer a global account of how this was possible, and in fact she did not have just one way of connecting the voice to her dead husband. In excerpts 6, 7, 12 and 13 she referred to the voice in several manners, as 'it', 'him', 'voice', 'husband who died', and as 'he', and each of these formulations was contingent on what was happening at the time in the interview.

So to summarise. Most of the contemporary voices recur. Some do not have crystallised identities, but those which do are *not* typically supernatural figures (like the daemon of Socrates) or bizarre (like Schreber's birds). Instead the voices tend to be mundane – aligned with individuals known and significant to the voice hearer. The identity alignments are not warranted only in terms of how voices sound, but also in terms of how they speak, and what they do with words. How the voice hearers actually refer to voices depends on the situation.

It should be noted that we have not attempted to interpret the voice identities which our informants presented us with. So did we miss, for instance, that TK's god-voice was really his stepfather, and did the doubt he expressed about whether it really was God in (18) reflect the power/hate ambiguities in their past relationship? We have already seen that almost all the past readings of Schreber's memoirs have been interpretive (Chapter 3). The analysts, from Freud (1911/1972) to Santner (1996), attempted to discover the *real* meaning of the supernatural agencies Schreber described in his memoirs. Schreber's supernatural reality becomes a destination of a practising solipsist, birds become girls, and the god becomes his psychiatrist Flechsig or his father Moritz. Should we have joined in and proposed, for instance, that Schreber's birds were really his stillborn children? Perhaps not. The point about interpretation is that it is not simply a substitution of one meaning (the true one) for another (the apparent one). Interpretation is a pragmatic act in which the patient's meaning is displaced by the interpreter's meaning, and in which the interpreter is semiotically privileged (Leudar and Antaki, 1997). Now clearly we were not in this position with our informants, and we would not want to be. We are not claiming that the voice-talk alignments cannot have symbolic meanings for the voice hearers themselves. Our aim is, however, to understand the voices in terms of voice hearers' own membership categories, and when one imports one's own categories (as one must), one must be absolutely clear what the pragmatic relationship between the two modes of understanding is. This was precisely why we focused our analysis of Schreber on the clash between his and psychiatrists' perspectives on his conduct in the Saxon Supreme Court.

Participant positioning of voice-talk

Speaking is not just saying things. The speaker also has to manage the position from which he speaks and others listen to him. This is captured in pragmatics by terms such as 'footing' (Goffman, 1981), 'participant role' (Levinson, 1988), 'positioning' (Harré and van Langenhove 1991) and 'dialogical positioning' (Leudar and Antaki, 1996a, 1996b). Traditionally the default dialogical participant format is taken to be that one participant in conversation (the speaker) addresses and targets another participant (the hearer). Other 'formats' are, however, also possible and common. For instance, I can speak for somebody who is absent or for a collective, and can do so to one person or to an audience (Leudar, 1998). I can align myself with one side of an argument and the other participants will judge what I say accordingly. I can address one person, but really intend my comments for somebody else who I know is overhearing us.

Earlier in this book we have seen that Schreber believed his voices were not aware of each other and spoke to him only and not to other people. The daemon of Socrates also only ever spoke to Socrates. It did so as a proxy of the divine, and Socrates in turn positioned himself as its proxy to fellow Athenians. Nothing *systematic* is known about the dialogical positioning of voice-talk, even though Schneider (1957) selected two particular formats to be first-rank symptoms of schizophrenia – voices talking to each other about patients overhearing them, and voices commenting on their actions or thoughts to the patients. There is, however, no reason to suppose that these are the major voice-talk participant positions, or those exclusive to schizophrenia (see Leudar *et al.*, 1997). But if voice-talk is a kind of unusual inner speech, the function of which is to regulate an individual's activities, one would expect the voices to be dialogically focused on the activities of voice hearers. One would not expect voices to attempt to participate in voice hearers' dialogues with others and to attempt to speak for themselves.

Most of our informants described their voices in one of two dialogical positioning formats. The first was for voices to speak one at a time, addressing the voice hearer, rather than another voice or another person, even when present ((19), lines 23–24 and line 72).

(19) DM and BI

23.   DM: Several, right. And do they, do they usually talk to you at one time, or all altogether?
24.   BI: Generally at one a (0.24) one at a time.
. . .
65.   DM: Right. Do they ever um do they ever kind of speak to you directly by name? Do they ever say?
66.   BI: Not by name no.
67.   DM: (informant's name)?
68.   BI: No, no, no, no. I've never heard 'em do that.
69.   DM: Right, right.
70.   BI: They probably will after this conversation.
71.   DM: (Laughs) Do they ever kind of refer to you as he or sh-she, or? Do they ever say?
72.   BI: They tend not to, um, refer to me in the third person. They tend to speak to me directly in the second person, but they just (0.77) use, in the first person rather (0.47), no (yeah?), I mean in the second person, I got (confused?) there. But, they say 'you', an' and all that, rather than (informant's name).

The second common participant format was to have several voices speaking at the same time, with each voice addressing the voice hearer. The informant TK, for instance, reported one voice urging one course of action, and another voice urging another course ((20), line 32)

(20) DM and TK

31.   DM: So do d'you ever hear more than one voice?
32.   TK: Sometimes I ge I can I can get in a psychosis about it, yeah, like, you know, it makes you go in a psychosis (s?), say you get about three voices at the same time and where they're coming from, you know what I mean (0.70), y'know, you you get a little worried in in your head and everything,

you know what I mean and you think oh, God, what's happening, y'know what I mean.

RO also reported hearing several voices at the same time together in a 'jumble' ((21), line 145). He does not, however, feel he is 'eavesdropping' (line 149).

(21) AG and RO

145. RO: Sometimes you get a bit of a jumble when maybe two, maybe three are talking at the same time. And often the exchanges, if there are any, are rapid and they talk over each other and it's all very hurried and impatient. A lot of interruption.
146. AG: They wouldn't ever speak on their own do you think?
147. RO: Oh. I think that it's easy to get confused here and imagine, you know, people talking all at once, but they are just sentences and often you get just one isolated sentence in one isolated voice and that will come and nothing more. But there may be other things going on around.
148. AG: Do they ever talk to each other with you overhearing them?
149. RO: There are exchanges back and forth but it's not like I'm eavesdropping or anything.

Finally, several informants reported hearing two or more different voices saying the same thing at the same time.

These two common participant arrangements were not mutually exclusive – some voice hearers reported experiencing both of them on different occasions.

So do voices tend not to speak to each other, contrary to Schneider's observation? The informant BN said that her father-voice and mother-voice talked to each other. On clarification it turned out, however, that her voices did not in fact address each other directly, but instead BN mediated between them. She would tell the father-voice about the mother-voice's criticism and then present the mother-voice with his reaction. Another informant, DS, reported hearing a male and a female voice whom he construed as a couple (22). He reported that the female voice occasionally backed the male voice in arguments, interrupting him, or censuring him for commanding DS. The two voices, however, did not talk *about* DS to each other.

(22) AG and DS

42. AG: Right. Do they each appear in different circumstances?
43. DS: Um (..) no they usually (..) it's usually him but sometimes she kind of interrupts.
44. AG: Is there any (..)
45. DS: not very (..)
46. AG: particular reason why she would?
47. DS: No, I don't know.
48. AG: OK. Um (..) and do they do different sorts of things?
49. DS: Um (..) like tell me different things?

50. AG: Yeah.
51. DS: Um (..) well (..) it's usually like him and then sometimes she's there and kind of backs him up in a way.
52. AG: Does each voice do different sorts of things? Like does one threaten and one be friendly and?
53. DS: Oh right, no you didn't ask me that. Um (..) well the man is usually like (..) um (..) bossing me about or giving me an order to do something. And the woman, I really don't know, she's kind of got a soft voice and she usually backs him up but sometimes tells me the total opposite but it's a much softer voice and it's much friendlier than the other voice.

TK was definite that her voices spoke to each other (23).

(23) AG and TK

203. AG. Right. Do they ever talk to each other with you overhearing them?
204. TK. They do talk together but um (. . .)
205. AG. What sort of things might they talk about?
206. TK. I don't know (. . .) here was one incidence when they were discussing things and I couldn't work out what they were talking about but it obviously wasn't for me to hear anyway. They were discussing something but they were waiting, they were deciding what they were going to show me so (. . .) it was (. . .) um (. . .) Well, yeah they were chatting (. . .) or communicating, that sounds better.

So overall, very few informants reported the format in which two or more voices address each other and the voice hearer is an overhearer and typically the voices were unclear.

So far we have considered the positioning of voices with regard to each other and the voice hearer. But how do voices relate to other people? Do they, for instance, attempt to address them? They could, so to speak, take control of the voice hearer's tongue (as is said to happen in spiritualist media and in other dissociative states) or they could use the voice hearers as willing proxies to convey messages to others. Such occurrences were simply never reported to us.

Voices are not, however, completely isolated from the social interactions in which the voice hearers take part. They comment on what others have said to voice hearers. This is what NJ reports in (24).

(24) PT and NJ

109. NJ: E:rm (0.53) in eh more more more recently (0.44) more recently (inaudible) my son got into trouble (0.46) erm in the last three weeks (0.65) a:nd (0.27) I actually s (dead husband's name deleted) oh wrong (0.23) (son's name), my son said to me 'Dad wouldn't have been impressed with this would he?' (0.35) and I heard him say (0.29) 'No, I wouldn't' (0.78).

110. PT: Oh right so (0.33) he does sometimes comment on other things
      | that people say | to you.
111. NJ: | Yea:h | yeah
112. and I didn't you know, apart from Jeremy reminding me of that (0.42) he
      would never even come into my mind but I heard him say it=
113. PT: =Ri:ght | right (inaudible).

NJ's narrative implies that her dead husband-voice was overhearing the conversation she was having with her son. This is consistent with NJ's view that it can be present even when it does not speak, but we cannot be sure whether NJ knew in this instance. She certainly did not say so or report any unusual bodily sentiments. Other voice hearers, however, also reported that their voices comment on what others have said to them, as well as on what they had said to others. This implies that voices are experienced as overhearers, known only to the voice hearers.

Our final consideration on the participant positioning of voices is whether voice hearers talk about voices to others or even *for* voices. Socrates spoke for his daemon, but Schreber only described his voices reluctantly. Most contemporary informants reported not mentioning voices to anybody, except occasionally to parents, psychiatrists or therapists. Hearing voices is a very private experience in this sense and reasons for this can vary. TK has a good reason to keep what his voices say to him from his friends (25).

(25) DM and TK

56. TK: I'd well (0.72), I get one saying 'you know', sometimes, or (0.85) 'you're evil' (0.59), or (0.48), 'slike 'cos it, with (0.40) someone, I ca- walk, I can walk into a room sometimes (1.05), I walked, like, for instance, last week I walked, last Sunday I walked into (0.52) smoke room an' Donna was sitting in there an' I got a voice as I was going in saying 'she's evil' (0.71), an' that to me was was terrible, I was sitting there like that, y'know sort of was like that, shaking, with me cigarette, y'know (0.70), 'cos I I don't I don't want people to (0.34), it's like a guilt thing as well (0.71), I don't want people to (0.56) to feel anything off me, you know what I mean y' don't (0.45) when you're getting me scared of people feeling (0.41) bad about you, y'know what I mean y s you get paranol ah paranoid about, that's why it's called paranoid schizophrenia you know I mean I think (0.83) you're just you're scared of people witnessing what you're going through, or hearing the voices. I've been through psychosis (0.46), because I've been scared of people being able to hear me voices.
57. DM: Yeah.

In other cases, voice-talk is mundane and concerns voice hearers' conduct, as we shall see in the next section. Such voice-talk is only interesting because it is voice-talk; otherwise it is not worth mentioning to anybody.

Sequential properties of voice-talk

The work in conversational analysis indicates that ordinary conversations are organised into sequential structures with adjacency pairs, for example, question–answer, request–refusal, assertion–agreement, and the different responses to the first parts of such pairs are normatively ordered in 'preference' (for example, agreement is 'preferred' to disagreement) with the 'dispreferred' responses marked, for instance, by pauses and pragmatic particles (Sacks and Schegloff, 1979). Taking turns in conversations is rule-governed (see Sacks *et al.*, 1974) and in general anybody can, for instance, ask questions, issue warnings or refuse to reply to a question. In some dialogues, however, the allocation of turns is notably asymmetric – doctors ask patients more questions in consultations and they recommend treatments; the right to give orders in the army depends on relative rank, and some children answer most questions in a class (see Marková and Foppa, 1991). Such asymmetries are not necessarily produced by prior institutional rules, and any two asymmetries in conversation may need to be explained in different terms (Drew, 1991; Schegloff, 1992).

What concern us in this section are sequential properties of voice-talk. The exchanges between Socrates and his daemon were restricted to what we might describe as forbid–obey pairs, with the daemon initiating, never Socrates. The reason for this asymmetry was their unequal wisdom – what could Socrates know that the daemon did not? And what could Schreber tell the supernatural about itself? With regard to the contemporary voice-talk, we need to know whether it is organised into the same sequential structures as ordinary talk, whether it displays the same preference organisation, and whether the positions of voices and voice hearers in it are equally distributed or asymmetric.

Most of our informants reported that the voices attempted to control their activities. Sometimes they would tell the voice hearer to carry out a particular action, which could be very mundane. BI reported voices which might tell him to 'push it (the door) open with left hand' ((26), line 46). His response would be to use his right hand.

(26) DM and BI

45.   DM: Right. Do they? I mean, how do you respond to the voice, if it says that to you?

46.   BI: Well, it depends what situation I'm in (0.83). If (0.98), if I've got any sense, I'll pay no attention to it. Oh, something that they do do (0.42) is things like, this (0.75) um (0.69) say you're walking along, or you're sitting somewhere, they'll try and (1.54) tell me what to do, as soon as I've made up my mind to do something, they try and tell me what to do, in some way. Or else, um, for instance I'm walking towards a door (0.52) and they might say something like 'push it open with your left hand' (0.75) so naturally I push it open with my right hand (1.19) and then they'd say 'told you', 'made you push it open with your right hand', 'knew you'd do that', and things like that, you know.

47.   DM: Right.

TK's voices told him to take a shower ((27), line 98).

(27) DM and TK

95.   DM: Oh. Do, um, do the voices ever, um, order you to do something?
96.   TK: Sometimes, yeah.
97.   DM: Do they, what what what might they say to you?
98.   TK: 'Have a shower', 'have a bath', or (1.32) they don't really bother me that much, though, I don't tend to get ordering voices, I just tend tend to get voices (0.94) that whisper to me, you know what I mean (0.59) er, not always whisper, what I mean is (0.95) I mean (0.54) they're only there if I listen for them as well, do you know what I mean Debs (0.84) they're only there if I listen for them (0.47) so. . . .

   In other cases the actions which voices urge are serious. RZ's voice tells him to injure himself in various ways, each of which is appropriate to his circumstances ((28), lines 88, 92), and sadly RZ sometimes obeys (lines 88–90)

(28) PT and RZ

85.   PT: Yeah. Could you give me an example?
86.   RZ: Well em (. . .) as as it was telling me to, like I say it was telling me to put a knife through me (. . .) you mean summat (. . .) summat like that, like er puttin' a knife
87.   PT: Yeah
88.   RZ: through me stomach. Going across the main road and actually jumping off (. . .) er (..) er (..) John Street car park. And it it (. . .) as, I'm pretty sure now that the voices were actually telling me to jump off this cliff.
89.   PT: Right. How long
90.   RZ: which I did do and that was t two years ago.
91.   PT: Two years ago. Right.
92.   RZ: And er (..) when I (.) when I was in here it was actually telling me to (.) to try and get some wires from the ceiling to electrocute myself. It were also telling me to climb up on the roof of this building to find to find the highest point to jump off of it and stuff like this, you see in ge in general. Even when I were here I thought I'm not even safe here it were like hiding trying to cope with it from me mind and telling it to just go away and leave me alone.
93.   PT: Right.

Note that RZ's reaction to self-destructive voice-talk is not always the same – he did obey the voice in the past but now he rejects the voice-directives.
   KL's voice tells her to assault others in ((29), lines 85, 91).

(29) RS and KL

82.   RS: OK, can you give me an example of when this might have happened when you, can sort of tell me what the voice actually said to you?

83.   KL: Err, There was one time when err (.) somebody had said something to me and which was not, somebody had made a comment about my arms and things like that, and

84.   RS: Ah ha

85.   KL: About the scars and that on them and I sort of ruded and that and the voice was saying 'hit her, hit her'

86.   RS: Right

87.   KL: And that's what it kept saying 'hit her' and then eventually I did hit her,

88.   RS: And when you did hit her did the voice then stop?

89.   KL: No,

90.   RS: What did the voice say then?

91.   KL: Just said, 'hit anybody'.

So the voices can issue simple commands which are relevant in the voice hearer's situation at the time. BI's voice in (26) regulated his current activity – he was about to open the door and the voice told him *how* to do so. RZ's voices in (28) told him to kill himself using electric wires which he had only just seen. KL's voice-directive in (29) was relevant to the insult she had just suffered and it could be understood as an encouragement rather than a command to do something which was alien to her. Note also that there are indeed voices which instigate violence – to oneself and to others – which as we have seen are foregrounded in the media. These are, however, clearly a minority of voice-talk.

Some informants also reported that their voices told them not to do something or discouraged them in more general terms. TL, for instance, reported that the voice of his deceased father tries to convince him that he cannot do things properly ((30), lines 16–18). So directive voice-talk does not necessarily only concern particular actions.

(30) AG and TL

11.   AG: And do you have a name for him?

12.   TL: Yeah, it's my father.

13.   AG: OK. Are there particular circumstances in which the voice will start?

14.   TL: Uh, yeah. When I feel (. . .) if I feel I can't do something I hear it then. If I feel I can do something with ease, I hear it then.

15.   AG: And what sort of things would he say?

16.   TL: He would (. . .) if I thought I couldn't do it he would convince me that I couldn't and if I feel I can do something very easily then he says it's kind of a waste of time or something similar to that.

17.   AG: Um (. . .) does the voice ever tell you to do things?

18.   TL: Yeah, not as specific actions but perhaps if I'm doing something he'll either tell me to give up and not carry on if that's what I really want to do.

In general, the voices managed our informants' activities by means of ordinary language, and the range of voice hearers' responses was what one finds in ordinary conversations. The preference organisation, however, seems not to be the same.

Statistically, the most frequent response to directive voice-talk was either to ignore it or to reject the particular directive, as RZ reported doing in (28) and again more colourfully in (31). Some reported challenging the right of the voices to judge them (see Leudar *et al.*, 1997).

(31) PT and RZ

110. RZ: (inaudible) that's what s beings said in me head. So when so when I'm like it said it it there were lights down the corridor and there were some wires erm like a loose loose light fitting and it was saying 'look up there' so I looked up there and it it said 'Pull some wires and electrocute yourself', but I said 'fuck off' (inaudible). I said 'fuck off and leave me alone'.
111. PT: Yeah.

The preference organisation of conversation is, of course, not a matter of statistics, but rather of norms. Many voice hearers reported to us that they never do what their voices tell them to *as a matter of policy*, and BI in (26) presented ignoring voices as a matter of good sense. But the rejection of a voice-directive need not be automatic, it can be reasoned – NI reported considering what the voices told her to do, and not carrying out the action (32).

(32) DM and NI

18. NI: It tells me to kill myself, you're the father, it say, things like that.
19. DM: What do you say to it – or do you talk back to it? ..
20. NI: Um, I think I think over it and try and think for it to go away 'cos I don't really like it.

But when voice hearers do as their voices tell them to, do they do so impulsively and without any consideration? Pierre Janet argued (see Chapter 4) that reactions to voice commands are automatic, and likewise the contemporary media some-times present voices as irresistible influences. It is in principle possible that voices could be in control of voice hearers' bodies in actions, impelling actions and putting voice hearers into positions of observers, as is the case in passivity experiences and dissociative disorders (see Putnam, 1989). This is of course not the mode of influence which is characteristic of ordinary conversation. Requests, for example, do not impel actions but rather provide reasons for acting in the way requested (cf. Grice, 1957; Searle, 1969). Whether or not one acts on a request is contingent on the situation and may depend, among other things, on how good the reason is, on the authority of the speaker and their mutual trust.

So how did our informants formulate the influences of voices on their conduct when they 'obey' them? Do they say that voices impel their actions without it being possible to resist, or do they see voices as advising, requesting or commanding in the ordinary sense? Do voice hearers say that their voices, not themselves, are responsible for their actions? The narratives we have provided so far indicate that voices do not inevitably, or even often, impel actions, and that the reasons for carrying out the voice-directives (or refusing them) are mundane. Some informants explained to us that they did what the voices told them because of the voice-talk's perseverance. KL's voice urged her repeatedly to hit somebody who made disparaging comments about her cut arms, and eventually she did. Other voice hearers said that they took the advice the voices gave them because it was good, or carried out their instruction because this was what they might have done anyway.

The problem is, however, that some informants indicated that voice-talk directives are difficult to resist, but why should this be so if voices are just talk, and the talk of madness at that? These voice hearers reported that their voice-talk was sometimes accompanied by irresistible urges. Let us return to KL: did she hit her abuser just because the voice told her to, or because this was also her own wish? We cannot say in her particular case but another informant, TR, formulated his dilemma to us. He knows that what his voices are urging on him is against his interests, but finds it difficult to resist (33).

(33) AG and TR

54.   AG: Does the voice ever tell you to do things?
55.   TR: Yes.
56.   AG: What sort of things?
57.   TR: Um (. . .) well when things get pretty heavy, I mean I don't know whether the voice or whatever you want to call it, when it comes on it tends to be telling me to do rather negative things. Urging me to act against my own interests, you know, doing things I shouldn't do.
58.   AG: Could you give me an example?
59.   It's not like commit a crime or anything like that but er I went through a particularly bad patch this summer and the start of this term when I was really depressed all the time um (. . .) and, you know, I can cope normally, but when something bad happens and you hit a real low and I just start getting urges to do things to my own body, not wise things if you know what I mean.
60.   AG: Right. So if they told you to do something would you normally do it?
61.   TR: No (. . .) not (. . .) sometimes (..) I don't know, I don't look at it in terms of them telling me to do something, it's not like little green men telling me to do this or that. It's kind of like this overwhelming urge to um (. . .) well I'm putting it in context like. A couple of weeks ago, a couple of months ago actually, I was sort of really depressed, you know for various reasons, and I started getting this urge to hurt myself. And a lot of the time I can sort of ride the storm out but a lot of the time I don't. I haven't had a really bad attack in ages but, yeah.

TR distinguished between coping with voices on a normal day from coping with them during personally difficult periods (when something happens and he is depressed and low ((33), lines 59, 61). Then he does not merely hear voices telling him to do 'negative things' (line 57) but he also gets 'urges to do things to his own body' (line 59). TR's problem is therefore that of resisting not the voice-talk, but his own urges ((33), line 61). Several other voice hearers reported urges accompanying voice-talk but, unlike TR, they did not see them as their own but as alien to them. The important point is that such urges are clearly not abstract cognitive phenomena that a computer could have. These urges are something very much embodied, what in NJ's case we referred to as bodily sentiments. (Remember that NJ said her voice was not simply an auditory experience but also a feeling of comfort and physical presence.) Should we separate formal pragmatic properties of voices from the accompanying bodily sentiments? This would be a step in a wrong direction because the two aspects are systematically related. We have observed three sorts of relationship: (1) the bodily sentiments can be used to establish the presence of voices even when they do not speak, (2) the spatial location of voices with regard to the voice hearers' bodies can be used as a cue to the status of a voice as a hallucination, and (3) the presence or absence of an urge must be considered when accounting for the effects of voice-directives. For these reasons we will not separate pragmatic and bodily aspects of voice-talk.

In any case, most voice hearers did not report conative urges accompanying voices, and the effects of voices on their activities were mediated, not direct. Most informants occasionally do as the voices tell them, but this is typically either because the actions indicated by the voices are reasonable and fit with their own plans, or because the voices are persistent and they are tired and want them to go away.

So far we have been concerned with voices telling voice hearers to do things. Voice hearers rarely tell voices to do things. This is not surprising since voices lack bodies, and our informants did not construe them as did Schreber, as supernatural agencies which could act in the world and affect it without bodies. Under this description what one can tell voices to do must be concerned with talking. Indeed, the most frequent thing our informants reported telling voices was to shut up and go away (see, for instance, the narratives 28 and 31 above). This rarely works. The conclusion, then, is that regulating actions in voice-talk is an asymmetric structure – voices regulate activities of voice hearers rather than the converse.

About half of our informants reported that voices judged them and their conduct. Voices would commend and even flatter (34) but as often they would be negative. NJ's voice ridiculed her and her conduct ((35), line 56).

(34) AN and KT

21. KT: I am not really good looking but I know that (0.66) there's a girl that I really fancy and she's very good looking
22. AN: ye:h

23.   KT: and y'd assume that I must be quite good looking to attract (0.46) this
       girl into my |li:fe (1.86)
24.   AN: |yeh
25.   KT: but I mean is the it's just an exaggeration (0.55) the voices just tell me
       that I'm orgasmatic that I'm really good looking (0.42) and that all girls will
       fall at me feet (0.60) and I and I hate that feeling 'cos it's not it's not the real
       me, the real me is | me
26.   AN: |mhm

(35) PT and NJ

54.   PT: So what what sort of things would would he say to you (1.34) | in those
       circumstances?
55.   NJ: | ((cough))
       erm
56.   I've got to think of an instance (0.40) uhm I can remember (0.26) there was
       quite some occasion I wasn't sleeping very well (0.46) and I would start
       (0.25) *missing* him and thinking of him (0.56) a:nd (0.52) remembering
       occasions where we were happy together (0.30) looking for comfort from
       him (0.38). But he would come and he would say 'you're being stupid, it
       never was like that' (0.53) 'you're being' erm (0.33) 'you're not being a
       proper mother' (0.28) 'you're neglecting things' (0.35) e:rm 'you're a mess'.
       It would be *very* derogatory to | me
57.   PT: | ri:ght
58.   NJ: you know he'd he'd say things like (inaudible) 'your hair's a mess' things
       that I really didn't want to hear at that time, 'cos I was hoping for some form
       of comfort | from him. (0.63)
59.   PT: | right

Nayani and David (1996) reported that abusive voices were the most frequent
in a sample of schizophrenics. Leudar *et al.* (1997) on the other hand found that
these were as common in informants with schizophrenia as in those without.
Leudar *et al.* also reported that voice-evaluatives usually targeted the voice hearers
and their conduct – we have seen that voices do comment on others but this is
reported relatively infrequently.

The reactions to these voice-judgements were like the reactions to voice-
directives. Most informants reported ignoring them, and a majority said that
occasionally they disagree verbally with voices. Some informants reported
rejecting voices' rights to judge them, but a quarter reported occasionally agreeing
with the voices' judgements, and telling them so. Overall, most of our informants
reported sometimes reacting to voices' judgements in words.

Voices therefore do not just tell the voice hearers what to do; they also judge
persons and their conduct. Schneider (1957) included voices commenting on a
person's thoughts and actions as a first-rank symptom of schizophrenia. In
pragmatic terms, the 'commenting' can mean that voices either critique plans and
intention and propose alternatives, or judge actions.

Leudar *et al.* (1997) reported that about half of the voice hearers reported that voices ask them questions. These questions are typically pertinent to voice hearers' mental states (36) and their ongoing activities (37), and sometimes they function as indirect requests.

(36) DM and TE

33. DM: Have the voices asked you questions ever?
34. TE: Many a time.
35. DM: Can you give me an example of one?
36. TE: 'Do you want a job, we'll get you a job, want a house, get you a flat.'
37. DM: Do you answer them back – what might you say?
38. TE. Yes.

(37) PT and NJ

121. PT: (0.54) Right. (2.23) Erm (0.64) do does does he ever ask you questions? (1.40)
122. NJ: Sometimes he'll say 'what are you doing now?' (0.52) 'Why are you doing this?' (1.11) a:nd e:rm ahm 'I don't like it.' (1.22)
123. PT: he says 'I don't like | it (why you doing it)?'
124. NJ: | mm:
125. PT: and when that happens, do you s: what do you, do you say anything back? or do you ignore it or? (0.30)
126. NJ: I ignore it. (0.43) | I try very hard to ignore it.
127. PT: | you i
128. PT: Right.

Voices were never reported to ask questions such as 'What time is it?', 'What is the weather like?' or 'Who won in the local elections?' Our informants also reported asking voices questions and being answered. According to cognitive theory of verbal hallucinations (e.g. Hoffman, 1986; Hoffman *et al.*, 1994), which sees them as fragments produced in the speech-planning process, there is no reason to expect that any questions addressed to voices would be answered. In fact Leudar *et al.* (1997) reported that only two of their informants were *never* answered by voices. The remaining informants reported receiving sometimes relevant answers from voices.

The final sequential structure we shall consider in voice-talk involves voices providing voice hearers with information. This structure was relatively less frequently reported than those we have considered already. In many cases the information provided would either be something known to the voice hearer but out of mind, or predictions typically concerning consequences of voice hearers' activities. Most voice hearers reported not providing voices with information, except in response to questions.

To summarise sequential regularities in voice-talk: it is centred on the regulation of voice hearers' present conduct. The experience is characterised by the same dialogical structures one finds in ordinary speech, and the activities managed by voices are most frequently mundane. Most of our informants did not report that their voices urged violence or that they were impelled to carry out the actions. In most cases the influence of voices and its lack were mediated by the voice hearers' will and reason. In some cases, however, voice-talk can be accompanied by urges which are difficult to resist. This might be a good moment to reconsider the presentations of voices and voice hearers in the mass media (see Chapter 8). They are hardly representative.

The properties of voice-talk are on the whole consistent with voices being a type of private or inner speech. This is what we have claimed elsewhere (Leudar *et al.*, 1997) and what Sass concluded about Schreber's voices – according to him, the 'birds' were Schreber's own inner speech which he misconstrued as a super-natural agency. The narratives collected in this chapter show that 'inner speech' is not, however, how any voice-hearers categorise the experience of hearing voices. Does this mean that they all therefore commit reality-testing errors? We shall see in the final section of this chapter that this is not so.

On mundane reality testing

The common explanation of hallucinations in cognitive psychology and psychiatry is in terms of reality-testing failures. In Chapter 1 we outlined the debate among French psychiatrists in the nineteenth century on whether there are psychological errors which are necessarily involved in hallucinations. The discussants singled out two kinds of error. One was to confuse different psychological processes; for instance, perception with fantasy or with memory. The other error was to believe that one's experience was caused by objects in one's environment when in fact it was internally generated. Freud (1923/1927) used the term 'reality testing' to name a process essential to the ego. This process allows a person to distinguish between what she perceives, and what she remembers or imagines. Pierre Janet (1925, p. 287) on the other hand thought that reality-testing errors were the least interesting thing about verbal hallucinations. Bleuler (1911/1966, pp. 102–103) accepted that some hallucinations 'are recognised as hallucinations' as they are experienced, but then he set these aside as 'pseudo-hallucinations'.

Rae Story has surveyed the recent conceptions of 'reality testing' in cognitive psychology and psychiatry, and found them to be surprisingly varied. First, they turn out to involve a family of distinctions, including those between:

- imaginary and real (Al-Issa, 1978);
- internal and external (Sarbin, 1967; Johnson and Raye, 1981),
- ideational and perceptional (Strauss, 1969);
- stimulus-intentions and plan-intentions (Frith, 1992).

The processes postulated by psychologists to allow persons to accomplish and maintain such distinctions are also varied. In psychoanalytic accounts poor reality testing is a matter of regression to childhood and 'an expression of instinctual, wish-fulfilment fantasies' (Sass, 1992, p. 273). In cognitive psychiatry or psychology, reality testing is usually defined as a meta-cognitive, inferential skill (Bentall, 1990). People are, for instance, said to use cognitive effort pre-consciously to establish that an experience has been intentionally produced, rather than evoked by environmental stimuli. Hallucinators, however, are said not to use 'cognitive effort' effectively as a reality cue (see Hoffman, 1986; Bentall *et al.*, 1991).

Perhaps it is obvious by now that many voice hearers hear voices and know that they are hallucinating. UN heard the words 'What do you want', thinking that 'he was hearing things' (43). His insight did not eradicate the experience, and this is so in general: knowing that one is hearing a voice does not make the experience go away. There is thus a problem for the account in terms of cognitive reality testing: according to it, the hallucinations presuppose reality-testing failures, and yet what the voice hearers say about voice-talk makes it perfectly clear that they are not confusing objective and subjective realities, or perception and fantasy. In our sample of about fifty voice hearers, of whom about two-fifths were at one time in their life or another diagnosed as schizophrenic, only one person, EF, reported what Bleuler would accept as a true hallucination: she integrated the voice into the environment and treated it as real. We have already proposed that it is easier to accuse Schreber of being deluded than of having reality-monitoring problems. Sass (1992, pp. 275–276) agrees that schizophrenics, in our terms, do not typically confuse voice-talk for real speech, and he explains this with the concept of double bookkeeping, which he refers to Bleuler (1911/1966, p. 127). Sass provides a useful critique of 'reality testing' but we would rather not apply the concept of double bookkeeping to hearing voices. It is a technical term which divides experience into two domains, pathological and normal, irrespective of the contingencies between two *for the patient*, and it can also allow the pathological chapters to represent the whole 'book'. Our own interests at this point are empirical: to establish what categories voice hearers use for their experiences, and what procedures they follow to accomplish the categorisations.

Most voice hearers certainly do not think that others share their experiences. The informant UN makes this clear to the interviewer (38).

(38) PT and UN

537. PT: Now (0.83) other people who would eh be around you when you're hearing the voice, would they be able to hear the voice? (0.45)
538. UN: Oh no=
539. PT: =No=
540. UN: =No.

KL also knows that others cannot hear his voice ((39), line 104), and he uses this knowledge to part-warrant his stance that the 'voice isn't real'. It is not real because it is in his head and because no one can hear it. John Austin (1962b) recommended that one should answer the question 'Is it real?' with 'Real what?' So what exactly is it that KL's voice isn't? What would it be were it to be real?

The voice is for KL a real *experience* (he hears it in his head (line 104) and if he did not, there would be no hallucination to consider). The voice is not a real *person* like KL (line 102). So KL's voice is not just an auditory experience, it has communicative agency – yet it is not a real person.

(39) RS and KL

 99. RS: You can't remember, OK that's fine, um (..) OK, um would you, do you see differences between the voice and yourself?
100. KL: Yeah,
101. RS: Like what?
102. KL: I am real, but the voice isn't real
103. RS: Right OK, and how do you know it's not real, how do you identify it as not being real?
104. KL: Because it is in my head and no one else can hear it.

But how do voice hearers know that other people cannot hear their voices? KL's warrant was that he heard the voice in his head. UN reported using another mundane procedure – when he started hearing the voice he simply asked his wife ((40), lines 541–546, 550–551).

(40) PT and UN

541. PT: Have you checked that out with people?
542. UN: Oh yeah=
543. PT: =Yeah?=
544. UN: =Well the with the wife you know.
545. PT: Yeah. (0.23) 'cos she said 'no well I can't hear it.' (0.89)
546. UN: I I asked her if if we'd got a bloody e:r wh er when I was in Spain, I said, 'Is this place wired for sound or what.' (0.44)
547. PT: Right. Did it sound like it was coming from a loudspeaker or s|omething like that?
548. UN: | Well, I that's all I could imagine, you know.
549. PT: Ye:ah (0.45)
550. UN: I said 'can't you hear it?' She said 'what you ta: | what you're talking about' y'know=
551. PT: | Yeah.

It is, of course, not our argument that *every* voice hearer is *always* clear that only he or she can hear the voice. Another of our informants, TK, does not actually think that others can hear the voice insulting his friend, but he is frightened by the possibility ((41), line 56).

(41) DM and TK

56. TK: I don't want people to (0.56) to feel anything off me, you know what I mean y' don't? (0.45) when you're getting me scared of people feeling (0.41) bad about you, y'know what I mean y s you get paranol ah paranoid about, that's why it's called paranoid schizophrenia you know I mean I think (0.83) you're just you're scared of people witnessing what you're going through, or hearing the voices. I've been through psychosis (0.46), because I've been scared of people being able to hear me voices.

57. DM: Yeah.

TK places the fear of people hearing his voices into the periods of psychosis (and into the past). Right now he is not frightened that others can hear his voices. In other words, his account allows for the reality-monitoring failure, but it is an aspect of psychosis, not of hearing voices. If this is an instance of double bookkeeping, then double bookkeeping is a contingent social matter, and KL accomplished it in the interview with the help of a now/then distinction.

So like Schreber, the contemporary voice hearers can know that only they hear their voices, and they know this on the basis of simple reality-testing procedures of which they are aware, and which they can report. These mundane reality-testing procedures are unlike the internal pre-conscious reality-monitoring devices, the failures of which are said to result in reality confusions.

This is not to say that hearing voices is not perplexing – we have seen this in many of the excerpts – but the puzzlement need not be dealt with by delusional interpretations, rather with the help of mundane procedures. One is to establish the source of the voice, and UN does this – he looked around for the source of the sound. The second procedure is to seek social consensus – UN asked his wife (40). Only then does UN report that he also thought that he was being tricked ((42), lines 53 and 55).

(42) PT and UN

45. UN: Yeah (0.86) Yeah (0.26) three or four people that's all, you know not many (0.31) just me. (1.25) and er (0.28) 'What d'you want? what d'you want'. (0.24)

46. PT: This ah and wh what did you do when that happen|ed?

47. UN: |I th I thought I was well I thought I'd say I thought I was *hearing things* which obviously I was, you know.

48. PT: Did you turn around to see where t | it was

49. UN: |Yeah to see where it were coming from.

50. PT: And where was it coming from?

51. UN: It wasn't (1.51) *nowhere*.

52. . . .

53.   UN: I *thought* it was something playing *games* to be quite honest.
54.   PT: | ri::ght |
55.   UN: | I thought it was | somebody having me on you know. (0.25) I w're I
      were looking round like this ((laughs)) here.
56.   PT: Right, Right

The informant NC follows the same procedures (43).

(43) PT and NC

25.   PT: OK, now just going back to the voices, how, what are the sort of
      properties, of the voices, I mean are they male or female?
26.   NC: The err one that the, the first one that I heard and I have heard quite
      a few times, *I don't know* I can't tell if that is male or female, it's clear but I
      can't tell, ehm (0.56) the: second one that I heard re:cently °right° ((asp)) *was
      my friend* (2.4)
27.   PT: ye your partner?
28.   NC: *Ye:h*=
29.   PT: =yeh
30.   NC: it was ↑*he:r*↓
31.   PT: °Right° (3.60) so, so you know very clearly that (0.67) em I mean it that
      it's: *her voice*, you can tell even if it | didn't (unclear) |
32.   NC: | Second one was | yeah yeah it was *it was
      definitely her* because I even had asked her if she'd come down to ma because
      I thought she might've come down to my *door*=
33.   PT: = ri:ght
34.   NC: has been and I hadn't eh I've been in the kitchen or something and I
      hadn't heard *the bell* (0.46) and she'd called me=
35.   PT: =ri:ght=
36.   NC: =y'know (0.70) °and eh° I even went to the front door thinking she
      was at the front door (0.30)
37.   PT: So it was very | real and vivid for you |
38.   NC: | (unclear) It was her | yeah yeah yeah (0.38)
39. | She said | no she hasn't=
40.   PT: | Did | =ri:ght so it didn't even need to introduce
      itself to you you just *knew* the change of her | voice because you knew her
      voice (??) |.
41.   NC: | Yeah °yeah°
            yeah |

NC's voice was sufficiently similar to that of her friend for her to go to the door to
check whether she was there calling her (43), and she phoned her for the same
reason. NC is reporting doing this to support her claim that the voice was so like
that of her friend. One could object that NC is confused; after all, she does go to
the door because of the voice. But the voice did not *tell her* to go to the door. She

went to the door to establish *whether* her friend was there (line 36). In other words, the experience is presented as being so lifelike as to afford reality confusion, but she resolves it by means of two simple procedures – she asked the voice analogue, and she established the absence of the voice-source. Note also that the distinction she is working with is between 'real person' and 'the voice', not between internal and external.

NJ's problem is different from NC's: her voice analogue is dead. Her problem is accomplishing a sensible relationship between the voice and the memories of her deceased husband. We have seen that she does not do this by formulating a theory or by becoming a spiritualist, but instead with the help of a family of linguistic referential devices: she refers to her voice differently in different contexts. Finally, NJ does not have to invoke any reality-testing procedures because she knows the voice. It seems therefore that the need to invoke a reality-testing procedure may depend on what kind of voice is being experienced. UN was describing the first time he heard the voices, NC was describing the first time she heard the voice of her friend, and NC was talking about a voice she knew for five and a half years.

It seems then that hearing voices does not necessarily involve making psychological or ontological errors. Voice hearers know that other people cannot hear their voices. This is in fact what is in part enigmatic about the experience. What is usually supposed to be an error causing the experience is actually a constitutive part of it.

So what have we learned in this final chapter about the present-day meaning of 'hearing voices'? It seems to be an *intrinsically* mundane experience. Voices do not reveal to voice hearers metaphysical secrets, nor do they give them privileged access to mundane knowledge. The foremost function of voice-talk is to regulate voice hearers' conduct, and it mainly accomplishes this through directing and judging. The agency of voices is primarily of a moral sort and the interesting point is that voice-talk is not fundamentally senseless. We have seen that voice-directives can be inimical to the voice hearer, instigating self-injury or suicide – but even then the voice-talk can make apt use of the resources which the current environment provides. (And we have also seen that not all voice-talk is necessarily intrinsically antagonistic.)

Voice hearers usually construe voice-talk as more than just sound – they typically invest it with at least a communicative agency. Should voices be considered to be the same sorts of persons as the voice hearers and other people? Perhaps not literally. The reasons for this clarification are threefold: voices lack social reflexivity, which is an essential characteristic of human individuals, and their social world is almost restricted to their voice hearers. Moreover, voices lack embodiment, even though they may be accompanied by bodily sentiments and urges that are alien to the voice hearer. These are, however, typically not considered to be their aspects.

Hearing voices, however, clearly carries an enigma and always did. It is an enigma which originates in two of its properties which are difficult to explain. The first is negative – the experience happens in the absence of a mundane source of sound. The second is that hallucinatory voices single out the voice hearer. How do they do this? The experience has never been common, and even though the voice-talk can be reported to others, only the voice hearer can experience it at the time. The voices thus stress the aloneness of a person. The enigma of voices is built as these two properties are explained: 'Why is the voice hearer singled out – is he a visionary or a madman? Are the voices a rare contact with the supernatural and its affirmation, or are they meaningless symptoms of insanity?' We have not even tried to answer these questions, and instead our aim was to understand what puzzles voice hearers themselves. The voice hearers who spoke to us did not just formulate general accounts of hearing voices – they also understood voice-talk as it took place in particular circumstances.

10 Conclusion

We began this book in ancient Athens, passed through nineteenth-century Paris and the *fin de siècle* Salpêtrière, through the Sonnenstein Asylum in Saxony and returned to Britain at the end of the twentieth century. So now we know what 'hearing voices' really is. Or do we? This depends on what kind of knowledge is sought.

If one asks specific questions, this book provides some definite answers. If you ask, for instance: 'What was it like to hear voices in the Sonnenstein Asylum in Germany at the end of the nineteenth century?', we can say that Daniel Paul Schreber took his voices to be of supernatural beings to which only he had access, but his psychiatrist Guido Weber thought them to be hallucinations and psychiatric symptoms of insanity. Schreber's privilege and his duty to act on what the voices told him were also his madness. You could also ask: 'What was it like for Socrates to hear the daemon?' According to Plutarch, the daemon was a voice and a bridge to the divine and the source of his wisdom. Only Socrates could hear it because of his virtuous life, and he and others heeded the daemon's advice. But again, even in Athens so long ago the experience was controversial – Plutarch conceded that some of Socrates' contemporaries thought that listening to voices and using them to justify deeds was superstition and humbug, but of course these were unwise young men who had no respect for tradition. In British newspapers at the end of the twentieth century the meaning of hearing voices is also definite. Voices are heard by people who are mentally ill, and they instigate violence and displace reason – Anthony Smith's voices were effective where reason and love for his family should have been. But again there is an element of controversy: the presentations of voices in British media often contrast two unequal versions of voices – the objective one of medical psychiatry and the irrational one of the insane. This inequality of status became stark in Schreber's case when the opposing versions met in a court of law. So there is a variety of answers as to what voices are – they are different matters in different historical places. Similarly, if one asks whether the voices somebody claims to hear are real, one will get a different answer depending on where one is asking – for instance, they are real (or false) gods, or symptoms, or experiences. (And this book probably underestimates the varieties of meaning of hearing voices available – we did not even look at the experience in contemporary cultures other than our own.)

This context-contingent knowledge may not be what you are after – 'But what are the voices like irrespective of all these historical contingencies?' you might ask. (After all, Galileo did not discover the moons of Jupiter just for sixteenth-century Florentines, Padovans or Romans, and Newton did not discover his law of gravity to apply just in England of the seventeenth century.) It is difficult to provide a definite answer to the timeless question 'what is it?', and this is not just because we do not know enough or because there is nothing to say which does not mention context. In fact, hearing voices does have some basic features through history – it is always an experience which only a few people have, they hear voices when the mundane sources (i.e. ordinary people) are absent, what the voices say typically pertains to the voice hearers' activities, and the regulative effect is achieved not by impulsion but authoritatively and by reference to moral codes. We have seen that more than two thousand years apart, Plutarch and Esquirol were perplexed by the same phenomenon – how can one person hear voices when others who are present do not, and when nobody is talking? But they solved the problem differently – Plutarch by reference to privileged access to the divine, Esquirol by categorising voices as hallucinations which he explained as being caused by the 'intense activity of the brain'. But of course not all the historically recurring properties of voices are psychological – we have seen that hearing voices has always been an experience with a socially contested meaning.

So can we not treat contextual variations as errors, combine the materials from all the different historical periods, and distil the real 'hearing voices' from them? We could then say that this is the core 'experience of hearing voices' and treat this as a phenomenon to be explained scientifically. Well, there is a logical problem with this – did we really discover that hearing voices had the same properties in all these times and places? Not quite – we identified these experiences in each of them on the basis of our contemporary meaning (or, as in the case of Socrates and the *Iliad*, this identification has been done for us previously by somebody else). So it is hardly surprising that they turned out to have some properties in common. What we actually discovered were the substantial differences between the phenomena we started by categorising as being the same. What we encountered were the limits to applying one's concepts in the past and the historical situatedness of our own thinking and psychology – this was very clear in the case of French psychiatrists who rewrote the past with the concept of hallucination with no regard for the local meaning.

The timeless and universal question 'what is hearing voices? period' is therefore not a happy one – it impoverishes the phenomenon studied. It impoverishes it because it treats as incidental and unimportant its context-contingent aspects. In psychology, which aims at biological and evolutionary explanations of mind, the timeless question implies that there is a basic, raw experience of hearing voices, which is given different clothes in different historical periods – but, like the Emperor, it is thought to remain the same underneath and sometimes it walks without them. This position is clearly not supported by the materials we have provided in this book. As there are no mechanical behaviours (except in abstractions) which become intentional conduct when combined with psychological phenomena, so there are no raw experiences which become meaningful under descriptions but can be lived without them. Conduct and experience are always lived under descriptions and these are historically specific. So the general conclusion is really that local concepts are constitutive of local experiences and there cannot be a psychology or psychiatry which can do without them.

You may say that if this is so, how does one explain voices, or can one not explain what they (and other psychological phenomena) are? We have deliberately not provided a theory of hearing voices in this book, even though we have partly done so elsewhere when we argued that hearing voices is really an ego-alienated inner speech (see, for example, Leudar *et al.*, 1992, 1994, 1997). In fact we began this book from that position, but in researching it and writing it, it became obvious that this point of departure barred us from understanding the experiences of voice hearers with conceptions different from our own. We have seen, for instance, that D.P. Schreber had a twofold 'outside' (one mundane and one supernatural) and so his distinction between what is inner and outer was very different from that which operates in cognitive psychology. This meant in turn that the notion of reality testing did not apply in any straightforward way, but we could not resolve the problem by saying that Schreber was wrong – we had to take on board his way of thinking to understand the logic of his experiences.

So we have avoided formulating a theory, not because it is not possible to provide historically contingent scientific explanations, but because formulating one's own theory may transform the phenomenon being explained – this was painfully obvious in the case of Pierre Janet, who provided a very apt account of hearing voices but also disbelieved what his patient Marcelle told him about her voices because he knew that they were impulsive *repetitions* of fixed ideas. We have therefore focused on what accounts the participants themselves provided for hearing voices and how this affected what they could do with them in interactions with other people.

So is hearing voices not an indication of insanity? Clearly not always in history. Voices become categorised as hallucinations indicating pathology in the work of Pinel and Esquirol, and as verbal hallucinations in the work of Pierre Janet. Certainly talking to the gods in the *Iliad*, and to daemons in Socrates' Athens, was not in itself madness. Does hearing voices, or if you like, auditory and verbal hallucinations, indicate mental illness nowadays? The fact is that it can, as the psychiatric diagnostic manuals such as the DSM-4 and the ICD-10 document. But should it? We have seen in Chapters 6 and 9 that there are many individuals who hear voices and yet have no psychiatric problems. Our argument has been that hearing voices in itself does not indicate mental illness any more than do thinking, remembering or any other ordinary psychological functions, even though *some* modes of thinking can indicate schizophrenia and *some* modes of memory imply trauma and abuse.

Notes

1 The daemon of Socrates

1   James (1995) provides an interesting analysis of how the medical sense of the word 'hallucination' entered the common French usage. According to him this was through the novels of Victor Hugo (*Notre-Dame de Paris*) and Honoré de Balzac (*La Comédie humaine*) who borrowed the concept.

2   Two kinds of self-directed speech are usually distinguished in developmental psychology – 'private speech' and 'inner speech'. The former is simply speaking to oneself aloud and can be overheard by others. The latter is conversing with oneself silently and so it cannot be completely co-experienced with others. In other respects, however, both inner and private speech use the ordinary lexicon and grammar of, say, English. We shall only use the term 'private speech' to avoid the implicit spatial metaphor, and the consequent implication that inner dialogues take place 'in the head'. In our sense 'privacy' of private speech is not somehow automatic but a situated accomplishment. We are not using the term 'private speech' to mean anything like 'private language', the notion savaged by Wittgenstein.

3   When we say that we *hear* somebody speaking, we imply that somebody has indeed said something which was or could have been heard by many. Hearing speech presupposes an author and medium. We can, however, bracket the author and the stimulation and talk about the *experience* (of hearing somebody speaking). Experience thereby achieves some mental autonomy. Plato, Xenophon or Plutarch (or at least their translators), however, do not use the word 'experience' in this mentalistic way – as 'just experience'. Plato talks about 'divine experience', which belongs to Socrates but is divinely caused.

4   Try the contrary exercise. Why is watching television not a hallucination? Try to imagine the grounds which would make it so.

5   We need to bear in mind that what we are told of the daemons at this point of 'On the sign of Socrates' comes from 'a voice', not directly from Plutarch, and neither is it presented as Socrates' own understanding of these matters. It is ambiguous whether this rhetorical strategy is meant to present the information as a conjecture or as something one can depend on – what the daemon tells Socrates is not doubted by him, but Plutarch also refers to 'the myth of Timarchus'.

2 The gods of Achilles

1   Neither of us reads Ancient Greek and so in our analysis we used two translations of the *Iliad* – by Rieu and Lattimore. The texts used in this chapter are Lattimore's translation.

2   Perhaps experiences are not just described but conceptualised through and through.

3   In Book XI: 555–557 Homer describes a battlefield retreat as follows: 'so Aias, disappointed at heart, drew back from the Trojans, much unwilling, but feared for the

ships of Achaians' (Lattimore trans.). Rieu uses two psychological terms in his translation – 'Thus in such discontent, Aias withdrew before Trojans, much against his will
and acutely conscious of the danger to the Achaian ships.'

4 This is how Rieu translated the passage: 'The man is raving mad. If he had ever learnt
to look ahead, he would be wondering now how he is going to save his army when
they are fighting by the ships.'

5 We have already seen that Homer used unique speech-reporting devices to indicate
that a hero was speaking to himself. Is god–hero talk also set aside from ordinary talk
in some way? No – Homer narrates the talk between the gods and Achilles using
exactly the same reporting devices that he uses to report the talk between mortals. For
instance, the phrases used in one episode are as follows: Achilles 'uttered winged words
and addressed her'. . . . 'Then in answer the goddess grey-eyed Athene spoke to him'.
. . . 'Then in answer again spoke Achilleus of the swift feet' (*Iliad* I: 188–221). Gods
come in the same sensory modalities as humans and their interactions are presented as
ordinary talk.

6 Compare this to the experience of John Bunyan, who heard 'a voice' 'from heaven'
while playing the game of cat. It offered him a choice: 'Wilt thou leave thy sins, and
go to Heaven? Or have thy sins, and go to Hell?' At the time he opted for sins as he
thought he was damned already (Bunyan, 1962, para 22: lines 16–25, and cf. Janet,
1903, p. 59; Royce, 1894).

7 But then rewarding with prizes in the *Iliad* is related to the heroes' honour.

8 Zanker pointed out that one must be analytically sophisticated – Homer and his
characters were not contemporary and his ethics were different from those of his
heroes. So it is necessary to distinguish between the practical ethics of Homer and
those of the characters. (Are they just *his* characters?) The narrator 'may construct his
characters to convey a background ethical scenario against which he may oppose
his own.'

9 So Achilles definitely does not have one of the first-rank symptoms of schizophrenia –
hearing voices discussing him in the third person. But then the participant positioning
corresponding to this Schneiderian symptom is uncommon even today, as we shall see
in Chapter 9.

3 The souls of Daniel Paul Schreber

1 Some passages in the *Memoirs* imply that Schreber may have heard Ariman/Ormuzd
or sensed him in nerve language. He complicates the issue for the reader. First, some
voices 'pretend' to be the god, and he hears them, not the god. At another point
Schreber writes that the god's distress at being in nerve fusion with him is evidenced
by 'continual cries for help which I daily hear in the sky from those parts of the nerves
which have become separated from the total mass of nerves' (1903/1955, p. 204).
These cries for 'help' are 'of those of god's nerves separated from the total mass, [and
they] sound the more woeful the further away god has withdrawn from me, and the
greater therefore the distance which those nerves have to travel, obviously in a state of
some anxiety' (ibid., p. 205). So these cries are again not those of Ariman/Ormuzd
himself. Schreber also mentions hearing a phrase 'We want to destroy your reason',
which he interprets as 'emanating' from 'the upper god' (Ormuzd). But again it turns
out that the contact is mediated – what Schreber actually hears is not the god, but his
proxies, the 'birds' (ibid., pp. 206ff., 86). One passage where Schreber unequivocally
reports hearing the god is as follows:

the lower God appeared. The radiant picture of his rays became visible to my inner
eye . . . that is to say he was reflected on my inner nervous system. Simultaneously I
heard his voice; but it was not a soft whisper – as the talk of the voices always was

before and after that time – it resounded in a mighty bass as if directly in front of my bedroom window. The impression was so intense, so that anybody not hardened to terrifying miraculous impressions as I was, would have been shaken to the core. Also what was spoken did not sound friendly by any means: everything seemed calculated to instil fright and terror into me and the word 'wretch' was frequently heard.

(Ibid., p. 124)

2   Schreber's double god Ariman/Ormuzd is in this respect much like Zeus in the *Iliad*. Achilles and Schreber do not talk to them directly but through proxies.
3   Schreber argued that psychiatric management increased the attacks of bellowing, rather than helping him. In his view the attacks were triggered by his forced stay in the Asylum:

The attacks of bellowing almost never occur when I am engaged in loud conversation, am in educated company or move outside the Asylum, on steamships, railways, public places, or in the streets of the town etc., but in the main are only observed when I am alone in my room or in Asylum's garden among lunatics with whom conversation is impossible.

(Schreber, 1903/1955, p. 416)

His position was that to return him into civil society was the best that could be done for him.
4   We have focused on the arguments in the court rather that on the social context of the case. This is clearly important. Lothane (1992, 284–291) describes contemporary attacks on the legal misuses of psychiatry, for instance in newspapers and in the Reichstag, and he reports that Weber responded for psychiatry in an article in 1902 (only a year before the *Memoirs* were published), claiming it is seldom that individuals are hospitalised without a good psychiatric reason. Moreover, it seems that Schreber's was not the only case in which Weber was involved.

4   Pierre Janet on verbal hallucinations

1   Janet described consciousness as 'that act by which multiplicity and diversity of states is attached to a unity' (1910, p. 56).
2   Janet accepts that there is a distinction between external and personal, and that his hysterical patients may confuse these. But this is something to be explained, not used as a basis for an explanation (1910, pp. 54–55). 'Psychasthenic patients ... are not completely insane and recognise the absurdity of their obsessing ideas' (p. 57).
3   Janet's stance on the evolution of language was consistently pragmatic. Speech was originally part of activities: 'The gestures which gave birth to language were nothing more than particular movements, which were an integral part of the action' and language separated from actions in commands: 'The chieftain learns to do no more than give the sign, and to stop there without continuing the action himself; the subordinate learns not to repeat the sign, but to complete the action of which the sign was the first stage' (1925, p. 233). For Janet the regulative function of language is historically basic and for him that language is essentially intersubjective – what was an individual action becomes distributed over the 'chief' and the 'subordinate'. Moreover, according to Janet the separation between actions and language is never complete: 'doubtless the separation between the word and the deed has never been complete; otherwise the word would have lost all meaning'. Janet does not regard the increasing autonomy of language as something good. According to him the result is loss of meaning (ibid., pp. 232–234).
4   Marie, terrified by her first period, stopped the blood flow by taking freezing baths.

She was successful, but the memory became a fixed idea which would emerge during her periods. Janet reports that she hallucinated the event subconsciously: 'she is normally conscious of nothing of this and does not even understand that the chill is the consequence of the hallucinations of the cold bath; it is therefore likely that this scene takes place below the surface of consciousness.'

5   Janet commended Bernheim rather half-heartedly for refusing physiological reductionism but criticised him in the same paragraph for a too inclusive definition of suggestion: 'for Bernheim the word suggestion is a synonym of the hoary general terms "thought", "psychological phenomenon", "phenomenon of consciousness"' (1925, p. 214).

6   Janet on the subconscious and pathology: 'clear cut phenomena truly comparable to subconsciousness of hysterics are infinitely rare in the normal mind' (1910, p. 68).

7   Janet has nothing against repetition in general, but repetition of an action must not be automatic if it is to be a complete action – it must fit into the current personal life of the doer and into the current environment. Indeed, repetition in these two aspects has an important function in bringing the past into the present.

8   Janet saw no need for interpretation: 'The poor patients whom I studied had no genius; the phenomena which had become subconscious with them were very simple phenomena, such as among other men are a part of their personal consciousness and excite no wonder' (1910, p. 62).

5   Pragmatists on self

1   It is important to bear in mind that James considered this to be a possibility and no more. It would be wrong to see the division as a cornerstone of his account of self.

2   Quoting Ribot perhaps expresses James' doubt about what the introspection revealed to him. Did he really equate 'feeling of life' with 'proprioceptions in the head'?

3   This is not to deny that speakers occasionally talk to themselves even when others are present. Such talk is, however, formulated in such a way that the self-addressivity is clear. It is also possible to use pronouns in such a way that it is clear that the speaker is also one of the addressees. The point is though that both of these cases are exceptional and must be accomplished.

4   The reaction is 'inner' but for Mead the word inner does not mean 'cognitive'. He does not divide acts into cognitive antecedents and mechanical executions. Rather, like Dewey (1896), he sees acts as having continuous private and external parts.

5   'The relative values of the "me" and the "I" depend very much on situation' (Mead, 1934, p. 199). Both aspects of the 'I' and 'me' 'are essential to the self in its full expression' (ibid.).

6   Mead allowed human experiences and actions which are not referred to self: 'self is not necessarily involved in the life of organism'. He implies, however, that habitual actions are the only modes of activity open to the 'lower forms of animal life' but humans can act both reflexively and habitually. The practical relationship between the two is not clear in his account.

7   What is the relationship between the 'generalised other' and the 'me'? Mead made more use of the former in *The Philosophy of the Act*, and of 'me' in *Mind, Self and Society*, and he did not explicitly compare the two terms. We note, however, that he discussed the 'generalised other' in terms of responses, and 'me' in terms of 'attitudes'. He also implies that the responses of 'generalised other' are based on attitudes of 'me'.

7   Working with voices

1   At the initial assessment (1994), Peg's ICD-9 diagnosis was schizophrenia (residual), with 'second person auditory hallucinations'. But there were problems with the diagnosis, because of evidence of dissociative phenomena. On one occasion she described what

appeared to be a fugue state while hearing voices, as well as unexplained perceptual disturbances in which she felt reduced in size in comparison with objects around her (her EEG was normal).

2 We shall examine this issue in detail in Chapter 9 where we provide the results of an empirical study of voice hearers, and consider the way in which people respond to instructions and commands given by voices.

3 On another occasion Peg said that she had often signed herself JCM in the past, indicating that this part of herself was still important to her.

8 Voices in British national newspapers

1 We used Internet and CD-ROM versions of the newspapers rather than the printed versions.

2 DoH (1998) Press Release, Department of Health, Tuesday, 8 December 1998.

3 DoH (1999) Press Release, Department of Health, Thursday, 21 January 1999.

4 In 1989 Sane (Schizophrenia – A National Emergency) was attacked for its use of negative and inaccurate images of people with mental health problems in an advertising campaign. This included negative and inaccurate statements such as 'He thinks he is Jesus; you think he's a killer; they think he's fine' alongside images of distressed-looking people.

9 Voice-talk

1 The two models receive some empirical support from our own past work. Leudar *et al.* (1992) found a relatively high frequency of speech errors in people with schizophrenia, indicating problems with planning speech. We also found that the voice hearers with schizophrenia had problems detecting such errors 'internally', in their 'mind's ear' so to speak.

2 This may seem to be the only possible arrangement if the informant hears only one voice. Yet even a single voice could refer to the voice hearer in the third person, apparently addressing somebody, so to speak, 'out of sight or hearing'. This possible participant arrangement was never reported by our informants.

3 Transcript conventions

?	rising intonation
.	falling intonation
,	continuing intonation
:	lengthening of the previous syllable
(2.35)	pause duration in seconds
(.)	a very short, still audible pause
(..)	a longer pause
(...)	a long pause
-	a cut-off of the prior word or sound
(but)	items enclosed within single parentheses are in doubt
((cough))	in double brackets there is a comment by the transcriber
talk	underlining indicates emphasis
| |	the onset and the ending of simultaneous talk between utterances (overlap)
=	indicates fluent turn change
°talk°	indicates decreased volume

Bibliography

Adkins, A.W.H. (1970). *From the Many to the One. A Study of Personality and Views of Human Nature in the Context of Ancient Greek Society, Values and Beliefs.* London: Constable.

Al-Issa, I. (1978). Social and cultural aspects of hallucinations. *Psychological Bulletin*, 84, 570–587.

Allen, H.A., Halperin, J. and Friend, R. (1985). Removal and diversion tactics and the control of auditory hallucinations. *Behaviour Research and Therapy*, 23, 601–605.

APA (1994). *Diagnostic Criteria from DSM-IV.* Washington, DC: American Psychological Association.

Austin, J.L. (1962a). *How to do Things with Words.* Oxford: Clarendon Press.

Austin, J.L. (1962b). *Sense and Sensibilia.* Oxford: Clarendon Press.

Ayer, A.J. (1968). *Origins of Pragmatism.* London: Macmillan.

Azam, E.E. (1882). *Hypnotisme, double conscience, et altération de la personalité.* Paris: Baillière.

Baker, G.P. and Hacker, P.M.S. (1983). *Wittgenstein's 'Philosophical Investigations'.* Oxford: Blackwell.

Baillarger, J. (1886). Physiologie des hallucinations. Les deux théories. *Annales médico-psychologiques. Journal de l'aliénation mentale et de la médecine légale des aliénés*, 4, 19–39.

Bakhtin, M.M. (1981). *The Dialogic Imagination.* Austin: University of Texas Press.

Bakhtin, M.M. (1988). *Problems of Dostoevsky's Poetics.* Manchester: University of Manchester Press.

Ball, M.B. (1882). De la folie religieuse. *Revue Scientifique*, 30, 336–342.

Bauman, Z. (1989). *Modernity and Holocaust.* Oxford: Polity Press.

Beck, A.T. (1952). Successful outpatient psychotherapy of a chronic schizophrenic with a delusion based on borrowed guilt. *Psychiatry*, 15, 305–312.

Bentall, R.P. (1990). The illusion of reality: a review and integration of psychological research on hallucinations. *Psychological Bulletin*, 107, 82–95.

Bentall, R.P., Baker, G.A. and Havers, S. (1991). Reality monitoring and hallucinations. *British Journal of Psychiatry*, 30, 213–222.

Bentall, R.P., Haddock, G. and Slade, P. (1994). Cognitive behaviour therapy for persistent auditory hallucinations. *Behaviour Therapy*, 25, 51–66.

Berrios, G.E. (1984). Descriptive psychopathology: conceptual and historical aspects. *Psychological Medicine*, 14, 303–313.

Berrios, G.E. (1991). British psychopathology since the early twentieth century. In G.E. Berrios and H. Freeman (eds), *150 years of British Psychiatry: 1841–1991.* London: Gaskell.

Binet, A. (1884a). L'Hallucination. I. Recherches expérimentales. *Revue Philosophique*, 18, 473–502.

Binet, A. (1884b). L'Hallucination. I. Recherches théoriques. *Revue Philosophique*, 18, 377–412.

Bird, G. (1986). *William James*. London: Routledge & Kegan Paul.

Bleuler, E. (1911/1966). *Dementia Praecox or the Group of Schizophrenias*. New York: International Universities Press.

Bleuler, E. (1924/1951). *Textbook of Psychiatry*. New York: Dover Publications.

Bowra, C.M. (1930). *Tradition and Design in the Iliad*. Oxford: Clarendon Press.

Brierre de Boismont, A. (1856). Report on two meetings of Société Médico-Psychologique, 29/10/1855 and 26/11/1855. *Annales Médico-Psychologiques*, Third Series, 2, 126–140.

Brierre de Boismont, A. (1861a). Des hallucinations historiques ou étude medico-psychologique sur les voix et les révélations de Jeanne d'Arc (Part 1). *Annales Médico-Psychologiques*, Third Series, 7, 353–376.

Brierre de Boismont, A. (1861b). Des hallucinations historiques ou étude médico-psychologique sur les voix et les révélations de Jeanne d'Arc (Part 2). *Annales Médico-Psychologiques*, Third Series, 7, 509–539.

Brierre de Boismont, A. (1862). *Des hallucinations, ou histoire raisonnée des apparitions, des visions, des songes, de l'extase, des rêves, du magnétisme et du somnambulisme*. Paris: Germer Baillière.

Briquet, P. (1859). *Traité clinique et thérapeutique de l'hystérie*. Paris: Crochard.

Brunet, (1863). L'enchanteur Merlin. *Annales Médico-Psychologiques*, Fourth Series, 1, 41–45.

Bunyan, J. (1962). *Grace Abounding to the Chief of Sinners*, ed. R. Sharrock. Oxford: Clarendon Press.

Button, G., Coulter, J., Lee, J. and Sharrock, W. (1995). *Computers, Minds and Conduct*. Cambridge: Polity Press.

Cacioppo, J.T. and Petty, R.E. (1981). Electromyograms as measures of extent and affectivity of information processing. *American Psychologist*, 36, 441–456.

Chadwick, P. and Birchwood, M. (1994). The omnipotence of voices: a cognitive approach to auditory hallucinations. *British Journal of Psychiatry*, 164, 190–201.

Charcot, J.-M. (1881). *Clinical Lectures on Senile and Chronic Diseases*. London: New Sydenham Society.

Charcot, J.-M. (1991). *Clinical Lectures on Diseases of the Nervous System*. London: Routledge.

Cleghorn, J.M., Franco, S., Szechtman, B. *et al.* (1992). Toward a brain map of verbal hallucinations. *American Journal of Psychiatry*, 149, 1062–1069.

Costall, A. and Leudar, I. (1996). Situating action I: Truth in situation. *Ecological Psychology*, 8, 101–110.

Coulter, J. (1973). *Approaches to Insanity*. London: Martin Robertson.

Curson, D., Patel, M., Liddle, P.F. and Barnes, T.R. (1988). Psychiatric morbidity of a long-stay hospital population with chronic schizophrenia, and implications for future community care. *British Medical Journal*, 297, 818–822.

Davies, P., Thomas, P. and Leudar, I. (1999). Dialogical engagement and verbal hallucinations: a single case study. *British Journal of Medical Psychology*, 72, 179–187.

Davis, J.M. and Caspar, R. (1977). Antipsychotic drugs: clinical pharmacology and therapeutic use. *Drugs*, 14, 260–282.

Davis, J.M., Schaffer, C.B., Killian, G.A. *et al.* (1980). Important issues in the drug treatment of schizophrenia. *Schizophrenia Bulletin*, 6, 70–87.

Dewey, J. (1896). The reflex arc concept in psychology. *Psychological Review*, 3, 357–370.

Dewey, J. (1909). *How do we Think*. London: D.C. Heath.

Diaz, R. and Berk, M. (eds) (1992). *Private Speech. From Social Interaction to Self Regulation*. Hillsdale, NJ: Lawrence Erlbaum.

Drew, P. (1991). Asymmetries of knowledge in conversational interaction. In I. Marková and K. Foppa (eds), *Asymmetries in Dialogue*. Hemel Hempstead: Harvester Wheatsheaf.

Ellenberger, H.F. (1970). *The Discovery of the Unconscious. The History and Evolution of Dynamic Psychiatry*. New York: Basic Books.

Ensink, B. (1992). *Confusing Realities: A Study on Child Sexual Abuse and Psychiatric Symptoms*. Amsterdam: VU University Press.

Ensink, B. (1993). Trauma: a study of child abuse and hallucinations. In M. Romme and S. Escher (eds), *Accepting Voices*. London: MIND Publications.

Esquirol, E. (1838). *Des maladies mentales considerées sous les rapports médicaux, hygiéniques et médico-légaux*. Paris: Baillière.

Esquirol, E. (1845). *Mental Maladies: A Treatise on Insanity*. Philadelphia, PA: Lea & Blanchard.

Fairburn, W.R.D. (1956/1994). *From Instinct to Self: Selected Papers of W.R.D. Fairburn*, Vol. 1. Northvale, NJ: Jason Aronson.

Falloon, I.R.H. and Talbot, R.E. (1981). Persistent auditory hallucinations: coping mechanisms and implications for management. *Psychological Medicine*, 11, 329–339.

Feyerabend, P. (1978). *Against Method*. London: Verso.

Feyerabend, P. (1987). *Farewell to Reason*. London: Verso.

Forrer, G.R. (1960). Benign auditory and visual hallucinations. *Archives of General Psychiatry*, 3, 119–122.

Foucault, M. (1967). *Madness and Civilization. A History of Insanity in the Age of Reason*. London: Tavistock Press.

Foucault, M. (1991). *Discipline and Punish: The Birth of the Prison*. London: Penguin Books.

Freud, S. (1911/1972). Psychoanalytic notes on an autobiographical account of a case of paranoia (Dementia Paranoides). In J. Strachey and A. Richards (eds), *Case Histories II*. London: Penguin Books.

Freud, S. (1917/1975). *Introductory Lectures on Psychoanalysis*. Harmondsworth: Penguin Books.

Freud, S. (1923/1927). *The Ego and Id*. London: Hogarth Press.

Freud, S. (1950). *The Interpretation of Dreams*. London: Allen & Unwin.

Frith, C. (1992). *The Cognitive Neuropsychology of Schizophrenia*. London: Lawrence Erlbaum Associates.

Frith, C. (1995). Functional imaging and cognitive abnormalities. *Lancet*, 346, 615–620.

Gaver, W.W. (1993). How do we hear in the world? Explorations in ecological acoustics. *Ecological Psychology*, 5, 285–313.

Goffman, E. (1981). *Forms of Talk*. Oxford: Blackwell.

Goldberg, D. and Huxley, P. (1980). *Mental Illness in the Community*. London: Tavistock Press.

Gould, L.N. (1949). Auditory hallucinations and sub-vocal speech. *Journal of Nervous and Mental Disease*, 109, 418–427.

Green, P. and Preston, M. (1981). Reinforcement of vocal correlates of auditory hallucinations by auditory feedback. *British Journal of Psychiatry*, 139, 204–208.

Grice, P. (1957). Meaning. *Philosophical Review*, 67, 377–388.

Hacker, P.M.S. (1996). *Wittgenstein's Place in Twentieth-century Analytic Philosophy*. Oxford: Blackwell.

Hacking, I. (1995). *Rewriting the Soul: Multiple Personality and the Sciences of Memory*. Princeton, NJ: Princeton University Press.

Haddock, G., Bentall, R.P. and Slade, P.D. (1993). Psychological treatment of chronic auditory hallucinations: two case studies. *Behavioural and Cognitive Psychotherapy*, 21, 335–346.

Hamilton, M. (ed.) (1984). *Fish's Schizophrenia*, Third edn. Bristol: Wright.

Harré, R. and van Langenhove, L. (1991). Varieties of positioning. *Journal for the Theory of Social Behaviour*, 21, 393–407.

Hester, S. and Eglin, P. (1997). *Culture in Action. Studies in Membership Categorisation Analysis.* Washington, DC: International Institute for Ethnomethodology and Conversation Analysis. University Press of America.

Hoffman, R.E. (1986). Verbal hallucinations and language production processes in schizophrenia. *Behavioural and Brain Sciences*, 9, 503–548.

Hoffman, R.E. and Satel, S.L. (1993). Language therapy for schizophrenic patients with persistent voices. *British Journal of Psychiatry*, 162, 755–758.

Hoffman, R.E., Oates, E., Hafner, J., Hustig, H. and McGlashan, T. (1994). Semantic organisation of hallucinated 'voices' in schizophrenia. *American Journal of Psychiatry*, 151, 1229–1230.

Homer (1950). *The Iliad*, trans. E.V. Rieu. London: Penguin Books.

Homer (1951). *The Iliad*, trans. R. Lattimore. London: Routledge & Kegan Paul.

Hughes, E.C. (1971). *The Sociological Eye: Selected Papers.* Chicago: Aldine Atherton.

James, T. (1995). *Dream, Creativity and Madness in Nineteenth-century France.* Oxford: Clarendon Press.

James, W. (1891). *Principles of Psychology*, Vol. 1. London: Macmillan.

Janet, P. (1889). *Automatisme psychologique. Essai de psychologie expérimentale sur les formes inférieures de l'activité humaine.* Paris: Baillière.

Janet, P. (1891). Études sur un cas d'aboulie et d'idées fixes. *Revue Philosophique*, 31, 258–287, 382–407.

Janet, P. (1901). *The Mental State of Hystericals. A Study of Mental Stigmata and Mental Accidents.* New York: G.P. Putnam.

Janet, P. (1903). *Les Obsessions et la psychasthénie.* Paris: Félix Alcan.

Janet, P. (1910). Chapter 4. In H. Munsterberg, T. Ribot, P. Janet, J. Jastrow, B. Hart and M. Prince, *Subconscious Phenomena.* London: Rebman.

Janet, P. (1919). *Les Médications psychologiques: études historiques, psychologiques et cliniques sur les méthodes de la psychothérapie.* Paris: Travaux du Laboratoire de psychologie de la Salpêtrière.

Janet, P. (1925). *Psychological Healing. A Historical and Clinical Study.* London: George Allen & Unwin.

Jaspers, K. (1963). *General Psychopathology*, trans. J. Hoenig and M.W. Hamilton. Manchester: Manchester University Press.

Jaynes, J. (1976). *The Origins of Consciousness in the Breakdown of the Bicameral Mind.* Boston, MA: Houghton Mifflin.

Jayyusi, L. (1984). *Categorisation and Moral Order.* London: Routledge & Kegan Paul.

Joas, H. (1985) *G.H. Mead: a contemporary re-examination of his thought.* Cambridge: Polity Press.

Johnson, F.H. (1978). *The Anatomy of Hallucinations.* Chicago, IL: Nelson Hall.

Johnson, M.K. and Raye, C. (1981). Reality monitoring. *Psychological Review*, 88, 67–85.

Kane, J., Honigfeld, G., Singer, J. *et al.* (1988). Clozapine for the treatment resistant schizophrenic. *Archives of General Psychiatry*, 45, 789–796.

Keary, C.F. (1884). The Homeric words for 'soul'. *Mind*, XXX, 471–483.

Kingdon, D.G. and Turkington, D. (1991a). The use of cognitive behaviour therapy with a normalising rationale in schizophrenia. *Journal of Nervous and Mental Disease*, 179, 207–211.

Kingdon, D.G. and Turkington, D. (1991b). A role for cognitive-behavioural strategies in schizophrenia? *Social Psychiatry and Psychiatric Epidemiology*, 26, 101–103.

Kingdon, D.G., Turkington, D. and John, C. (1994). Cognitive behaviour therapy of schizophrenia: the amenability of delusions and hallucinations to reasoning. *British Journal of Psychiatry*, 164, 581–587.

Klein, M. (1975). Notes on some schizoid mechanisms. In M. Klein (1988) *Envy and Gratitude and Other Works 1946–1963*. London: Virago.

Lattimore, R. (1951). Introduction. In *The Iliad of Homer*, trans. R. Lattimore. London: Routledge & Kegan Paul.

Lavy, E.H. and van den Hout, M.A. (1990). Thought suppression induces intrusion. *Behavioural Psychotherapy*, 18, 251–258.

Leiman, M. (1994). Projective identification as early joint action sequences: a Vygotskian addendum to Procedural Sequence Object Relations Model. *British Journal of Medical Psychology*, 67, 97–106.

Lelut, L.F. (1836). *Du démon de Socrat*. Paris: Trinquart.

Leudar, I. (1991). Sociogenesis, coordination and mutualism. *Journal for the Theory of Social Behaviour*, 21, 197–220.

Leudar, I. (1995). Reporting political arguments. In F.H. van Eeemeren, R. Grootenderst, J.A. Blair and C.A. Willard. (eds), *Reconstruction and Application. Proceedings of the 3rd International Conference on Argumentation*, Vol. 3. Amsterdam: Sic Sac.

Leudar, I. (1998). Who is Martin McGuiness 1: On contextualizing reported political talk. In S. Cmejrkova, J. Hoffmanová, O. Müllerová and J. Světlá (eds), *Dialogue Analysis 6*, Vol. 2, Tübingen: Niemeyer.

Leudar, I. and Antaki, C. (1996a). Discourse participation, reported speech and research practices in social psychology. *Theory and Psychology*, 6, 5–29.

Leudar, I. and Antaki, C. (1996b). Backing footing. *Theory and Psychology*, 6, 41–46.

Leudar, I. and Antaki, C. (1997). Participant status in psychological research. In T. Ibáñez and L. Íñiquez (eds), *Critical Social Psychology*. London: Sage.

Leudar, I. and Costall, A. (1996). Situating action IV: Planning as situated action. *Ecological Psychology*, 8, 153–170.

Leudar, I. and Nekvapil, J. (1998). On the emergence of political identity in the Czech mass media: the case of the Democratic Party of Sudetenland. *Czech Sociological Review*, 6, 43–58.

Leudar, I. and Sharrock, W. (1999). Multiplying the multiplicity. *British Journal of Psychology*, 90, 451–455.

Leudar, I. and Thomas, P. (1995). *The Guide-lines for Establishing Pragmatic Aspects of Voice-talk*. Manchester: Department of Psychology, University of Manchester.

Leudar, I., Thomas, P. and Johnston, M. (1992). Self-repair in dialogues of schizophrenics: effects of hallucinations and negative symptoms. *Brain and Language*, 43, 487–511.

Leudar, I., Thomas, P. and Johnston, M. (1994). Self-monitoring in speech production: effects of verbal hallucinations and negative symptoms. *Psychological Medicine*, 24, 749–761.

Leudar, I., Thomas, P., McNally, D. and Glinski, A. (1997). What voices can do with words: pragmatics of verbal hallucinations. *Psychological Medicine*, 27, 885–898.

Leuret, F. (1834). *Fragments psychologiques sur la folie*. Paris: Crochard.

Levinson, S. (1988). Putting linguistics on a proper footing. Explorations in Goffman's concepts of participation. In P. Drew and A. Wotton (eds), *Goffman. Exploring the Interaction Order*. Oxford: Polity Press.

Lothane, Z. (1992). *In Defense of Schreber: Soul Murder and Psychiatry*. New York: Lawrence Erlbaum.

Luria, A.R. (1961). *The Role of Speech in the Regulation of Normal and Abnormal Behaviour*. Oxford: Pergamon Press.

McGuire, P.K., Shah, P. and Murray, R.M. (1993). Increased blood flow in Broca's area during auditory hallucinations in schizophrenia. *Lancet*, 342, 703–706.

McGuire, P.K., Silbersweig, D.A., Wright, I., Murray, R.M., Davis, A.S., Frackowiak, R.S.J. and Frith, C.D. (1995). Abnormal monitoring of inner speech: a physiological basis for auditory hallucinations. *Lancet*, 346, 596–600.

McGuire, P.K., Silbersweig, D.A., Wright, I., Murray, R.M., Frackowiak, R.S.J. and Frith, C.D. (1996). Abnormal monitoring of inner speech: a physiological basis for auditory hallucinations. *British Journal of Psychiatry*, 169, 148–159.

McInnis, M. and Marks, I. (1990). Audiotape therapy for persistent auditory hallucinations. *British Journal of Psychiatry*, 157, 913–914.

McKellar, P. (1957). *Imagination and Thinking*. New York: Basic Books.

Margo, A., Hemsley, D.R. and Slade, P.D. (1981). The effects of varying auditory input on schizophrenic hallucinations. *British Journal of Psychiatry*, 139, 122–127.

Marková, I. and Foppa, K. (eds) (1991) *Asymmetries in Dialogue*. Hemel Hempstead: Harvester Wheatsheaf.

Maudsley, H. (1867). *The Pathology of Mind*. New York: Appleton.

Maudsley, H. (1897). *Natural Causes and Supernatural Seemings*. London: Kegan Paul, Trench, Trubner & Co. First published 1886.

Maury, A. (1855). Les Mystiques extatiques et les stigmatisés. *Annales Médico-Psychologiques*, Third Series, 1, 157–176.

Mead, G.H. (1934). *Mind, Self and Society from the Standpoint of a Social Behaviourist*. Chicago, IL: University of Chicago Press.

Mead, G.H. (1938/1972). *The Philosophy of the Act*. Chicago, IL: University of Chicago Press.

Mellor, C.S. (1970). The first rank symptoms of schizophrenia. *British Journal of Psychiatry*, 117, 15–23.

Micale, M.S. (1994). Henri F. Ellenberger: the history of psychiatry as the history of the unconscious. In M.S. Micale and R. Porter (eds), *Discovering the History of Psychiatry*. Oxford: Oxford University Press.

Miller, G., Galanter, E. and Pribram, K. (1960). *Plans and the Structure of Behavior*. New York: Holt, Rinehart & Winston.

Muhlhäusler, P. and Harré, R. (1990). *Pronouns and People: Linguistic Construction of Social and Personal Identity*. Oxford: Blackwell.

Myers, F.W.H. (1903). *Human Personality and its Survival of Bodily Death*. New York: Longmans, Green & Co.

Nares, R. (1782). *An Essay on the Demon or Divination of Socrates*. London: T. Payne.

Nayani, T.H. and David, A.S. (1996). The auditory hallucination: a phenomenological survey. *Psychological Medicine*, 26, 177–189.

Niederland, W.G. (1974). *The Schreber Case. Psychoanalytic Profile of a Paranoid Personality*. Hillsdale, NJ: Analytic Press.

Nietzsche, F. (1872/1991). *The Birth of Tragedy*. London: Penguin Books.

Nietzsche, F. (1878/1994). *Human, all too Human*. London: Penguin Books.

Pavlov, I.P. (1928). *Lectures on Conditioned Reflexes*. New York: International Press.

Pennings, M.A.H. and Romme, M.A.J. (1996) *Hearing Voices in Patients and Non-Patients*. Maastricht: University of Limburg.

Pinel, P. (1818). *Nosographie philosophique ou la méthode de l'analyse appliquée à la médecine*. Paris: Brosson.

Plato (1993a). Crito. In H. Tarrant (ed.), *The Last Days of Socrates*. London: Penguin Books.

Plato (1993b). Apology. In H. Tarrant (ed.), *The Last Days of Socrates*. London: Penguin Books.

Plato (1996a). Euthydemus. In E. Hamilton and H. Cairns (eds), *The Collected Dialogues of Plato*. Princeton, NJ: Princeton University Press.

Plato (1996b). Republic. In E. Hamilton and H. Cairns (eds), *The Collected Dialogues of Plato*. Princeton, NJ: Princeton University Press.

Plato (1996c). Phaedrus. In E. Hamilton and H. Cairns (eds), *The Collected Dialogues of Plato*. Princeton, NJ: Princeton University Press.

Plutarch (1959). On the sign of Socrates. In P.H. de Lacy (ed.), *Plutarch's Moralia*, Vol. 7. London: William Heinemann.

Posey, T.B. and Losch, M.E. (1983). Auditory hallucinations of hearing voices in 375 normal subjects. *Imagination, Cognition and Personality*, 3, 99–113.

Price-Williams, D. (1989). Communication in therapy with emotionally disturbed mentally retarded individuals. In M. Beveridge, G. Conti-Ramsden and I. Leudar (eds), *Language and Communication in People with Mental Handicap*. London: Chapman & Hall.

Prince, M. (1920). *The Dissociation of Personality*. London: Longmans, Green & Co.

Putnam, F.W. (1989). *Diagnosis and Treatment of Multiple Personality Disorder*. New York: Guilford Press.

Putnam, F.W. (1994). Dissociative disorders in children and adolescents. In S.J. Lynn and J.W. Rhue (eds), *Dissociation. Clinical and Theoretical Perspectives*. New York: Guilford Press.

Rees, W.D. (1971). The hallucinations of widowhood. *British Medical Journal*, 4, 7–41.

Renfield, J.M. (1975). *Nature and Culture in the Iliad: The Tragedy of Hector*. Chicago, IL: University of Chicago Press.

Ribot, T. (1885). *Les Maladies de la mémoire*. Paris: Baillière.

Rogoff, B. (1990). *Apprenticeship in Thinking. Cognitive Development in Social Context*. Oxford: Oxford University Press.

Romme, M. and Escher, S. (1989). Hearing voices. *Schizophrenia Bulletin*, 15, 209–216.

Romme, M. and Escher, S. (1991). *The Metaphoric and Interpersonal Sense of Hearing Voices*. Maastricht: University of Limburg.

Romme, M. and Escher, S. (1994). *Accepting Voices*. London: MIND Publications.

Romme, M., Honig, A., Noorthoorn, E.O. and Escher, S. (1992). Coping with hearing voices: an emancipatory approach. *British Journal of Psychiatry*, 161, 99–103.

Rose, N. (1989). *Governing the Soul*. London: Routledge.

Royal College of Psychiatrists (1999). *Press release: New Study Reveals Fall in the Contribution of People with Mental Illness to National Homicide Figures for England and Wales*. London: Royal College of Psychiatrists, 5 January.

Royce, J. (1894). The case of John Bunyan. *Psychological Review*, 1, 22–33, 134–151, 230–240.

Ryle, A. (1994). Projective identification: a particular form of reciprocal role procedure. *British Journal of Medical Psychology*, 67, 107–114.

Sacks, H. (1992). *Lectures on Conversation*. Oxford: Blackwell.

Sacks, H. and Schegloff, E.M. (1979). Two preferences in the organisation of reference to persons in conversation and their interaction. In G. Psathas (ed.) *Everyday Language: Studies in Ethnomethodology*. New York: Lawrence Erlbaum.

Sacks, H., Schegloff, E. and Jefferson, G. (1974). A simplest systematics for the organization of turn-taking in conversation. *Language*, 50, 696–735.

Sacks, H., Schegloff, E. and Jefferson, G. (1978). A simplest systematics for the organisation of turn-taking in conversation. In J.N. Schenkhein (ed.) *Studies in the Organisation of Conversational Interaction*. New York: Academic Press.

Santner, E.L. (1996). *My Own Private Germany: Daniel Paul Schreber's Secret History of Modernity*. Princeton, NJ: Princeton University Press.

Sapir, E. (1957). *Culture, Language, and Personality: Selected Essays*. Berkeley: University of California Press.

Sarbin, T.R. (1967). The concept of hallucination. *Journal of Personality*, 35, 355–380.

Sass, L. (1992). *Madness and Modernism. Insanity in the Light of Modern Art, Literature, and Thought*. Cambridge, MA: Harvard University Press.

Sass, L. (1994). *The Paradoxes of Delusion. Wittgenstein, Schreber and the Schizophrenic Mind*. Ithaca, NY: Cornell University Press.

Schatzman, M. (1976). *Soul Murder*. London: Penguin Books.

Schegloff, E.A. (1992). On talk and its institutional setting. In P. Drew and J. Heritage (eds), *Talk at Work: Studies in the Interactional Order*. Cambridge: Polity Press.

Schneider, K. (1957). Primäre und sekundäre Symptomen bei Schizophrenie. (Primary and secondary symptoms in schizophrenia.) *Fortschrift für Neurologie und Psychiatrie*, 25, 487.

Schreber, D.P. (1903/1955). *The Memoirs of my Nervous Illness*. Cambridge, MA: Harvard University Press.

Searle, J. (1969). *Speech Acts*. Cambridge: Cambridge University Press.

Seglas, J. (1888). De l'hallucination dans ses rapports avec la fonction du langage, les hallucinations psychomotrices. *Progrès Médical*, 18 August, 124–137.

Seglas, J. (1889). Deux cas d'onomatomanie, echolalie mentale. A report to 'Société médicale des hospitaux', 12 April.

Sidgewick, H., Johnson, A., Myers, F.W.H. *et al.* (1894). Report on the census of hallucinations. *Proceedings of the Society for Psychical Research*, 34, 25–394.

Slade, P.D. (1972). The effects of systematic desensitisation on auditory hallucinations. *Behaviour Research and Therapy*, 10, 85–91.

Slade, P.D. (1974). The external control of auditory hallucinations: an information theory analysis. *British Journal of Social and Clinical Psychology*, 13, 73–79.

Slade, P. and Bentall, R. (1988). *Sensory Deception: Towards a Scientific Analysis of Hallucinations*. London: Croom Helm.

Slater, E. and Roth, M. (1969). *Clinical Psychiatry*, Third edn. London: Baillière Tindall.

Snell, B. (1953). *The Discovery of the Mind: The Greek Origins of European Thought*. Oxford: Blackwell.

Sodi, T. (1995). A call to become an indigenous healer: an integrative or disintegrative experience. Paper presented at the Hearing Voices Conference. Discourse Unit, Manchester Metropolitan University, 8 July.

Strauss, J.S. (1969). Hallucinations and delusions as points on continua functions. *Archives of General Psychiatry*, 21, 581–586.

Suzuki *et al.* (1993). Ch. 9, p.1 (cited by Hoffman)

Szasz, T. (1996). 'Audible thoughts' and 'speech defect' in schizophrenia. A note on reading and translating Bleuler. *Traduttori, traditori. British Journal of Psychiatry*, 168, 533–535.

Szasz, T. (1997). *Insanity. The Idea and its Consequences*. Syracuse, NY: Syracuse University Press.

Taine, H. (1878). *De l'intelligence*. Paris: Hachette.

Taylor, P. and Gunn, J. (1999). Homicides by people with mental illness: myth and reality. *British Journal of Psychiatry*, 174, 9–14.

Thomas, P., Romme, M.A.J. and Hemmelinjk, J. (1996). Psychiatry and the politics of the underclass. *British Journal of Psychiatry*, 169, 401–404.

Tien, A.Y. (1991). Distributions of hallucinations in the population. *Social Psychiatry and Psychiatric Epidemiology*, 26, 287–292.

Voltaire, F.M.A. (1773/1994). *Letters Concerning the English*. Oxford: Oxford University Press.

Vygotsky, L.S. (1934/1962). *Thought and Language*. Cambridge, MA: MIT Press.

Vygotsky, L.S. (1978). *Mind in Society: The Development of Higher Psychological Processes*. London: Harvard University Press.

Walker, C. (1988). Philosophical concepts and practice: the legacy of Karl Jaspers' psychopathology. *Current Opinion in Psychiatry*, 1, 624–629.

Wegner, D.M., Schneider, D.J., Carter, S.R. and White, T.L. (1987). Paradoxical effects of thought suppression. *Journal of Personality and Social Psychology*, 53, 5–13.

Weir Mitchell (1888). *Transactions of the College of Physicians of Philadelphia*, 4 April (cited by W. James, 1891, p. 381).

Wertsch, J.V. (1985). *Culture, Communication and Cognition: Vygotskian Perspectives*. Cambridge: Cambridge University Press; London: Harvester Wheatsheaf.

Wertsch, J.V. (1991). *Voices of the Mind*. London: Harvester Wheatsheaf.

Westen, D. (1990). Physical and sexual abuse in adolescents with borderline personality disorder. *American Journal of Orthopsychiatry*, 60, 55–66.

Whorf, B.L. (1956). *Language, Thought and Reality: Selected Writings of Benjamin Lee Whorf*. Cambridge, MA: MIT Press.

Wilshire, B. (1968). *William James and Phenomenology. A Study of Principles of Psychology*. Bloomington: Indiana University Press.

Winch, P. (1964). Understanding primitive society. *American Philosophical Quarterly*, 1, 307–324.

Wittgenstein, L. (1976). *Philosophical Investigations*. Oxford: Blackwell.

Xenophon (1990a). Memoirs of Socrates. In R. Waterfield (ed.), *Conversations of Socrates*. London: Penguin Books.

Xenophon (1990b). Socrates' defense. In R. Waterfield (ed.), *Conversations of Socrates*. London: Penguin Books.

Xenophon (1990c). Dinner party. In R. Waterfield (ed.), *Conversations of Socrates*. London: Penguin Books.

Young, A. (1995). *The Harmony of Illusions. Inventing Post-traumatic Stress Disorder*. Princeton, NJ: Princeton University Press.

Zanker, G. (1994). *The Heart of Achilles. Characterization and Personal Ethics in the Iliad*. Ann Arbor: University of Michigan Press.

Index